THE DEMOCRACY TRAP

THE
DEMOCRACY TRAP

The Perils of the
Post–Cold War World

by Graham E. Fuller

A DUTTON BOOK

DUTTON
Published by the Penguin Group
Penguin Books USA Inc., 375 Hudson Street,
New York, New York 10014, U.S.A.
Penguin Books Ltd, 27 Wrights Lane,
London W8 5TZ, England
Penguin Books Australia Ltd, Ringwood,
Victoria, Australia
Penguin Books Canada Ltd, 10 Alcorn Avenue,
Toronto, Ontario, Canada M4V 3B2
Penguin Books (N.Z.) Ltd, 182–190 Wairau Road,
Auckland 10, New Zealand

Penguin Books Ltd, Registered Offices:
Harmondsworth, Middlesex, England

First published by Dutton, an imprint of New American Library,
a division of Penguin Books USA Inc.
Distributed in Canada by McClelland & Stewart Inc.

First Printing, November, 1991
10 9 8 7 6 5 4 3 2 1

 REGISTERED TRADEMARK—MARCA REGISTRADA

LIBRARY OF CONGRESS CATALOGING-IN-PUBLICATION DATA:

Fuller, Graham E., 1939–
    The democracy trap : perils of the post-Cold War world / by
Graham E. Fuller.
        p.   cm.
    Includes index.
    ISBN 0-525-93371-9
    1. World politics—1989-   2.Democracy. 3. United States—
Politics and government—1989-   I. Title.
D860.F85   1991
327'.09'049—dc20   91-16979
                                                                        CIP

PRINTED IN THE UNITED STATES OF AMERICA
Set in Times Roman

This book is dedicated to my own children, Samantha, Melissa, and Luke, and to my nieces and nephews Dylan, Laura, Elijah, Erin, Grayson, Laurel, Matthew, Richard, Philippa, and Rosemary—all of whom, as members of the next generation, must find their way in the challenges of the post–Cold War world.

CONTENTS

ACKNOWLEDGMENTS

This book is the product of many years living abroad—mostly in the Third World, during which time I became interested in problems of democracy. For me, as for so many other people, the stunning collapse of the Berlin Wall in 1989 was the chief signal of the new opportunities for democracy in much of the former totalitarian world. Despite the joy of that occasion, I rapidly became concerned for the problems that democracy itself can pose, not just in new democracies, but also in the new post–Cold War America.

The ideas in this book have been formed by an immense variety of inputs over the years. It is not a study of the problems of democracy per se, but rather of the problems of democracy as they can be observed in the current world situation.

I have profitably discussed many of these ideas with friends, colleagues, and family members, including my father, Edmund Fuller, my daughters, Samantha and Melissa, my brother, David, and my sisters, Meredith and Faith—all of whom had insights to offer into various substantive areas of the book. Several good friends kindly consented to look at the manuscript in its earlier stages; I particularly want to thank Charles Waterman for his comments. My father read and critiqued the manuscript at several stages of writing and provided extremely sound counsel as well as consistent encouragement. I would also like to thank Terrance and Patricia Murphy and Paul

Henze for their useful ideas, as well as numerous other friends whom I cannot mention here. My friend and RAND colleague Frank Fukuyama and I have often discussed problems touched upon in this volume in the past; indeed, Frank's well-known article "The End of History"—which I found stimulating and provocative, but with which I profoundly disagree—provided the immediate stimulus for setting forth my own views on why history has not ended at all, but in fact has just begun.

Naturally I bear full responsibility for all the ideas in the book. The book was written independently of the RAND Corporation, and it does not necessarily represent the thinking of RAND on any issue. I wish to thank too my editor, Laurie Bernstein, for her initial support for the concept of the book, and for her useful editorial critiques at various stages. Lastly I thank my family, and especially my wife, Prue, for her patience and support, technical and otherwise, during the writing of the book.

Thousand Oaks, California
1991

Many forms of Government have been tried, and will be tried in the world of sin and woe. No one pretends that democracy is perfect or all-wise. Indeed, it has been said that democracy is the worst form of Government except all those other forms that have been tried from time to time.

—Winston Churchill

Our worst enemies today are our own bad qualities—indifference to public affairs, conceit, ambition, selfishness, the pursuit of personal advancement, and rivalry. There is the main struggle we are faced with.

—Vaclav Havel,
New Year's Address, 1989

THE DEMOCRACY TRAP

INTRODUCTION

It is the thesis of this book that the end of the Cold War—
magnificent victory for liberal democracy as it was—opened
the door to new challenges that exceed in complexity those
of the past era. The new openings to democracy—symbolized
most vividly in the collapse of the Berlin Wall—will nonetheless present those peoples liberated from communism, ourselves, and the rest of the world with more intractable
problems than the Cold War era ever did—although we did
not know it then. Indeed, we are facing what I call the
"Democracy Trap," a series of potential pitfalls that spring
from the character of democracy itself.

In principle, the news of the past few years from Eastern
Europe and the Soviet Union, despite immense problems
there, is still overwhelmingly good compared to the past. Who
cannot be in favor of democracy? And yet, as I watch these
events I cannot help but feel that we in America may be
heading toward an even more trying period: a crisis in ourselves and in our own system. Our release from the Cold War
has impelled us out of the long-term certitudes of the East-
West struggle and into a new era where those familiar,
finite—even comforting—demands of global struggle are no
longer valid.

What is the Democracy Trap? Democracy is not, of course,
a trap in itself. But it can become so in our casual and uncritical confidence that the process will spontaneously alleviate

1

major social ills. Democracy can become a trap when it stimulates the erroneous belief that with the passing of the Cold War we are emerging into a new and automatically more promising world.

Democracy is a superb form of government—the most desirable in human history. But it contains its own serious pitfalls that we have usually overlooked in times of long preoccupation with other economic or political goals, as during the long era of strife with communism. Yet, ignored, these pitfalls grow more serious as our own democracy continues to explore new horizons of democratic practice that were never visible in a less leisured, less wealthy, less permissive, less option-laden past.

The Democracy Trap is the possibility that democracy may not simply go on getting better, but may contain the seeds of its own decline, possibly spurring an eventual authoritarian response from within our own society. Indeed, the Democracy Trap may lie in the very nature of postindustrial American democracy itself: its tendency to intensify the disorders of an increasingly unstructured and possibly decaying society—one in which the traditional binding social institutions of the past are falling by the wayside. Uncritical extension of the frontiers of democratic society and practice could mark the deterioration, rather than the maturation, of American society. The successful practice of democracy will require increasingly complex decisions and a constant awareness of alternatives and trade-offs, lest the system indeed become a trap that can damage the unwary, uncritical, or paralyzed society.

We no longer have the luxury of defining our own system against the moribund and bankrupt systems of Marxism-Leninism; there really was no contest there anyway, although the outcome was not in fact certain for several decades. But democracy at home must be judged against a far harsher criterion—that of our self-imposed aspirations—now that there is no longer any external excuse of "national security" or "the communist threat" for falling short of our goals.

The Democracy Trap suggests that the new era of "peace" exposes us to a range of exceedingly complex problems abroad, stemming both from the collapse of Cold War structures and from the dilemmas of democratic transitions in dozens of countries:

• The collapse of totalitarian rule and new aspirations toward democracy will unleash profound forces of both neonationalist and radical religious movements that will destabilize large regions of the world. American values—such as the principle of national self-determination and our insistence on human rights—will serve to exacerbate these forces.

• The inability of many newly liberated societies to manage their problems under fledgling democratic orders will cause many of them to revert to some authoritarian alternative of unknown character. The transition to democracy may in fact prove to be only transient, a halfway house for new unstable orders that will routinely unsettle the world.

• The nationalistic and religious movements and local wars of the new century are unlikely, however, to carry the kind of global ideological character that local wars did in the Cold War period. Both the United States and Russia will be sitting many of them out.

• Problems of ethnicity are rising worldwide. Historically, these problems were kept suppressed in the major authoritarian states. While our own "melting pot" philosophy encouraged us to think that we in America were immune to major dilemmas of ethnicity, those same problems are beginning to affect us as well, as we struggle with evolving concepts of minority rights, ethnic quotas, and ethnic entitlements under democracy.

• Democracy faces severe testing from the new demands of ecology that will require sacrifices from Americans, Chinese, and Brazilians alike. Will the need to meet ecological imperatives be "successful" at the polls in all countries? It is conceivable that the United States might come to believe military action a necessary means of dealing with other countries that threaten the very future of the planet in exercising their own democratic freedom of choice. But our democracy also might opt not to devote the necessary attention to the ecological future of our planet.

This book posits that American society as a whole is drifting toward increasing acceptance of a latter-day, romantic view that is based on the Rousseauean vision of the essential perfectibility of Humanity and the corrupting nature of society.

For several thousand years there was a philosophical vision of Humanity throughout diverse world societies that saw people and not society as the problem. I will argue that the American abandonment of this vision is the source of much of our confusion on issues of freedom, morality, and discipline today.

These are a few of the issues that constitute elements of the Democracy Trap. This is emphatically not to say that democracy is no longer a viable concept. It is a seminal and indispensable concept. The problem is that democracy will now be challenged in ways that we have not previously foreseen, ways that will test our national—and international—will more sorely than the Cold War Century did. (I say "Cold War *Century*" because the struggle began in 1917 with the challenge to the capitalist world posed by the Bolshevik revolution.)

Because the Cold War dominated all of our lifetimes, we have in a sense come to view it as a "normal" state of affairs. Yet I submit that the Cold War was not a normal period of international relations but an exception, one in which the world had come to be unnaturally polarized—and disciplined—by the face-off of two huge ideological powers, America and Russia, both of which went on to develop nuclear capabilities that remain capable of incinerating the planet. But, as wonderful as the tidings of victory of liberal democracy over totalitarianism are, we do not yet seem ready for life in a world in which the stabilizing features of the Cold War are no longer present even though the balance was a balance of *terror*. This book is an attempt to identify the challenges of the next era, most of which will spring from some facet of democracy: problems stemming either from its practice at home or from the implications of our support for it abroad.

History may eventually record that the Cold War had greater impact through its demise than it did in its heyday. For the world had grown accustomed to the long-term presence of ideological strife and the focus that comes with permanent coexistence with an adversary.

But now, the collapse of the Russian collectivist experiment has left both Russia and the Western world ideologically spent. Worse, both countries now seem at ideological loose ends. Nobody knows how Russia will eventually sort itself out without its worldwide, almost century-long mission of Marxism-Leninism. We in America, too, have also been struck with uncertainty about the nature of our future national interests and directions, and to some extent even about our very national purpose. If the long struggle for maintenance of Western democracy has been "won" with the collapse of Soviet totalitarianism, where do we go from here?

It's not just a question of what to do, but where everything is going. Amid all this swirl of change, who can feel any sense of confidence in his ability to foresee the future course of the world? There has probably been no period in the entire twentieth century in which the paradigms of world politics have shifted so profoundly and rapidly as to cast doubt upon most of the active operational precepts by which we normally judge world events. Marchers in Moscow denounce seventy years of "Red Fascism," the Berlin Wall is torn down by cheering East Berliners, Ceausescu in Romania moves from absolute supremacy to a riddled corpse of absolutism within days, the Sandinistas hold free elections in Nicaragua and lose, South Africa releases Nelson Mandela and starts talking about a new order for blacks, the Soviet Union collapses and NATO is soon to be history. Old political verities melt in front of our eyes on the nightly news; our credulity has been stretched to the point where almost any news about developments from anywhere around the world is now believable.

The genesis of this book really stems from my own "crisis" in political understanding, from my own temporary loss of a political and ideological compass as the uncharted dimensions of the Gorbachev era unfolded. Having been a longtime student of Russian language, history, and culture, I had been steeped professionally in the Cold War. As an American Foreign Service officer overseas for nearly two decades, I had encountered hundreds of Soviets and had engaged in tortured sparring matches and Jesuitical arguments about the global Cold War more often than I care to remember. As a senior-level intelligence officer responsible for long-range National Estimates at the Central Intelligence Agency (essentially crystal-balling the future of strategic issues for policymakers at the White House and the State and Defense departments), I had been regularly required to think about global issues and trends as the heart of my daily work for the Director of Central Intelligence. There were always surprises; surprise is endemic to politics. But surprise, by definition, is usually infrequent. By the end of the eighties, surprise in international politics had become no longer surprising.

Gorbachev was the initial source of most of this strategic *bouleversement*. Within two years of the accession of this key figure of the twentieth century, most of my working assumptions about the nature of Soviet power and behavior were shattered. While still at CIA, I struggled to evolve for myself a new set of standards, a new criterion, indeed a new vision, of what the new Russia was all about. As my old and trusty working assumptions about Russia and the Cold War no longer proved reliable, many other assumptions about the way the rest of the world worked under this international Cold War order also began to be infected. This book thus emerges out of my own personal intellectual crisis in trying to maintain some coherent picture of the international order—so professionally necessary for projecting future trends within strategic issues worldwide.

My personal vantage point on American domestic politics was uncommon. My family and I lived in eight very different countries overseas in Europe and Asia over nearly twenty years, with long visits to many more, but periodically returned to the United States for several months or even a year. After living in such diverse places as Germany, Lebanon, Yemen, Afghanistan, and Hong Kong, the culture shock on reentering the United States on each occasion was palpable, rendered more intense for me when I found myself thrust into the passionate debates among old friends back home about the current political coloration of American politics. As much as I valued my friends' intensity of views about the nature of life and the future of political movements in America during the chaotic late sixties and early seventies, I also felt a sense of distance from the problems. Coming from a professional discipline in which daily preoccupations involved analysis of Turkish, Yemeni, or Chinese politics, social trends, and cultures, I found I looked at American issues with slightly different eyes. I was usually less harshly critical and somewhat more sympathetic than my friends who lived in the daily hurly-burly of anti–Vietnam War protests, peace movements, the Grateful Dead, bus-riding to the South, women's lib, and Watergate.

This book therefore reflects the advantages—and disadvantages—of regularly comparing American culture and political life with the environments I was living in abroad. I feel lucky to have experienced the exposure to repeated, intense, sharp, personal, firsthand impressions upon my visits to the United States every two years, when I would steep myself in television and other forms of media to absorb the current *Zeitgeist*, travel around the country, and hear friends and relatives tell me what was on their minds.

This book also reflects a lot of thinking over many decades about what makes many Third World cultures tick. Living for so long in various places around the world, undertaking the study of many foreign languages and cultures, I was acutely conscious of the contrasts among political cultures—an understanding of which was essential to doing accurate political reporting from abroad.

Lastly, as a senior political scientist at the RAND Corporation for the past several years, I have had further opportunity to think and write about broad political and social trends at work in various parts of the world.

This book, then, represents a composite of professional experiences. If it has a particular strength it is in the cross-cultural exposures that have made up my life, and that let me see America in sharp contrast to the political, cultural, and philosophical norms of Russians, Arabs, Persians, Chinese, and others. Indeed, I have been subjected to a regular (and sometimes unsought) barrage of what Indians, Russians, Turks, etc. think is wrong with the United States.

This book is intended neither as prediction nor as prescription. It instead concerns *how to think about* the new era ahead of us—particularly those problems that are related to the spreading character of democracy. While all of us have our political preferences on various issues, the book contains no conscious political agenda. Unlike many popular "futurist" books, *The Democracy Trap* looks beyond the "technological good news" down the road; it tries instead to assess the new forms of classic human political problems that will emerge in the political and social arenas of tomorrow.

In most cases the problems discussed in this book are not

so much "problems" as "dilemmas." While problems may well have answers, dilemmas usually do not. They really involve *trade-offs* between conflicting aspirations. Americans tend to be uncomfortable with trade-offs. We are a society that prides itself on problem-solving, a society imbued with a historical sense that progress is inevitable and that things will go on getting better, despite a few bumps along the way. This book suggests that things do not always go on just getting better—and at least posits that ever harder choices must be made.

While much of the book may be pessimistic in character, I too am a child of democracy. I believe in it, and have some reasonable confidence that it is the best way for both America and the rest of the world to proceed into the next millennium. But it will take a lot of serious thinking about what we are about, where we are going, and what we hope to "do" with our democracy. We may indeed be testing the very viability of democracy in an era of new conditions that no democratic society has yet experienced. To believe that we can put democracy on automatic pilot, and just cruise on into the third millennium, is to fall into the Democracy Trap.

ONE

Perils of the Post–Cold War World: The Argument

The victory bells were pealing. Self-congratulation was in the air. We had passed out of the long night—seventy years long, to be precise—of struggle with communist totalitarianism into the new dawn of victorious liberal democracy. As inhabitants for three generations of an ideological bomb shelter, we rubbed our eyes in the new light, looked around, and seemed to have won.

The end of the struggle came as a surprise to nearly all of us. Of course, we've always had faith that our Western model of democracy and free enterprise was in fact the superior system. It has delivered more to its citizens than any combination of "rational" centralized planning, radical social engineering, "vanguard parties," and "people's democracy" put together. In new, free elections, ungrateful publics have been staying away in droves from communist candidates, from Moscow to Managua. The Berlin Wall—the physical, ideological, and psychological barrier between East and West—has fallen, ideologically shattered by the collapse of its erstwhile architects, and physically breached by the sledgehammers of Eastern Bloc citizens whom it was designed to "protect." No more vivid symbol of change could be found than the images of freed peoples of the East surmounting their wall to hail the new era. And nowhere else have antidemocratic forces proved themselves so bankrupt. "Seventy Years on the Road to Nowhere" and "Workers of the World, Forgive Us!" read the signs now carried through Red Square on May Day. Fall 1989, which marked the fall of communism, brought a fulfillment of aspirations that few in the West over the last forty years ever thought they would see in their lifetimes. And the process was capped by the self-destruction of the Communist Party in its attempted coup against Gorbachev in August 1991.

Of course, the initial *élan* of perestroika in the USSR has collided with the desperate realities of getting the Soviet economy, state, and society to work again. We watched with dismay as the challenge of Russian politics moved Gorbachev to the right, forcing him to reverse course. Indeed, Gorbachev had fulfilled his historic mission—"still shining as a burnt-out comet in the sky," as Gavril Popov, the mayor of Moscow, observed in early 1991—unable to carry his mission forward when it called for the final *coup de grâce* to the old system. There remain deeply disturbing signs of backsliding in many walks of Soviet life—in the role of the military and the KGB. But these are, in the end, dying forces. They may again hobble or even halt the reform process for a while, but they cannot turn the clock back. The collapse of communism as an ideology, as a system, and as half of the old international order is complete, despite spasmodic resurgences in its death throes. The Russia of the future may yet prove nettlesome, but the Cold War is history.

But the ambivalence toward this collapse of the communist world that we encounter in America does not spring from these lingering doubts about the durability of Soviet reform. This ambivalence runs far deeper, reflecting some unconscious unease at what the "fruits of victory" might involve. Indeed, we should be uneasy. Our problems are just starting. If we have just trashed our adversaries of over half a century—in a confrontation often cast in terms of political Good vs. Evil— we now face our own shortcomings, the built-in weaknesses and contradictions of democracy, which may yet prove more daunting than Marxism-Leninism ever was. It may ask more of us and bring us greater anguish and moral uncertainty than did our international mission in defense of Western liberal democracy against the East of the commissars and the gulags.

What Happens When You Get Your Wish?

By almost any judgment, we should all be thrilled that the Cold War has been resolved in favor of democracy—however long it takes Russia to fully join the club. But the sweetness of success, perversely, does not seem to be universally gratifying. Acceptance of victory does not come easily to many. Could it be that, upon reflection, it is not the news that we really wanted after all? For the collapse of the Cold War has kicked the struts out from underneath the strategic, moral, political, and military orientation the United States has had for nearly half a century. As we turn to the gradual shaping of a new order, the stakes are high for a vast spectrum of American life—private, corporate, professional, cultural, political, military, and strategic. Our national conception of the new world order, whatever that is, will determine the allocation and focus of a huge range of national resources—intellectual, economic, technical, and ideological. The very role of the United States in the world is now open for reevaluation across a broader spectrum of debate than we have seen since World War II.

Such ambivalence about the end of the Cold War may be in order. Uncertainty about the nature of our victory may reveal some inchoate, unconscious awareness of deeper problems, some hidden anxieties that we have not yet had time or desire to probe or articulate. The mixed reactions toward what should be a demonstrably positive development reveals much about where our political culture—from right to left—stands today. Indeed, this ambivalence may be a healthy sign, for it suggests at least a partial premonition of the broader systemic crises down the road for our own democratic system. It is these potential democratic crises—or traps—that form the main subject of this book.

Let's take a look at the ideological ambivalence, or sharply differing agendas, of diverse ideological groups toward the end of the Cold War. However narrow much of their thinking may appear to be, each element may give us a little extra insight into our own political values and where our democracy may be going. Their fears and concerns are not without weight and validity. They will help us to formulate what I see as the ultimate challenge to our democratic society: our own internal societal shortcomings so deeply rooted in the special conditions of modern democracy itself.

"The Merchants of Death"

At the most obvious level, there are those whose very livelihood has directly depended on the existence of the Cold War—not exactly your classic "merchants of death," but, yes, the arms manufacturers and defense contractors, the Pentagon, the armed forces, and the Cold War strategists. All are suddenly faced with the prospect that the predictable, nourishing engine of defense requirements may now coast to a halt. To some this may seem like an end to the American way. This is understandable: the American economy may never have depended on war to prosper—however the left-wing pundits would tell it—but there is no doubt that the transition to a new era involves a lot of dislocations for a lot of people. Layoffs worry communities from San Diego to Boston. M1-A1 tank production cannot be converted to off-road Suzuki Samurais overnight. Indeed, the mission of an M-60 stirs souls more deeply; it calls forth greater visions of patriotic action and national self-sacrifice than an off-road foray in the Suzuki for a romp in the dunes. The war we were girded for—so as never to fight it—we must now ungird for, since we will not be fighting it.

The Cold War Scholars

But the challenges cut even deeper, invading the "softer" realm of the intellectual and the academician as well. Scholars and researchers who have spent entire careers examining the deployments in the order of battle at Fulda Gap or the obscure tea leaves of Kremlinology, discerning minute shifts of policy and personnel among the leaden-faced geriatric figures standing on the Kremlin wall in review, have now lost control of their arcane science. For glasnost has dethroned the high priests of Kremlinology. Today the Soviet Union is accessible to everyone; all you have to do is turn on CNN to see what thousands of Russians now tell us in embarrassing detail about themselves and their ordeal, sharing with us yesterday's horrors of Stalin's blood orgies and fears of KGB footsteps in the hall, and the grimy realities of today's failing economy, empty shops, stinking rivers, and ethnic rage. Harvard Soviet specialists are displaced from the op-ed pages of the *New York Times* in favor of unheard-of professors from some city in Siberia, emerging from decades of silence, who can now tell it like it is from Novosibirsk—a great deal more accurately and knowledgeably than can be done from Cambridge. Specialists on Soviet foreign policy all over the globe are losing their calling, for who cares now about Soviet policy toward Africa? French policy toward Africa probably has greater salience.

The Intellectually "Even-Handed"

Then there are those whose sensitivities are such that the very idea of declaring Western victory is aesthetically unpalatable. In one sense, of course, they are right: to win should not be to gloat. However great the vindication of Western liberal democracy, we all have good reason not to want to rub the Soviet Union's nose in it; after all, we are now more interested in the peace than in the victory. But for others, the thought that our less-than-perfect society has triumphantly succeeded against the adversary is intellectually repugnant. Operating out of a misguided sense of moral balance and moral equivalence between the Soviet Union and the West, many had come to talk fashionably about the Eastern Bloc as an "alternative way" of development; both systems, you see, had their own up- and downsides, enabling reasonable men to differ in their preferences.

Long used to this rationale, which cropped up even in the mainstream pages of *Time* in the seventies, we have trouble now accepting that, yes, it was pretty awful what happened in the Soviet Union for nearly fourscore years of the twentieth century. The "socialist alternative" turns out not to have been an alternative after all. But according to this line of once fashionable reasoning, "victory" is an unseemly term because it suggests that we are not bearing enough of the moral blame ourselves for what has been wrong between East and West. These observers are even more discomfited when the Soviet Union itself now reveals grim details that only a few Western researchers like Robert Conquest in his work on Soviet collectivization had talked about. Conquest, who was for decades dubbed "hard right" by many scholars in America for his unfashionable presentation of harsh Soviet realities, has now been vindicated by formal Soviet recognition of what he and others had been saying about the excesses of Stalinism, the failure of the command economy, the deterioration of life, ecological rape, and the deep wellsprings of discontent among dozens of Soviet nationalities that aren't Russian at all.

The Enemies of Moral Ambivalence

Segments of the left itself were able to participate richly in the polarized values of the Cold War drama. The existence of the Bomb actually enabled a half-thought like "Better Red than Dead" to become a respectably arguable prospect. Whole careers were built on apocalyptic visions of "nuclear winter" and other perceptions of the madness of the nuclear arms race. What do those movements, which spoke with such ringing clarity about "five minutes to midnight" on the clock of mankind, now have to talk about? What other issues possess quite such moral clarity as the struggle for Life and Peace in the face of nuclear holocaust?

And it was not just elements in America that participated in this ideological reductionism of values—on the right and the left—stimulated by the Cold War. Indeed, look at the Soviet Union's own desperate struggle for decades to find some genuine, clear-cut values amid the murky Hegelianistic abstracts of Marxist thought; it was in this context that frustrated Soviet artists found to their immense relief that war was the best of all possible creative materials for art under the watchful eye of the Soviet Filmmakers' Union. It is not surprising that virtually the only decent films that ever came out of the Soviet Union officially until the 1980s were war films. Why? No one either in the socialist motherland or abroad would have been able to thrill to the official ideology of Boy Meets Tractor, but there was no doubting that war occupies a central place in the human dilemma. In the polarization of wartime values, life and peace become nearly the sole absolute values. Soviet filmmakers could draw upon these unchallengeable universals to appeal to an international audience. The theme was unexceptionable. But once war is over in a socialist state, peacetime presents a far more complex and shaded range of values that do not lend themselves to ready slogans of the cultural commissar. Zealots of all stripes are now rudely deprived of the absolutes of Cold War conflict.

"Don't Vindicate Reaganism"

The left, in fact, seems to be profoundly ambivalent about the whole new era before us. The idea of Western victory makes leftists uncomfortable because it might lend some support to those who claim that Ronald Reagan was right in his simplistic vision of the world. They do not want to give the right anything to crow about, nor grant the American system the laurels of victory, given their own deep misgivings about the nature of American capitalism, sharp inequities in the distribution of wealth, and the frequent lack of distinction and intellectual elegance in our national leadership. Intellectuals as a class, in fact, tend to be pained by the collapse of socialist systems in general—systems that, however bad, must by nature always grant pride of place to intellectuals, ideologists, and paternalistic planners within the system. As *The Nation* gruffed:

> Many Americans would like to see Gorbachev surrender in the manner of the Japanese on the deck of the U.S.S. *Missouri*, with bows and scrapes and swords delivered to triumphant generals. The Russians would immediately forswear state ownership of the means of industrial production and disarm unilaterally once and for all. Perhaps cold-war-crimes trials for the defeated leaders would be held in a Soviet city, and all party members would be required to enroll in de-Communization classes run by the American Enterprise Institute.[1]

The Fair-Minded

In these circles, too, then, it is not easy to be comfortable with the idea that we have won. And Americans, ever sporting and fair-minded, instinctively like to share some of the blame for what was wrong with the Cold War years. Yet how much blame can we, as earnest and fair-minded Americans, take upon ourselves for seventy years of hostility with the Soviet Union? It is sobering to recognize that virtually *all* the stunning changes that transformed the world in 1989–90 derive from one sole source: the decision of the Soviet Union to change. It speaks eloquently about the root cause of the original problem when the world is revolutionized in a few short years *solely* by the actions of the Kremlin—as all the rest of the world simply sits by in rapt fascination. Of course, the West remained steadfast in its principles through this period, but the changes are strictly "made in Moscow." And as we reflect upon it, arguments about the true significance of the collapse of communism run deeper yet.

The Philosophical Right: The End of History?

At a far more sophisticated level of discourse, we hear from my distinguished former RAND colleague Francis Fukuyama that it may not be just communism that has come to an end, but perhaps history itself. Fukuyama wrote a fascinating essay in 1989 in which he brilliantly expounds the argument of an obscure Russian émigré—with a nod to Hegel—that "history" has in fact come to an end. Fukuyama is arguing in the philosophical sense, of course, that the grand dialectic of ideas— ceaselessly churning out a new antithesis to challenge each reigning thesis, thereby producing a new reigning synthesis— has now emerged with the new synthesis: the decisive victory of liberalism over communism. He argues that the dialectic may now be over: that there are perhaps to be no more serious philosophical challengers claiming to offer a superior form of governance than victorious liberal democracy, now that the last reputable challenger, communism, is physically broken and brain-dead.

But, astonishingly, some of the right are not comfortable

with this ringing reaffirmation of the victory of their cherished values either. Many (including Fukuyama) betray a hint of nostalgia for the Cold War epoch, not out of sheer love of strife, blood, and violence, but for some of the qualities evoked by that struggle: dedication, self-sacrifice, clear moral purpose, national identity and mission—all evoked and highlighted by the existence of the antidemocratic enemy. These thinkers reveal a love for the elegant philosophical simplicity of the Cold War period, when the enemy seemed to be relatively easy to identify, when the nature of the challenge to the West seemed quite clear, and when meeting the challenge seemed a distinguished cause available to engross one's energies. Fukuyama, at the end of his essay, betrays his own bias when he admits that life may now be much more, yes, boring:

> The end of history will be a very sad time. The struggle for recognition, the willingness to risk one's life for a purely abstract goal, the worldwide ideological struggle that called forth daring, courage, imagination, and idealism, will be replaced by economic calculation, the endless solving of technical problems, environmental concerns, and the satisfaction of sophisticated consumer demands. In the post-historical period there will be neither art nor philosophy, just the perpetual caretaking of the museum of human history. I can feel in myself, and see in others around me, a powerful nostalgia for the time when history existed.[2]

For much of the right, questions of human purpose and moral fiber are thus evoked in the struggle of the Cold War; they betray a suspicion that without the great challenge of communist totalitarianism, our nation will have a problem in reaching consensus to gird itself for any other grand issue. Did Saddam Hussein in Baghdad come along just in time? However gratifying it was to exercise American military leadership once again against the tyrant of the Tigris, Saddam was hardly the stuff of sustained grand challenge to Western society that American world leadership may require.

The right senses—but never really articulates—that external ideological challenge creates an internal discipline in our society that is a good in itself, providing focus and organization

that might otherwise be missing in a fat, lazy, sassy, and functioning society. In the absence of discipline, conservatives
espy the seeds of libertarian collapse. They may not be all
wrong.

As sophisticated an insight as the thinking right encapsu-
lates in its concern for moral purpose, it fundamentally
betrays a classic authoritarian characteristic: the "need for an
enemy." While Toynbee may have spoken of the essentiality
of challenge for societies to rise to their full potential, it is
unsettling to think that such challenge must come in the form
of an external enemy, as some of the right seem to seek. This
book readily accepts that democracy and the nation indeed
do require challenge to rise to greatness. But the supreme
challenge comes in the form of the enemy within ourselves,
in the contradictions of our society and democracy, rather
than in the more readily convenient, objectifiable, vanishable
foreign enemy. In short, this war against the external enemy—
which many of the right embrace as a morally redeeming process—in fact has presented us all along with a relatively simplistic challenge. The contradictions and dilemmas of democracy
at home are of a quantitatively and qualitatively new character in their demanding late-twentieth-century forms. They
demand vastly more introspection, wisdom, discrimination,
and patience than ever before if we are to cope with the
frustratingly subtle categories of the struggle on which our
success or failure as a society will rest.

The Return of History

Fukuyama's intriguing propositions notwithstanding, history
is not over in any sense, because history is not linear, even
as the Hegelian dialectic evolves. In fact, if we must assign
geometric similes, it is circular. Fukuyama is fundamentally
wrong. Ideas, including the grand hoary concept of political
collectivism, never die. They simply are recycled, and come
around again and again, in ever newer cultural garb and par-
ticularistic vocabularies to feed on the failures of democratic
and individualistic government. Leninist communism may be
dead, but collectivism in some form will surely be back again
with us, challenging our failures, sooner than we think—

maybe not as an ideology controlling half the world in an armed camp, but nonetheless waiting in the wings to redress our fundamental democratic failings. It is the permanent counterweight to libertarianism, the indispensable foil against which our own concepts of democracy are measured, the collectivist Yin to the libertarian Yang. No victory is permanent. History won't go away.

The Peace Dividend, or, Did the Berlin Wall Ever Really Exist?

But forget philosophy. A grand debate has broken out about what the momentous events at the Berlin Wall truly mean for us in a practical sense. Many Americans see unadulterated good news in this epochal turning point in history, especially as it translates directly into money in the bank, though not in any crass terms of self-gain—in fact, much was lost in the collapse of defense industry shares. For them, the end of the Cold War may resemble the end of a dark rainbow, where lies the Great Peace Dividend, the immense financial *deus* out of the industrial-military *machina*, enabling us to apply the enormous resources once squandered on arms to the needs of the people and the correction of all that afflicts America. Just like those who espouse cruder and more naive forms of social materialism, those who wish to cash in the peace dividend cling to the dangerously false hope that our problems can be alleviated by the application of yet more massive financial resources. In this sense, the peace dividend is the cruelest hoax of all, for it marvelously ignores the internal and systemic nature of our problems while proffering the cheapest of all solutions: money.

Such peace dividend as we ever do get will, of course, be extremely welcome. We have squandered billions on arms. Much of it was necessary in an age of a virile communist military challenge, but much of it, too, was wasted. The campaign to destroy Saddam Hussein cost—possibly unnecessarily—tens of billions more, delaying further the hoped-for dividend check. Nonetheless, in their eagerness to address the resource problem, and in the rush to redistribute wealth, a smaller handful of nonthinkers are already developing rapid retroactive ideological amnesia: always opposed to the commitment to major defense expenditures over the decades, some are now suggesting that Gorbachev's stunning turnaround of the Soviet behemoth shows that the Soviet Union was really just a cornered, frightened, hissing pussycat all along; that we had allowed ourselves to slip into financial impoverishment from a Cold War that need never have been—and perhaps never was.

One need not even dignify this perception with much comment. If the 1930s collectivization process, or the Polish officers' mass graves in Katyn Forest, or the Russian tanks in Budapest in 1956, or the rolls of concertina wire against the background of grim Soviet watchtowers on the Czech border, or the invasion of Afghanistan, or the largest standing army in the world, or the biggest defense budget in the world, or the putrid Volga waterway, or the unispeak Soviet media for nearly a century—if none of this can restore memory of the heyday of communism to these impoverished ideologists, then nothing will avail. Yes, Virginia, there was a communism. But it's going to go on getting harder to convince newer generations that such an ugly challenge could ever really have existed.

Thus do the right and left react to the monumental events of our time. It is easy to pillory some of these views—and some deserve pillorying. But in another sense, nearly all of these people are right. In groping in the philosophical dark at the predawn of a new era, we are all grasping at different parts of the peace elephant, each of us perceiving radically different features of the phenomenon. A new era has indeed emerged, huge segments of the old challenges are gone, and by all rights we should have huge new dollops of mental, physical, financial, and psychological resources at our disposal to lavish upon the creation of a new domestic and world order.

The Old Challenges of the Cold War

Not only was there a communism, but one of its nastiest features is what it did to distort our own agenda. Indeed, one of the great "virtues" of the Cold War was that it set before us a relatively finite challenge. The goal was to contain communism—an affliction both of postdemocratic societies in the West and of developing societies in the Third World. Our first response was that the challenge of communism could be dealt with primarily through military means. Of course, an idea can never be stifled by military force. But it wasn't only the idea but the military challenge of communism as well that was quite real, was implicit in Marxism-Leninism. All is moral when it serves the interests of the revolution and the inexorable advance of history. War, conquest, coups d'état, class slaughter, mass executions, purges, and sedition—all serve to hasten the millennium, and time is on the side of the revolution.

Communism broke out of its confinement after World War II to extend to all of Eastern Europe and North Korea, China, and much of Indochina in the few years after 1945. Confronted with this challenge—in which the Soviets amassed the greatest land army capabilities in the world in order to help history along—the West was thus justified in turning to the military instrument as one of its tools in the effort to contain the totalitarian clarion call of communism. We proclaimed that there was to be no more communism delivered at sword point by a Red Army and its allies.

The Distortion of American Priorities
  ## Overseas

Whatever value the Cold War had in helping keep the West's ideological socks up in Europe and at home, it was exceptionally damaging to American ability to form a coherent policy toward reform and change in the Third World. Every single American president clearly recognized that there was a dilemma: that we could not afford to be guilty of "mindless anticommunism," as Carter said, or to ignore the fact that Third World peoples had many legitimate aspirations that deserved American support rather than suspicion. But in the end, American policies were heavily informed by the application of the instant "Soviet-interest touchstone"—a device that enabled the user to immediately determine the geopolitical importance to the United States of a Third World country by establishing the degree of the Soviet presence and challenge to Western interests there. By such means were the Afghanistans, Nicaraguas, and Angolas of the world vaulted to front and center on the American foreign policy agenda.

While it is easy to write in a belittling fashion of these ideological dilemmas, they were nonetheless real—and far from simple-minded. Where did one draw the line between "mindless" anticommunism and "mindful" anticommunism? Genuine efforts at real reform by fledgling democracies were at peril from Leninist parties to whom the slogan "the worse, the better" was the tactic of choice: indeed, for such parties, the greater the mindless violence and mayhem that could be wreaked in these societies, the greater the likelihood of a harsh right-wing crackdown, native-style. Any sharp right-wing reaction would fatally compromise the democratic character of the nascent democratic regime, leading many in the given country, and in the United States as well, to reject the legitimacy of the struggling democratic regime in power. America has faced these problems in Vietnam, El Salvador, Nicaragua, Chile, the Philippines, and elsewhere. This dilemma for the United States was never resolved. Indeed, it continued unabated, right down to the first tremors in Eastern Europe under Gorbachev.

The Warping of Domestic Priorities

The Cold War not only served to distort our approach to the entire Third World, but also warped our priorities. Confronted with the magnitude of the communist challenge, we shortchanged a whole host of other international and domestic questions—the dilemmas of Third World development, democratic reform, debt, equitable and stable commodity prices, fair trade, and ethnic self-determination—all in the certainty that those issues, at least to some extent, had to take a backseat to what we were trying to accomplish globally for the preservation of the Western democracies and the noncommunist Third World.

Our vision of ourselves was further distorted by the fact that we were able to feel good about our own society and system, for it demonstrably delivered. It delivered not by some abstract measure but by direct comparison with the ideological competition in the Eastern Bloc. Even when not all Americans—especially intellectuals—were convinced of the magnitude of the failure of Soviet communism (more delicately referred to as "socialism"—never mind what the European democratic socialists felt about that appellation), we knew that the differences were great. It is only now, when the corpse of communism's failure worldwide lies naked on the political marketplace, that we have proof positive of what the Western system—democracy and free enterprise—can accomplish relative to all competition. A Russian political theoretician recently acknowledged that capitalism tends to produce both very rich countries and very poor countries; but under communism, he said, all countries are poor.

Living Without an Enemy

But now communism has a kind of final revenge upon us from its grave, for the collapse of the Soviet Union has deprived us of a great deal more than we realize. Georgi Arbatov, former head of Moscow's Institute of the U.S.A. and Canada, said in the late 1980s, "We are going to do a terrible thing to you, we are going to deprive you of your enemy." While Arbatov understood what the Cold War meant in terms of the maintenance of the whole Cold War structure, he certainly did not understand the grander dimensions of the democratic dilemma implicit in his statement. Indeed, died-in-the-wool anticommunists may now find that this final act by Moscow will have inadvertently served to cast more confusion onto the American scene than any piece of mayhem from Lenin's amoral political calculations, his Red Army, or his KGB. Even latter-day backsliding by these instruments of the dying Soviet order are not of an order to reverse the grand trend, however much some on the hard right might wish to restore the enemy.

For with the collapse of the communist model, we no longer possess a comfortable target against which to measure ourselves and our own performance. Compared to the grim bastions of the Kremlin, the gray austerities of Moscow, the Siberian mud wastes, the Appalachia-like dilapidation of the Russian village, the horrors of Lubyanka prison, the regular spate of killings in the ethnic republics, and the fear-inspiring, bristling Soviet arsenals of missilery rolling through a May Day Red Square—compared to all this, the United States looks awfully good. We will miss the competition, for it served us well.

The disappearance of the classic communist model now leaves us with no ready elements of comparison by which to reassure ourselves of the strengths of our own system. The measure of the quality of American life—and its foreign policy—must now be found elsewhere. We must now pit our accomplishments against our own expectations of what we want from ourselves and our own society. To be sure, we can still compare our life and society with that of other developed or less-developed nations, but the comparison becomes less comforting all the time. Americans are no longer able to feel as good about themselves as before, and the criteria are shifting fast.

I do not mean to belittle the American accomplishment. It is remarkable, by almost any of a vast range of indicators. Indeed, the Cold War seems now to have played to our strengths. Or perhaps the Cold War brought out certain strengths in us. Our military strength and technology were formidable, and our ability to project force overseas to support allies was critical to their security and the deterrence of radical adventurism. Our economy not only remained robust in spite of—some would say with the help of—the defense industry; it was an economy that served as the engine to drive the economies of most of the rest of the free-market world. The overall American standard of living was astonishing. Technology blossomed. The world sought to emulate America in myriad ways. Furthermore, major progress was made at home in the area of human rights and racial and gender equality. Our sense of idealism helped to rally others in what was not just a military confrontation with the USSR, but also a struggle about values. But now we are left with the hard part.

The New Challenge

Alas, history is not over, not even in the Hegelian or philosophical sense. Nor does the Cold War resemble a World Series—we all get to go home when it's over. Rather, we are out of one phase of history and into another. Worse, inherent in all this good news is a trap, a trap emerging from the very essence of the democracy that has been so critically important to this nation and to the West. For now, for the first time in perhaps a century, we are not only free to turn our attention to new issues, we are compelled to do so. We are facing social decay at home, even while we tout our system abroad as the wave of the future. We have no further excuse to tarry from ministering to massive problems—some classic, some new— that surround, even overwhelm us.

Of course, problems of democracy are not new to the world. Athenians discussed them in the *agora*. Many of these dilemmas are discussed in some of the classic dissections of democracy, including Alexis de Tocqueville's perceptive *Democracy in America*, written in 1835. Indeed, American politics over the past several decades have had to cope with many challenges to the democratic system, and to ourselves. How did we treat such challenges then? And what is so different now? Why may the challenges be greater at this phase? Indeed, what are some of the hidden traps of democracy that we were able to overlook before?

Our democracy in some senses is entering political and social terra incognita. Many of these problems are the products of a mature postindustrial society and its massive freedoms of option, never before encountered in the earlier eras of American democracy and social development—not even during the American cultural revolution of the 1960s and 1970s. Hence the nostalgia for the past: we may not like what we are now confronted with. We may have liked better the challenges that we had before. Worst of all, we seem to have lost all concept of the philosophical bases of democracy and the complex trade-offs of values that democracy entails. We tend to view its freedoms as a straight-line path—the farther you can get on it, the better. Herein lies the Democracy Trap.

We confront the tough dilemma of making democracy—and the free-enterprise system that it so closely linked with it—

work better. And work better in an era in which demands and problems—many arising out of democracy itself—are growing: inequities of race and gender, the deterioration of the family, a trend toward the use of mechanical quotas as a measure of social justice, a sclerotic Congress that fears any new initiatives that will cost at the ballot box, the declining ecosphere, increasing disparity in the equal distribution of material goods and services, declining productivity, corporate greed, the NIMBY Factor (Not in My Back Yard), the dilemma of proper limits to individual freedoms, the problem of the proper place for religion in society, the existence of a seemingly intractable permanent underclass, rampant individualism and growing individual selfishness toward broader social problems, burgeoning population and the concomitant inability to contrive effective social controls, lagging education, increasing confusion over values and their proper sources in a secular society, a culture of self-gratification formally celebrated by Madison Avenue, out-of-control drug usage, rampant sexual freedoms, AIDS—and hosts of other issues that stem essentially from the maturation of society in the democratic post-industrial age. Worst of all, we are less certain about the *purpose* to which all our social instruments and mechanisms should be put. The shadow of Japan across our nation insistently raises the specter of American failure as much as it does Japanese success. Where is the country going? Is the mechanism that has produced such immense accomplishments and innovations in past decades and centuries finally breaking down?

For the new issues are vastly less clear-cut, involving ever more complicated political, social, and economic—indeed, moral—trade-offs. In our seemingly losing struggle to call forth sufficient national will, national vision, and sense of values to meet the challenge, we seem to be experiencing great confusion about national purpose. Yet, is it the business of democratic government to define a "national purpose," except in times of great national peril? Should that be the business of government—or rather just to provide the conditions whereby everyone can do his or her own thing? Have Americans thrown away the compass with the Cold War Confrontation Kit?

In the chapters ahead we will take a closer look at a number of these ills that seem to spring from the very character of democracy in rapidly evolving, postindustrial America. We will also examine some of the key sources of crisis abroad in the coming decades, many of which are profoundly related to the challenges and pitfalls of democracy. The purpose of this book is not simply to catalog ills, however, for most of them are well known to all of us. Nor is this book simply a plea to return to certain established values. An understanding of these ills requires recognition that in most cases we are not talking about pursuit of an *absolute* value—recognition that instead our society is made up of *conflicting* absolute values that invariably entail painful balancing acts: freedom vs. discipline, the individual vs. society, justice vs. equality, freedom vs. social values.

Hooked on Linear Thinking

It would seem to be a feature of the positivistic culture of the West that we think in terms of absolutes, of linear progression toward Progress and the Good. Life moves inexorably forward. It is one of the shortcomings of Western society that we have never developed a strong cultural sense of complementary virtues, of the Yin and Yang of existence so meaningful to Asian society. Qualities cannot be absolute, but are in tension with other values, or complementary to other values. Relentless pursuit of one value invariably leads to the loss of another. This is sometimes—unsatisfyingly—referred to as the "dialectic" in the West, but is hardly part of our popular consciousness. And even the dialectic suggests forward motion rather than eternal tension and balance. The concept of "trade-off" comes closer. We need to be more conscious of the Yin and Yang, the concept of complementarity and balance of virtues that seems somehow alien to our American culture. We ignore the concept at our peril. Our school textbooks have never heard of the idea.

If the nature of these trade-offs in values is not better understood, publicly recognized, and regularly articulated, the nation is likely to devolve in the direction of greater frustration and rage as each man's absolute is seen as a Holy Grail that deserves defense at all costs—against another man's Grail, or society's Grail. How do we accommodate a proliferation of Grails? By just downgrading all Grails to simple administrative rights adjudicated by hungry lawyers?

Indeed, it is precisely because our society is so advanced that the problems become more intractable. Simpler societies have more obvious needs; the wise statesman can readily ascertain the greatest good for the greatest number. As societies grow more complex, however—as Gorbachev is learning—it gets harder to speak of "the good of society" as some *kollektiv*; interests split like amoebae, ever more discrete and specialized, making it harder to meet anybody's needs without ignoring, or harming, the needs of others. And popular government is ever less inclined to risk the retaliation of the ballot box by making the hard call on the tough issues. Democracy is seemingly flagging in the face of increasingly exacting calls for decisions. Public debate shies from talk of the hard issues. One wonders now whether indeed the system can summon up the decisive leadership to carry us successfully into an ever more complex era. Or whether there is even any consensus about what that leadership should be. And Richard Reeves has suggested that maybe Americans do not want leadership at all, but prefer to keep presidents on a tight leash, with weekly polls and periodic referenda determining the course of our national agenda.

Gored by the Sacred Cow of Individualism?

As our society plumbs new frontiers, the role of the individual becomes more problematic. It is harder to be an individual under the pressures of mass culture and the restrictions that the state and society impose upon the individual. On the other hand, the legal demands of the individual against society in our modern court proceedings have strongly favored the individual to an extent that has weakened the structure of society. To champion the "rights of society" over those of the individual is distasteful to all of us, precisely because it smacks of collectivism, "The People," or Hitler's *Das Volk*.

At the same time, the pluralistic nature of society makes it harder to reach consensus on much of anything, leading directly to a weakening of social cohesion. The values of the pioneer days, the "village town meeting," and the community orientation of the expanding West are a thing of the past. Americans move, communities splinter. Americans divorce, families splinter. Life in New York City would seem to be totally fractured, with almost no sense of personal responsibility or community cohesion left. *Suave qui peut.* Every man for himself. How does democracy fare under such circumstances?

Deriving Secular Values

The ultimate challenge to democracy, of course, lies in our greater freedom of choice and the determination of our values. American values have moved decisively away from the "God-given" values that spring from the moral codes of the world's great religions such as Christianity, Judaism, Islam, and Hinduism. Historically, "God-given" implies fundamentally nonnegotiable value systems that are taken as a given, and do not need to be explained or justified. Today such value systems have largely given way to the courts, which are now our primary arbiters of morality and ethics. Indeed, values and ethics have become highly negotiable and situation-oriented. Under such circumstances, American society has naturally been probing the limits of the licit, exploring the final extremes of public morality—and it is increasingly difficult to determine anymore what is morally "wrong." Indeed, the modern field of psychology has weighed in; the term "wrong" is becoming quaint and archaic, to be expunged from any functioning place in therapy.

The dilemma does not go unnoticed. A *Los Angeles Times* poll at the end of 1990 showed 71 percent of Americans as dissatisfied with moral values in American society.[3] Nearly every American possesses a disquieting sense of ethical decline in America, reflecting perception of social decay in broad areas, malfeasance in the federal government and on Wall Street, cheating in the schools, on taxes, and in welfare, increase in theft everywhere at all levels of society, and lack of regard for property and stewardship of the land and our resources. That the success of capitalism derives from its engine of greed might suggest that this is the source of the problem—were not every one of these problems even worse in the authoritarian socialist societies now in a state of collapse.

And America is the pioneer in probing these new horizons, for better and for worse. The paths traversed by America will to a large extent be the paths that other nations will eventually and ineluctably follow themselves as their societies reach similar stages of "advancement"—eventually entering the same syndrome of democratic dilemma we now face in America. For America did not invent these new characteristics of postindustrial modern democracy, but simply *discovered* them first as a natural outgrowth of economic and social development under democracy, industrialization, and postindustrialization.

Islamic fundamentalism comes as a reaction to these realities. Its burgeoning power is a profound philosophical and ethical retort to the West. Islamic fundamentalism may be no less perceptive in its diagnosis of the faults of the West than Marx was—although certainly no better in supplying any answers. Islam takes a conservative view of people's ability to handle their freedoms. So does Christianity. So does Confucianism, for that matter. In fact, can we handle our expanding individual freedoms, or will they lead inexorably to the unraveling of the social fabric? Where do the individual and national interests diverge?

All these problems are exacerbated by an explosive quality of ethnic unrest and racial anger. The great melting pot experiment of America is under threat, particularly as it seems to melt less and less of everything except tempers. As we move toward more demands from aggrieved and deprived minorities for "rights"—rights that we are not sure were ever part of the Constitution in the first place—anger builds on all sides. If we are in doubt about the legitimacy of the "rights" of minorities, we can be in no doubt about the actuality of their plights. American concepts of ethnicity differ from the experience and principles of ethnicity in other multiethnic, multisectarian, and nondemocratic societies such as the Soviet Union and Lebanon: are we perhaps unwittingly moving in that direction?

Ethnicity abroad will manifest increasing shrillness in the new environment of post–Cold War democratic expectations and the ambiguous blessings of human rights. These trends are inexorably leading in the direction of a new century of ethnic and religious wars, in which the United States will find itself caught in an agonizing choice between stability and freedom. Indeed, the final chapter of this book explores the degree to which democracy may be the American ideology, and suggests that America might do well by adopting a foreign policy that grants a "pro-democracy ideology" a more significant role.

The latest entry onto the ideological scene in the late twentieth century is ecology—the topic of a key chapter. The "ideology" of ecology is already fanning out into a huge range of subideologies that tangle directly with democracy: eco-capitalism, eco-fascism, eco-libertarianism, eco-feminism, eco-authoritarianism, eco-socialism, and even eco-terrorism. When the state was able to justify harsh or peremptory actions against opponents in the name of freedom during the Cold War, how much greater harshness of action will be justified by the need to save the planet? Will American B-52s bomb Brazil to save the rain forests and to heal the ozone layer?

Lastly, this book will take issue with the Rousseauist vision of the inherent goodness of Humanity. This latter-day philosophical heresy, which flies in the face of most of the "wisdom" of nearly all cultures over the course of human existence, establishes the groundwork for a vague acceptance of the perfectibility of Life and Humanity. The shallowness of this view is leading to deep frustrations in the American body politic as we view the seeming intractability of a wealth of social problems, and to an increasing obsession with the unique "stresses" of modern life, which, in terms of material well-being, are less than ever before in history. Only a broader and deeper view of Humanity and its "tragic destiny"—diagnosed so repeatedly by great writers of the past such as Dostoyevsky—will begin to illuminate our understanding of our current social problems and dilemmas. It is the very tension of the material accomplishments of modern society, versus the moral, psychological, and spiritual failures we increasingly sense, that has contributed in part to a worldwide resurgence of religious expression and practice. What are these religious phenomena? Opiates? Solace? Or insight and guidance?

This book will explore these and other challenges to democracy, both at home and abroad. Indeed, not only do they represent challenges to democracy, but they often constitute dilemmas that spring *from* the very extension of democracy itself. The conservatives may have been right: we may come to look back with nostalgia upon the Cold War era.

Yet it is morally and intellectually outrageous to suggest that such an era, characterized by balance of terror, was preferable to one in which human beings are freed of the nuclear menace and granted options to explore their own aspirations. It is indefensible to seek to have an enemy simply for the moral backbone that an enemy provides. This book is about that dilemma and paradox.

The diagnoses of this book will be of little cheer to those who believe that the closing of the post–Cold War era automatically opens a positive new age. As a society we have never been less well equipped to engage these problems, for their solution will lie in categories of thinking partially foreign to those of contemporary America. There are no liberal or conservative panaceas at hand to which we can turn; neither right nor left in America, nor the church, has come to terms with the broader nature of the moral and ethical problems before us—a set of problems that basically spring from the classical dilemma of the limits of freedom, the role of the state and the alienation of the individual, and the place of morals in society.

While the dilemmas are classical, these modern metamorphoses are quantitatively and qualitatively new. We delight in passionate debate over the minutiae of symptoms and palliatives. As a society we are still talking about having it all. It is politically "risky" to talk about root causes. We can afford to offend no one in hard talk about fundamental issues. Public discourse studiously ignores the nature of the painful trade-offs before us.

Can we go on this way? We may yet discover that we have reached limitations of democratic form and expression, producing crises that will close out the golden age of democracy through a public call for some more disciplined or authoritarian approach that deals directly and abruptly with the social demand for solutions. The dialectic of history is not over. How do we know that liberal democracy must eventually emerge on top when it may be signally failing to meet a growing social crisis in America? If the problems are tough now, the dilemmas will get even tougher as we move into the next millennium. Nothing less than explicit recognition of these dilemmas and a frank discussion of choices will suffice. Otherwise we fall into the Democracy Trap.

NOTES

1. "Beyond Summitry," *The Nation*, June 18, 1990.
2. Francis Fukuyama, "The End of History?" *National Interest*, Summer 1989, p. 18.
3. *Los Angeles Times* poll, January 1, 1990.

TWO

Civics Lessons from the Ashes
of Communism

Lessons from Moscow

Whether we realize it or not, we are privileged to be witnesses
to the tumultuous and revolutionary events in Eastern Europe
and the Soviet Union of 1989–91. While every generation is
given to viewing its own age as unique, the transition in the
Soviet Union and Eastern Europe is truly unprecedented in
history: never before has the world experienced the internal
collapse of totalitarianism—and virtually overnight at that.
(Many weighty pundits of the right, including Jeane Kirkpat-
rick, said it could not happen.) These events have added
extraordinary new pages to the annals of political science.
Ironically, we have learned more about the nature of totalitarianism from its collapse than we have from its existence; political scientists will feed off these events for decades to come.

The meltdown of the communist world offers us a short,
living refresher course in civics and the origins of democracy.
We would be well advised to absorb the lessons of this course,
for they remind us where our own political system has come
from—remind us of processes that we, in our political ennui,
have largely forgotten. In the short space of less than five
years, Gorbachev's Russia has basically telescoped major features of the history of democratic evolution, compressing cen-

turies of political experience into digestible chunks that even we can painlessly absorb on our TV screens, without ever having to go to the barricades ourselves. It is a textbook model of the organic emergence of democracy virtually from scratch, since seventy years of totalitarianism had virtually destroyed the everyday political processes that we take for granted in most of the rest of the world.

Russia is reinventing the democratic wheel. Typically, the Russians do not have it right yet, and there is a lot of slippage, occasional distressing backsliding, and a whole lot of turmoil ahead of them. But what has already happened is vastly more important than what has not yet happened. Gorbachev and Boris Yeltsin helped revitalize our own Western understanding of what the dynamics of democracy are, and, indeed, of why we do what we do. An emergent democracy is a joyful, moving, sobering, and refreshing spectacle for a Western world that has sometimes grown weary or even cynical about the negative features that have crept into our own practice of democracy. It is sad that Gorbachev is no longer the man who can carry the reforms through to fruition. But the spirit of what he started is carried on by a now vast cadre of reformers, headed by Yeltsin, who clearly understand the task at hand, thanks to the revolution begun by the now spent Gorbachev.

As we view this spectacle, we must consider whether we too can draw upon the excitement of these moments in order to deal once again with the grand issues that face our own mature, if not graying, democracy. If the new leaders emerging in the world catch the imagination of our public, why cannot our leaders too seize this historic moment to talk about the core issues that affect our democracy as well? Will we let this fulfilling moment of history pass—remaining mere silent witnesses to the power of an idea at work far away from our shores? Will it be wasted on us as we sit passively at home? Or will it renew our own determination too, to think in terms of what democracy is supposed to mean in our own culture and democracy in the post–Cold War era?

Russia and the East European states have really done little more than set forth on the new democratic odyssey. Democracy obviously consists of more than the mere establishment of institutions, as praiseworthy as such establishment is; it is continuity through periods of internal duress that gives democracy its meaning and importance. Along with the Russians, we marvel over the course of recent events, but are left in no doubt that the process of democratization in the largest country in the world is hardly over. Whatever the excitements and blessings of early democracy for Russia are, that country is not out of the woods, and the economic chaos still to be borne by most citizens promises to be traumatic. Indeed, will democracy triumph in Russia in the end? Or will it be overwhelmed by staggering problems on all sides? Is democracy the right medicine? It would be very dismaying to conclude that our democratic system is no more than an American home brew that has only a limited export market.

The World's Debt to Russia

Russians now regularly speak of their historical sufferings as a result of the seventy-year communist experiment: the mass deaths, the gulag systems, the blood, the deprivations, the lies, the distortion of human relations, the shattering of the economy, and the grimness of daily life. Could anyone have seen it coming? Numerous Russian writers of the nineteenth century such as Dostoyevsky and Herzen often depicted with uncanny prescience a tragic view of Russia's role in history, a role filled with suffering. For Dostoyevsky there were even strong parallels between Russia's travails and Christ's suffering upon the cross in order to redeem Humanity.

While we may not share this messianic vision of the Russian mission in history, has Russia or the rest of the world learned anything from the Russian experience? Has this dreadful human tragedy of prolonged dimensions simply been an aberration in human political experience, or have any lessons been learned from it? One approaches the issue of "the lessons of history" with extreme trepidation, for human beings have strong tendencies both to forget history they have never lived through and to never forget history, blinding themselves to the possibilities of change and future opportunity.

Is it possible that Russia's near-century on the ideological cross has meaning and value for the world? Was Russia's own suffering in vain? Perhaps the world was in fact predestined to explore the implications of Marxism with Leninist teeth, of radical socialism and social experimentation devoid of any state values higher than "the revolution." Perhaps the political rationale of the radical left had to be explored before it could be laid to rest. Perhaps it had to plumb the ultimate limits of political horror, and failure, before it was clear to the majority of the world that this is a path never to be followed again.

Unfortunately, as we noted earlier, ideas are rarely permanently vanquished, regardless of their flaws; the chances are good that the concept of collectivism in some form will revisit the world soon, in response to failings of other systems. We can only hope that this particularly virulent, bloody, Russian form will not readily be forgotten. If some memories of the Russian experiment persist in the world's mind, then perhaps Russian suffering will not have been entirely in vain.

Paralysis: The Totalitarian Legacy

A look at the chain of events whereby democracy has reemerged in Russia reinforces for us the strongly pragmatic rationale behind our own commitment to a democratic order.

To begin with, democracy is not chosen by societies for the beauties of its ideals. Democracy must meet real gut needs of significant segments of the public. Democracy is usually taken, rarely given. In the Soviet Union there were real, pressing, intractable political problems born of totalitarianism that needed to be overcome. Indeed, "totalitarianism" is a word often misused and misunderstood. Totalitarianism never meant that the state was able to control the totality of a person's existence. Even George Orwell's *1984* state did not quite manage that. But the unique characteristic of the Soviet system was the state's total preemption of every facet of civil society. No entity had formal existence outside of what the state created and monitored.

While many in the West had come to take this depressing totalitarian reality as an almost permanent fact of life, few realized how utterly corrosive the totalitarian structure had become to the functioning of Soviet society itself. Seven decades of Marxist-Leninist communism utterly froze the evolution of society in most respects. To be sure, education increased apace, and urbanization brought massive changes to the character of Soviet society, even under Stalin. But society had come to lose nearly all ability to chart the course of its own evolution. The most shocking single feature of the new Gorbachev era of glasnost and perestroika has been the way Russians now seem to struggle in political and economic helplessness, uncertain how to function now the fetters are lifted, like a long-caged bird that has lost the secret of flight.

Among the dismaying powers of communism had been its ability to inflict the entire society with collective amnesia about how free societies might operate under freedom of choice. It is astonishing that communism, ineffective in so many other respects, had such success in rooting out nearly all vestiges of civic-mindedness among such a gifted people as the Russians.

Reinventing the Democratic Wheel

We in the West had inevitably come to take a great deal of our own democratic system for granted. The unusual character of our Constitution, the meaning of political parties, and the role played by civil institutions had largely become second nature, no longer viewed as "anything special" in the eyes of most citizens. Thus watching Soviet politics crawl toward its first few steps in parliamentary and civil life provided us with an enriching lesson in civics, serving to highlight the strengths of our own society and political system.

Indeed, what the Soviets had come to discover by the end of 1990 is that democracy is not just simply a beautiful idea, or even a means to signal reconciliation with the West by accepting its political system. Before our very eyes the Russians are writing a pocket version of the history of democratic institutions. They are groping their way to the gradual revelation that democracy is pragmatically a necessity if the Russian state is to function successfully in the modern era.

Ironically, the "secrets" of the American Constitution were one thing the KGB couldn't steal; there is something about the process of "getting there" over several hundred years that provides a value added that can't quite be bought. The Russians must learn the Constitution and the Bill of Rights step by step, by themselves. They were not, of course, starting from square one: Russian intellectual history of the nineteenth century had absorbed vast amounts of Western democratic theory, and Russians were beginning tentatively to apply such principles after their 1905 parliamentary revolution, until the process was so decisively broken off by Lenin and buried for nearly a century.

First Things First: Truth—Not Pravda

Gorbachev's remarkable adoption of glasnost or "openness" was the first sign of recognition that the rational state must be grounded in truth rather than in the ideological fantasies of seven decades. In Gorbachev's eyes, liberalization of speech and public expression was the first chosen instrument to liberate the state from the morass of state-created lies and distortions and the self-serving inventions of a bloated "what-me-worry?" bureaucracy, and to reverse the impoverishment and desiccation of individual thought that deprived the state of critically needed creative input.

While Stalin was able to build the Leviathan state (admiringly referred to in public as "Soviet power") on the basis of the Big Lie and total suppression of information, this edifice was constructed only at massive cost—social, economic, human, and psychic. As the Soviet Union moved toward the age of information, it was clear that a society in which the photocopy machine was literally viewed as subversive and the computer as a dangerous antistate instrument, the Soviet future had simply become untenable. If information had truly become the basis of national power in the world in the dawning computer era, then the Russian state had no option but to give up its monopoly of information. (State-controlled computerization, such as it was, had provided triumphant vindication of the classic computer verity: "garbage in, garbage out." The State Planning Commission, already deserving of a Heritage Foundation prize for having rendered the Soviet economy unworkable, was about to stoke its massive new computer power with whole archives of false statistics that could only hasten the exponentially burgeoning implosion of the state system.)

In short, an eternally cherished virtue, the truth—not its Russian version, *Pravda*—turns out to have been more than just an abstract political virtue. The Marxist-Leninist state itself had been brought down by the very absence of this virtue.

The Ambivalent Blessings of Congress

We in America love to hate our Congress. Gorbachev and his colleagues may be following suit. But in the evolution of the Soviet parliament, Russian leadership came to realize yet other truths. If the state wants to keep its policies effective and on course, then regular criticism of existing policies will provide the best check on ministers and their bureaucracies. The new Soviet leadership suddenly grasped the brilliant idea that the ministries must be answerable to someone else outside the bureaucracy or else they would feel little pressure to perform.

Individual members of parliament speaking out independently—once a total no-no—now came to be seen as desirable as well. Such expressions were perceived to be useful and constructive pressures on the bureaucracy. But of course there should be no parliamentary factions, because Lenin had long established that factions lead to divisions of the monolithic ruling party that would vitiate its vanguard role in the state. Yet within a few months we then discover in the Soviet press that whereas one parliamentary deputy can have a lot of good ideas, it isn't enough, because no single individual can come up with comprehensive alternative programs all by himself. How to handle this? Well, maybe factions in a parliament do have some benefit after all.

And within months of this revelation we learn that the concept of factions inevitably leads one more short step toward acceptance of the idea that political parties actually possess systematic strength beyond that of individual factional programs. Next, the existence of nascent parties serves to draw together not only like-minded members of parliament, but also segments of the public at large, serving to express public needs and aspirations. Suddenly the communists no longer had any justification for the "leading role" of the party in society; its "Lenin-given" mandate to monopolize the governing process was running out. The virtues of the legislature—often readily overlooked in the tediousness of congressional and parliamentary logrolling—is once again evident even to doubting Westerners.

Here too, we can watch the subversive character of free speech and organization at work. The party conservatives were right: once you open the door a crack, a floodwave rushes in, swamping party control and the entire edifice of the authoritarian state. Democracy takes on the power of a truly cleansing agent, sweeping away all vestiges of the "old thinking."

The subversive, revolutionary character of democracy has of course always posed a threat to authoritarian power. Indeed, those in America with slightly more ideological sympathy for at least the egalitarian goals of the Soviet state—certainly not the methods—often suggested that one reason the Soviet Union often threatened the West militarily was that Moscow itself felt threatened by the West. Those who would cast the arms race into a chicken-and-the-egg mold nonetheless had lost sight of the fact that it was Marxism-Leninism that challenged the future of the West, declaring the West doomed to ultimate communist revolution.

These liberals were right in one sense: the West did threaten the Soviet state. But it was an ideological threat, threatening precisely through its abiding external presence as functioning democracy. Soviet conservatives were absolutely right too: the West stood as a permanent ideological threat to the communist state; Western ideas are truly subversive to the concept of monolithic party control. And sure enough, when the Soviet Union opened the doors to glasnost, the collapse of the ruling political structures was not far behind. And once the communist ideology was gone and a semblance of democratic process had moved to the fore in Soviet society, the East-West confrontation was largely over, all those nuclear weapons notwithstanding.

Wanted: An Interlocutor Who Doesn't
Always Agree

The logic of democracy continued to play itself out in a Soviet Union already reeling with change. Indeed, one of the most startling turnarounds of the history of the Soviet Communist Party was its terrifying moment of realization sometime in 1988 that it had an explosive crisis of communications on its hands, symbolized in the mounting unrest all over the country on dozens of different issues. Indeed, the very concept of Empire began to come under assault as the party saw increased restiveness among the various non-Russian nationalities: Lithuanians, Georgians, Armenians, and Azerbaijanis. Angry coal miners with deep grievances in the Donbass region added their weight to the assault on the system. As the mood grew more explosive, Moscow was required to come to terms with it quickly.

Yet communication with angry minorities proved extremely difficult to attain; the system had been effectively hoisted by its own petard. Moscow was devastated by the ultimate irony of all: the party's very success in establishing itself as the unchallenged spokesman for "the people" had suddenly become a dangerous liability, for there was no mechanism by which to consult with the real people. Docile, discredited state-controlled trade unions could not speak for the workers, so no reliable dialogue could take place through existing structures. The worse the local situation got, the more the local Communist Parties were rejected by the public, who perceived them as corrupted groups of yes-men interested only in serving Moscow. At the very time Moscow needed to negotiate with genuine public opinion to keep the lid on, the local parties had become worthless instruments for negotiation. What Gorbachev needed more than anything else was truly representative local bodies that could deal with Moscow authoritatively, empowered by their public-at-large and able to commit themselves for the public-at-large—something the local Communist Parties had never been able to do.

Thus, in the short period of a year or two, Soviet politics, once released from the rigidities of ideology, found itself traversing the political logic of many centuries of Western political development. Indeed, the "secrets of the Constitution" could not really be exported: constitutional software travels poorly without the societal hardware. It is only living with democracy for prolonged periods that gives it its gloss and patina. But, remarkably, Russia so far has implemented a number of key tenets of democratic governance, showing a genuine understanding of their true pragmatic value.

Recreating a Civil Society

Politics are only the superstructure of the democratic republic; Gorbachev's reforms are doomed if they are limited solely to the establishment of political mechanisms and parliaments. Perhaps perceiving this, or bowing to public desire, Gorbachev began the process of relaxing state controls, permitting a civil society to gradually crawl its way back into existence. The process of private citizens meeting to pursue and orchestrate the manifold private interests of society has always been anathema to the one-party state, in which the State alone undertakes to articulate and fulfill all of society's needs.

The critical importance of a vibrant civil society to the successful functioning of democracy is often forgotten in the West, where we tend to take the existence of civil society utterly for granted. Indeed, it is astonishing to realize how much civil society has become an essential clement of life. We are likely to overlook the incredible collective impact of innumerable private organizations—PTA, Rotary Club, League of Women Voters, Young Democrats, American Medical Association, B'nai Brith, United Auto Workers, American Association of Retired Persons, National Rifle Association, Sierra Club, Young Republicans, PEN Club, Knights of Columbus, National Association for the Advancement of Colored People, American Civil Liberties Union, Arab-American Anti-Discrimination Organization, Daughters of the American Revolution, Matachine Society, Friends of the Earth. Hundreds of thousands of private organizations play an integral role in American democracy in framing public opinion and channeling it in political directions. Thus is public opinion articulated, sometimes leaving Congress as nothing more than the recipient of the aggregated views of the nation, all beset with thousands of differing and often competing agendas.

But where and how is Soviet public opinion articulated? This is the dilemma of the totalitarian state. If the Communist Party is the handmaiden of the rulers of the state, how does the state even know what public desires are? How does the public express its desires and grievances to a leadership that in Stalin's day as often as not quite literally shot the messenger? Ironically, in the Soviet state, the KGB was in a position to end up being one of the more "liberal" organizations in that it alone was tasked with reporting "the real truth" on both foreign and domestic issues—in a state where no premium was placed on "truth" outside of revealed party truth.

Today the Soviet Union is undergoing an exquisitely painful process in seeking to establish—or at least permitting the establishment of—civil organizations, or "nonofficial organizations" as they are called. (Indeed, the very concept seems to be expressible only in negative terms, as that which does *not* belong to the state.) Gradually, thousands of private civil organizations are developing throughout the USSR, gingerly feeling their way through the maze of legal stumbling blocks in the new world of perestroika. Many of them, especially the private-enterprise efforts, meet bitter public condemnation, outrage that private groups are seeking to better themselves, establish a position, or even earn money that elevates them out of the common swamp of misery. Indeed, the Soviet state was nothing if not egalitarian, helping all groups to share the misery—except for the party, of course.

Citizens are struggling to create new public organizations, parties, platforms, and the articulation of needs. Networks of allies, partners with common agendas, all must be created. Rudimentary private businesses can scarcely be established because the state system has no mechanism for the admission of private orders and requisitions. Telephone lines by which to conduct business with the outside world are not there in Hungary. Furniture for private offices cannot be purchased in Poland. The currency of one of the largest economies in the world, the Soviet Union, once considered a superpower, is all but worthlesss outside its own borders. Barter is a key form of commercial survival within the Soviet system, and for foreigners as well. PepsiCo now swaps its syrup and sets up bottling plants in the USSR in return for all the Stolichnaya vodka it can peddle abroad. Some might argue that the Americans got the better deal. Or was it part of Gorbachev's plan to get the Russians to come off vodka cold turkey and onto Pepsi?

Communism's "Success"

But to witness this process is to understand retrospectively the full enormity of the communist system. What other system in the world has been capable of stifling nearly every single aspect of human political, social, and economic behavior, to the degree that people hardly know how to proceed once the doors to the cage have been opened? Faced with the demands, complications, and responsibilities of a new rudimentary democratic state opening the doors to free enterprise, it is no wonder that many citizens feel they would rather scurry back into the security of the cage—where at least there are regular feeding times and few surprises. No other system in history seems to have so successfully extirpated the very concept of civil society for so long, reducing Soviet political culture to utter infancy.

The Pitfalls of Democracy

Despite the astonishing first five years of Gorbachev's reforms, no one can be certain that democracy is firmly established anywhere in the old Communist Bloc. But the bad old days of Brezhnev are surely gone. Communism is dead. There is no going back to the old bankrupt ideology; the Communist Party is now utterly discredited in the public's eyes and can only desperately cling onto waning privilege in its final collapse. Eastern Europe is gone, and the ethnic republics of the Soviet Union have shattered the myth of the Soviet state and are launched on a process of independence.

But the old guard will fight to retain every last drop of power and privilege that it long enjoyed. And the historically unprecedented transition to a free-market economy is already wreaking havoc; law-and-order figures—albeit not totalitarian—are waiting in the wings to seize the reins of state in the event of utter chaos and anarchy. The greatest misfortune of all is that Gorbachev, the remarkable figure who in five years brought about the greatest change in the international order in the century, has now largely fulfilled his historic mission. His skills lay in keeping the USSR together through the most stunning stages of transition, but he is not the man to build the new order. To do so requires the letting go of the pretense of political unity; it requires giving the *coup de grâce* to the dying party. He cannot bring himself to do that. New figures have already sprung up around him in the process, figures now more capable of the next stage of the revolution. One can only hope that Gorbachev will show his extraordinary ability to recognize the inevitable, graciously acquiesce to these new forces, and not destroy his remarkable name by allowing the undoing of the great good that he has done.

Thus it is premature to celebrate the safe arrival of a democratic order in the old communist world. Even while the old order is gone, the success of the new cannot yet be assured. Indeed, its success can only be measured in terms of a sustained democratic process, bumps and all.

But what does this say about democracy itself? What are its complications, if Russia and its East European neighbors may yet trip and fall? The uncertainty of democracy's future reminds us, first of all, that under circumstances of extreme hardship, deprivation, and anarchy, democracy does not seem to fare well. For much of the world, democracy may only be a fair-weather plant. It may not permit the decisiveness required in periods of turmoil.

Gorbachev has repeatedly sought "special powers" to enable him to implement the necessary reforms. Other Soviets, such as liberal political commentator Andranik Migranyan, have argued that such special dictatorial powers are necessary in order to "save democracy." While the irony of this formulation is apparent, it may also be true that only an iron hand will get Russia through the worst of the economic transition to a market economy. The historical pitfalls, of course, are that the iron hand will never let go, or that the iron hand may become monstrous in the process.

To assess the pathologies of Russian democracy would require a special book in itself. For our purposes it is enough to note the nature of democracy's genesis in the Gorbachev era. The world is rarely witness to the workings of such a political laboratory in full public view. After seven decades of communism, Russia had become almost a political *tabula rasa*. Russian "discovery" of the virtues and mechanisms of democracy—the reinvention of the wheel, Soviet-style—is invaluable to us in understanding the strengths and weaknesses of democracy as an operating mechanism.

Morning After in Russia and Eastern Europe

But it is the very triumphalism in the air, the feeling that they may now be entering the Promised Land, that constitutes a grave pitfall for these refugees celebrating their recent escape from totalitarianism. The West has acclaimed their rebirth—appropriately—but now the hard work begins. The Bulgarian Tsvetan Todorov has spoken of the "posttotalitarian depression" that is now afflicting Eastern Europe. Can democracy "work"? Already political apathy has struck in many parts of the old Eastern Bloc, brought on by a sense of the enormousness of the problems. Nobody seems to have any answers. The public no longer trusts anyone. But democracy, after all, is not a solution to anything, it is merely a facilitator. If the wisdom, the bureaucratic skills, the foresight and imagination—the wherewithal of success—does not lie within the population, democracy cannot magically bring it into being.

Politics Are Filthy: Eastern European Style

Politics is not a good word for most Eastern European refugees from the communist experience. They understand better than anyone else the horrific implications of the state run wild. They have suffered directly and egregiously from the social engineering of the Nazis (in East Germany, Poland, and Czechoslovakia) and of the Marxist-Leninist-Stalinists. They have no stomach for slogans that talk of the will of the people, class struggle, the vanguard of the proletariat, and advances of socialism. Such populations will be intensely suspicious of governments and politicians that seek to usurp power in the name of "the people."

On the other hand, Eastern Bloc populations have supped at the public trough for seven decades, and the ethic of individualism—perhaps never strong in Russia anyway—has been sharply weakened. The public under any circumstances will demand from the state certain kinds of social guarantees, even if they are delivered at a low level of competence—such as in medicine, food, and guaranteed employment. These new publics thus may prove more demanding of social services and "security nets" than any Western state, including Sweden.

But the enormity of the communist system has created a revulsion against politics, a gnawing, visceral distaste for the endless corrupting accommodations and compromises that nearly every individual of a communist state was forced to engage in to one extent or another in order to survive. "Compromise" in all these cultures is an ugly word. It is mainly in America that the word has strongly positive political connotations—in addition to a few negative ones. The victims of communism crave some true purity, true values to displace the sham values so long forced down their throats and cynically parroted. The victory over communism has heightened a belief in the critical character of political morality, the need to stand tall for one's principles. Havel stated in his New Year's address in the first new year of freedom:

> Let us teach both ourselves and others that politics does not have to be the art of the possible, especially if this means the art of speculating, calculating, intrigues, secret agreements, and pragmatic maneuvering, but that it can also be the art of the impossible, that is, the art of making both ourselves and the world better.[1]

Yet herein lies the dilemma. Riding on a justifiable moral high after years in the amoral underground maze of communist politics, Eastern Bloc citizens find the concept of "compromise" distasteful. But compromise also lies at the very heart of democracy; constant accommodation must be made with those whose views we don't share. Those whose political views and values are derived from religion (or communism) find this compromise morally repugnant: how can one compromise true, ultimate values when that very process tarnishes them? How will those citizens of the old Eastern Bloc, having escaped from lifelong tawdry compromises with communist power, now feel about compromise in the Western and democratic sense, compromise that is essential and good? This lesson will come hard indeed.

New Heroes for Old Times

In 1990, America fell in love with several foreign visitors who represented something of the spirit of the "new order." Vaclav Havel, dissident playwright and new president of Czechoslovakia, and Nelson Mandela, newly released head of the African National Congress, led the list. Gorbachev and Poland's Lech Walesa were not far behind. All of these leaders captured the imagination of the American electorate in ways that no domestic leader had done for years. Was this because they represented values we can no longer find in America? Or did we just feel a rush of adrenaline as we watched our commonplace democratic values suddenly impassion and invigorate once-desperate societies? How much should we compare ourselves to them, wondering what has gone wrong with our own leadership that it does not equally command the hearts of our citizenry?

The Tediousness of Mature Democracy

In fact, no society can maintain itself at permanent white heat, at full throttle of exciting change and conquest of idealistic new frontiers. All celebrations come to an end, forcing us to return to Monday morning's world of reality, to sweep up after the festivities, to come to terms with the less glamorous but ultimately more important virtues of perpetuating those ideals whose success we celebrated. And it's less inspiring yet when it is no longer heroes and supermen, no longer men of the hour, who lead the nation, but average workaday practitioners who lack charisma or brilliance but do keep the engines running.

Indeed, the real skill comes precisely in the long-term

implementation of these ideals after the cheering has faded. The choices grow less compellingly stark, right and wrong play lesser roles in complex political calculations. As societies grow more sophisticated, they become increasingly diverse in character; what is good for one segment of the population is less likely to be good for another. Yet, the heroic new democracies of the world still grapple with the basic issues of society: food, housing, freedom, law and order, and political equality. These issues involve the basic physical and moral sustenance of society. These issues are as basic as they are grand.

In America we too face these issues, but they are not quite of the same magnitude. Shamefully, our consciences are less pricked because the great majority of us have already achieved most of the grand material requirements, making it easier to overlook the needs of a minority. American problems are increasingly subtle, involving more painful trade-offs among competing values and competing needs of widely diverse segments of the people. To reach national consensus in this area is far more challenging, but also far more exacting—even tedious—because of the detailed craftsmanship of legislation and the subtlety of adjudication called for. But our society too cannot fall back comfortably on the belief that all we are left with is the fine tuning; we too still need to think in terms of grand issues that challenge us.

We may draw sustenance from the idea that the countries now struggling to assert some democratic order are in fact following in the ideological footsteps long ago laid down by America. Indeed, in some senses we are the future, for better and for worse. Our democracy as a model is now on the line: its failings may send a message to those who think of following in our footsteps. The world will still be watching us, precisely because so many of the serious social problems that confront us today derive specifically from the very freedom of the democratic order and its political culture.

Conclusion

While we passionately hope that our new foreign heroes will emerge crowned with success, we do not know whether even Yeltsin will in fact be able to achieve economic and political stability in the new Russian order. We cannot tell whether Havel will show wisdom in the pursuit of the exacting tasks of formulating legislative compromises on myriad small issues that make up the totality of a functioning, equitable economic and political mechanism in Czechoslovakia. We do not know whether in the end Mandela will be able to bring the radical members of his movement to sit down with the South African government and the Zulu opposition and reach statesmanlike solutions to the persistence of apartheid and tribal rivalry. Walesa may have fulfilled his mission best as a symbol of national resistance and liberation rather than as president and architect of a new Polish free-market system and a developing democracy.

But in the end, does their eventual success or failure tarnish what they have already accomplished? Is success the final criterion for our view of their accomplishments? Of course it matters immensely whether Russia, Poland, Czechoslovakia, and South Africa make it in the end. But even if they do not this time around, even if the soil on which democracy has been planted there proves still too inhospitable without further fertilizing and watering, is the triumph of their initial victories without meaning for them—or for us?

For them, failure would be bitter. It would basically consign these new leaders to history as inspiring leaders, but not founders of a new order—yet. They will have established important precedents for their countries, perhaps bringing their countries closer to another, more successful round at establishing a democratic order.

For us, Gorbachev and Havel, Mandela and Walesa—all represent the inspiring breakthrough, a living reaffirmation of the revolutionary spirit and idealism that have characterized much of the American experiment. We can partake of the excitement of the grand affirmation of values that we share. Our politics rarely are granted the opportunity anymore to embrace the grand moral moments that currently galvanize the ex-communist world. Perhaps the civil rights movement of the sixties is the last somewhat comparable experience. The fall of the Berlin Wall should be the second grand political affirmation, summoning forth from us our own response, our own new burst of idealism and of self-examination.

For we have grown bored, blasé, or cynical about the foi-

bles, weaknesses, and failure of our politicians and our political system. We turn away from the voices that offer broader
debate and deeper perspectives, the politicians who move
beyond tactical positions carefully hedged against the latest
Gallup Poll. Democracy is, of course, meant to reflect public
opinion, but public opinion occasionally needs to be shaken
up by genuine choice and debate.

Jesse Jackson has offered one moral vision and political
program; Pat Robertson has offered a different moral vision.
Ronald Reagan brought a sense of new vision to politics when
he challenged decades of conventional political thinking, however disappointing much of his administration was. John
Silber in Massachusetts ran a Democratic campaign for governor that involved many looks at the hard issues—to the discomfiture of much of the electorate. Gary Hart flirted with
some original thinking, but it was not new thinking that
brought him down. None of this is to say that any of these
men should be elected, but their positions are all welcome
contributions to a serious, philosophically grounded debate.
Apparently much of the public does not want this, and the
ground rules of TV sound bites are such that departure from
the usual pablum of political rhetoric can mean sudden death
in the next negative commercial against you. It may be that
our society is incapable of the rousing grand debates—until
the wolf is truly at the door, and social issues beckon the
political man-on-horseback.

This is where we need the Gorbachevs, the Havels, the
Mandelas, and the Walesas to assist us in the reaffirmation
process. This is the emotional and psychic fuel that should
help us slog on through the evermore complex trade-offs of
our current political dilemmas. We envy them for the moment
for the charged power of their victories, and wish that we
could import that electric quality into our own political travail.
The maturity of our political system, the complex demands of
our uncertain society, should not deter us from renewed vigor
of approach. As American society declines in broad areas, we
need to be invigorated by strident debate of the grand issues
of democracy that we no longer consider. They are all still
there—freedom vs. responsibility, equality vs. egalitarianism,
the individual vs. society, morality vs. liberty. They exist in
endless concrete cases, and they need broad, contentious dis-

putation if we are ever to deal with them. Alas, our media are bored with such issues. World politics now comes in thirty-minute segments, carefully wrapped in the fluff of human interest stories that deflect our vision from the hard issues. And when it comes to elections, most Americans would rather go fishing.

As the old communist world debates the bedrock issues of society in its new flush of enthusiasm, we have ample reason to do the same. We need to do it because our society needs it. We also need to do it because we claim that our democratic system is the way for the world to go. We had better start living up to that system and demonstrate that we still have something to offer as a modern model, not just a historic principle enshrined in a glass case in Washington. So far we seem more content with smug observation of the struggles of the new democracies, allowing the spirit of their enthusiasms and contentions to fall unheeded on the sterile ground of our complacency and self-absorption.

These, then, are the civics lessons from the ashes of communism—ones not to be missed, for such high drama is not likely to be played out for our benefit more than once a century, if then.

NOTES
1. "Vaclav Havel's New Year's Address," *Orbis*, Spring 1990, p. 258.

THREE

America, the Exporter of Culture—for Better and for Worse

The United States may be suffering from a trade deficit, but in one area of exports it is winning hands down: the export of culture. Mass culture. Mass culture is the direct product of our democratic society and its free-enterprise economy. If we have pioneered mass culture, we are also pioneering the social and political dilemmas that spring from our system, which produced it. Our future is in many ways the future of much of the rest of the world. The world had better take note.

The Invasion of American Culture

In the eyes of much of the world, America has long been foisting its own culture on overseas audiences, facilitated by its extraordinary wealth and power to influence the rest of the world. This culture has been alternately welcomed and excoriated by audiences worldwide; intellectuals have historically tended to sneer at it, while the masses have often been seduced by it. American fashions and passions have enjoyed immediate international reception, often even crowding out local cultures.

The world has already been for many decades "Disney-literate": Mickey Mouse is at least as well known in China as

Chairman Mao, and more enduring. Today Berbers sitting in their tent villages in Algeria watch *Dallas* with total involvement. At one point the French considered banning *Sesame Street* in favor of some French stand-in. *Batman* has been an international sensation. American films have set the standard—not usually for art, but for popularity among world moviegoers—and regularly inform the work of foreign directors. Rambo has now entered the international political lexicon. In its sincerest form of flattery, the American Western film is imitated widely, leading to the creation of that special genre the "spaghetti Western." American film stars have as large an international following as royalty anywhere.

Music is at least as influential. Elvis enjoys a firm niche in the pop music culture of the world. Jazz, a uniquely American phenomenon, has powerfully influenced the world's music, and now there are some very gifted foreign jazz musicians. It was American rhythm and blues, also of black American origin, that gave way to rock and roll, ultimately spawning its British imitation that enriched international rock through the Beatles and the Rolling Stones—who largely imitated and embellished American musical styles.

The American invasion has gone beyond the ears to the stomach. Colonel Sanders enjoys a brisk business all over the world, including in Bali, even though Kentucky can't cut the mustard when it comes to Balinese-style red-hot peppers. McDonald's restaurants spring up like mushrooms to purvey the once lowly hamburger "with everything" to the hungry crowds of the world; the American hamburger's crowning achievement was its recent invasion of the very citadel of communism—"Beeg Meks" are served in the very heart of Moscow. Would Lenin have had his with everything? Pizza Hut opened simultaneously in Beijing and Moscow—two capitals that these days share very little else. Coke and Pepsi project their corporate rivalry and secret syrup war abroad for domination of obscure Third World markets. There is no remote desert oasis left that cannot offer the latter-day Lawrence the pause that refreshes. And if the American hamburger poses no threat to L'Escoffier, California cooking—perhaps the world's most creative and imaginative cuisine today—is successfully blending culinary cultures from Asia, Mexico, India, the Middle East, and Europe into inventive new dishes that are revolutionizing the whole concept of ethnic cooking, even in Paris.

The Queen's English may be the time-honored international standard of excellence for formal English, but it is already moribund in England—even on the BBC. Indeed, standard spoken American English is now the norm of English-as-a-foreign-language classes the world over. The American idiom, which cedes nothing to British English in its higher forms, is rich with contemporary informal expressions that reflect not only America, but the advance of America into ever new regions of political, economic, technical, scientific, sociological, and other areas of life in which new concepts are coined first in America. American media have helped render the American dialect the most accessible international language anywhere. American English, however abused by many of its citizens, is by far the most vital tongue in the world today.

International advertising now leans heavily on some form of American flavor to push products. Foreign firms carry out their marketing campaigns in the context of some American backdrop or setting. The image is powerful. America sells.

Even the very uniform that dresses the world population of the new age is made in America. Lenin could not succeed in standardizing the garb of the Russian work force, but American Levi's have now become the international garment of choice of the proletariat—and of the not-so-proletariat as well. While fashions from all over the world continue to inform American haute couture, popular American clothing styles usually dominate the exchange, especially among youth. After a predictable time lag, popular American hairstyles can be found adorning the heads of international youth, moving out like concentric circles from the American source, despite the influences of Paris and Rome as well.

But why stop with the international hairstyle and clothing of the teenager? The very teenager himself is an American invention. I would leave it to social historians to determine when the teenager was invented, but it was most likely within the last fifty years that the adolescent appeared as a distinct social, cultural, and economic class—or perhaps tribe. That class has been growing in America, occupying the countryside as well as the city, recruiting at ever tenderer ages.

The invention of the teenager was not, of course, some

brainstorm of Madison Avenue, or even of Dr. Frankenstein the sociologist. The teenage class developed out of the socioeconomic syndromes of American life: lengthening school years, gradually extending well up into college for the majority of American youth; increased communications, allowing the tribe to self-consciously discover itself and communicate more effectively; the growing tolerance of parents, permitting increased teenage freedom; and the growing job market for teenagers, which turned them into a permanent economic force, stimulating a formidable commercial interest in this distinct new market.

The invention of the teenager, in fact, is probably one of the most far-reaching acts of American social creativity. A contemporary, more "hip" Marx might have observed that the teenage "class" developed spontaneously out of definable socioeconomic conditions of capitalism, and that it would develop in other countries as soon as the same socioeconomic conditions were replicated there, installing that class as a virtually permanent social institution. Mercifully, Marx might not have spoken of a final victory of the teenage class— although it is quite possible that all other classes might wither away in the class struggle if faced by such a prospect.

The Discovery of Mass Culture

But has it actually been American power and wealth that have allowed us to peddle our culture and tastes—in food, clothing, films, TV shows, music, language, soft drinks, and even class formation? Are guardians of native cultures abroad right in complaining that America is imposing its products, as well as the implied American commercial values that accompany them? Is it the power of the dollar and the force of the American presence that led to this stranglehold on cultural exports? Even Japan, with its astonishing sweep of the world market of consumer goods, has only managed to peddle "hardware," not the Japanese cultural "software" that goes with it. A growing rage for sushi and some challenges to management practices notwithstanding, Japan has barely made a nick in insinuating the exotica of Japanese culture and outlook into the marketplace of international culture, despite Japan's massive commercial presence.

So what is this American cultural imperialism, so often derided by foreign intellectuals and guardians of the gates of culture? What is the instrument by which the United States is able to impose its wares on the rest of the world, even in countries like Brezhnev's Russia or the Ayatollah's Iran, where America was formally proclaimed the enemy? Can it really be our vaunted marketing techniques, which are now so conspicuously failing to sell American hardware abroad? Is it the numbers of American servicemen and tourists abroad, promoting these products by example? Is it some kind of insidious American monopoly of world power that has enabled American culture to get a head start on the products of other states? Or just sheer commercial hustle and New World brashness? Or the power of bad taste?

There are elements of truth in most of these hypotheses, but the heart of the answer lies elsewhere. The reason American culture has had such sensational success abroad is not that it is *American* culture, but that it is *mass* culture. America did not, in fact, invent mass culture. America *discovered* it. If we had not discovered it, some other large democratic state would eventually have done so. The United States, for a variety of reasons, was the first country in the modern era to discover the essence of mass culture, a phenomenon that grew, like the teenager, out of specific socioeconomic stages of development. Crowds in Beijing, Zagreb, Lima, Amsterdam, Marrakesh, and Lagos respond to something inherently and generically universal about American mass culture, something that prompts them to consume it and then emulate it.

Mass culture is what strikes a universal response. All countries may contribute to it, but America gloms it up from around the world and reprocesses it—from Andean and Nigerian music to Mexican and Asian popular food, now becoming part of the international scene, largely via America. Even sushi did not reach Europe from Japan, but from America. Asian martial arts really received their entree to the world through American "discovery" of them. It is America's discovery of mass culture that continues to give America the international lead in this area, to produce the cultural exports—even if we have fallen short in recent years in producing exports of anything else.

For Sale: The American Spirit

It was not, of course, only the material goods of America themselves, but the spirit that went with them that gave American-produced mass culture its impetus. Americans from early days have maintained an indomitable sense of optimism about the vast promise of the New World. Freedom from history can be immensely liberating, and this has been one of the great liberating elements of American life. Our history is relatively recent; we thus wrestle with few ghosts of the past— at least compared with other nations of the world. Starting from a *tabula rasa*—a new continent—everyone was in theory equal and opportunity was present for all. There are few scores to be settled from ancient historical grievances such as infect the rest of the world—though the grievance of Native Americans are an important exception. Palestinians and Israelis argue today over landownership claims going back well over two millennia. Shiite and Sunni Muslims still reflect almost daily awareness of a decisive battle of A.D. 680 that created Shiite Islam. But in America, class backgrounds were largely left behind in the old country, and everyone had opportunity to start afresh upon arrival in the Promised Land. Each new arrival represented an individual who was free to embark on a new life without reference to some collective membership. This, at least, was the ideal, the compelling myth that powered early settlers. It reflected large elements of reality. Although America has fallen woefully short of its ideals in many respects, even today the dream has not lost all its drawing power.

Thus much of the appeal of American society and culture came from its implicit promise: the romance of vast, virtually unpopulated lands waiting to yield their bounty; the technological accomplishments that produce rafts of consumer goods specifically for mass, not elite, tastes and needs, at an affordable price—epitomized by Henry Ford's Model T; the freedom of a supposedly classless society in which money created the only meaningful class. Money, the universal leveler, was a commodity accessible to all, regardless of background.

The American experience has also pioneered other major developments that had impact upon the world.

• Mass affordable housing after World War II developed in reaction to population growth and a perception that the suburban life was the wave of the future for those working in the urban and industrial environment.

• The automobile as a way of life has brought untold social change to America in opening up horizons, permitting wide travel to virtually every single American, liberating the individual from narrow localities, and increasing an overall sense of nationhood. The car has also come to symbolize personal freedom, the ability to escape, to get out, to get on the road. Auto glut was only to come later.

• Fast-food restaurants developed in response to the phenomenon of the working couple, in which neither had great amounts of time for cooking. The emphasis was on attractiveness of food reflecting customer preference, rapidity of service, and affordable price. The appeal was to the mass palate, and not to the demands of a classic culinary tradition, an imperial kitchen, or even the dictates of a dietitian.

• The concept of consumer convenience engulfed the nations: stores open twenty-four hours a day, supermarkets with a vast array of produce. The whole concept of serve-yourself stood in stark contrast to the most conspicuous characteristic of the all-powerful state-run economy: waiting in line for "service." Shops open till nine at night and on weekends for customer convenience are still almost unknown in the rest of the world. In Europe most shops close at noon for lunch and close promptly at five. Stores are usually shut on Sunday, and often on Saturday afternoon too.

• The hardware "supermarket" has had profound class implications. These vast warehouses with their assortments of every known type of tool, construction materials, paints, and plumbing and electrical fixtures have done away with all sense of class. Nobody is too good to do home repairs. Indian women in saris can be seen pushing carts laden with plumber's helper, two-by-fours, and bags of nails, thrust into the American work ethic from a culture in which the upper class historically prided itself on not engaging in any physical labor.

Customer Is King

All of these developments emerged not as a result of any government policy but in almost total absence of government interest. There were needs to be met. Simple enough in conception, but why did these phenomena not emerge in other countries first? After all, much of Western Europe was equally industrialized, with potentially similar needs.

The clearest answer seems to be that America was attuned to consumer wants and needs. Much money was spent researching consumer desires. Some charge that consumer needs are actually created. But this proposition is really rather questionable in view of the remarkable response that most consumer-oriented innovations seem to have met almost anywhere in the world. It suggests that basic "needs" are being met, some kind of longing within mass publics for certain kinds of services, diversions, and consumables. Sugar is instantly recognized as a "need" by primitive cultures that have never had it before.

Why did Europe and other countries lag in meeting customer needs? Perhaps one reason was the weight of shopkeeper tradition, custom, and maybe less emphasis on service, the meeting of needs: a shopkeeper has his profession and goes home at five just as do the lawyer and dentist. It is not his job to search out what new things others may want, but simply to provide them with what they have always needed. Perhaps there is even a diminished entrepreneurial spirit there: American shops, after all, stay open not as a selfless act of public service, but because there is money to be made. And also because the American life-style—especially one encompassing working wives as well as husbands—requires a kind of service that an earlier age did not.

Interestingly enough, the idea of convenient hours and sense of "service" seemingly always existed in the Third World. There merchants do stay open long hours, perhaps closing down at a universal siesta time, and then staying open till late at night. In these societies merchants perhaps represent not just a profession but a *class*, one that does not yet aspire to the hours of the professional bourgeoisie. And the functioning of the bazaar transcends the merely mercantile; it represents the hub of social and even political intercourse of the country. But the bazaar demonstrates no search to meet or develop new tastes among the public.

American Culture: The Tidal Wave of the Inevitable

America, then, has captured the sense of mass international taste, and pioneered much of the terrain of future trends. The American experience is the advance wave for what much of the rest of the world will also inevitably come to experience. The deeper significance of this phenomenon is that indigenous culture in the rest of the world—however deeply rooted in geography and history—is itself highly susceptible to sharp and rapid change under the onslaught of new cultural exposures and the new economic relationships that they betoken. (This is what Islamic fundamentalism is all about—the "corrupting" character of the Western cultural invasion.) In fact, the world's embrace of so much of American mass culture reflects an even broader international trend toward global cultural homogenization, along lines first discovered by America. These processes are basically "natural" and reflect a more general course of human aspiration. America has been the first society to experience many of these new cultural, political, economic, and social stages of development. We have put an American accent on it, but they are not American "inventions," they are "discoveries." American mass culture was not created, it "happened." And it will happen elsewhere as the conditions that created it spread abroad.

American mass culture thus springs from several different facets of American life. Its roots lie first in the major economic processes of urbanization, industrialization, and postindustrial development that has produced the wealth that enabled a strong consumer-oriented society to arise. It has been powerfully fueled by the existence of a free-enterprise system that has given rein both to creativity in the marketplace and to the ability of enterprise to chase consumer dollars and interests. American democracy and political freedoms, too, encourage the variegated preferences of a free society.

In other words, the public at large has the money, leisure, and options to pursue its goals. Affluence itself has its social effects: researchers suggest that individualism develops out of affluence, from the increased ability to express personal choice. (Japan's strongly social orientation is beginning to give way to a process of individualization on just such a basis.) Lastly, a society that has treasured individualism has inevitably come to encourage the individual quest for the good life as a fundamental part of the American birthright.

A number of these social and economic conditions do not necessarily obtain in the majority of countries abroad, at least right now. But most of these aspirations toward the American model are ultimately universal in character and are in the process of arising overseas, propelling other countries to follow in the wake of the American experience. Indeed, if the consumer society encounters any hindrances in arising spontaneously in most countries abroad, as in China and Eastern Europe, the very existence of America and the draw of its consumer culture and style will hasten the popular quest for similar benefits.

America: Glimpses into the Dark Future of the World

But if there is a relentlessness to the spread of American mass culture abroad, the downsides of that spread are relentless too. Most of the current ills that beset America flow out of the very economic, social, and political conditions that we have discussed above—the conditions that led to the discovery and exploitation of mass culture.

The pathology of American society today must therefore preoccupy the rest of the world as well, for the world will inevitably come to share many of America's problems. In fact, it already does. We can see this taking place as we read of the disastrous state of British mass education today, paralleling many of the worst features of American education, with more and more students seeming to know less and less. The same goes for crime and race relations. In Japan there are already signs that the vaunted sense of social discipline is beginning to slacken with newer generations that demand higher standards of living, greater social freedom, and a less rigid, hierarchic business culture. Pick up any popular magazine abroad today and recognize emerging social problems that we have long been dealing with here.

It is not that America-discovered culture brings specific problems in its wake. That would be to confuse symptoms with causes. It is the socioeconomic and political conditions that produced the mass culture in America in the first place that are replicating themselves overseas, thereby spawning the problems of modern mass-culture democracy—problems America is currently experiencing. We are exporting the future, for better and for worse.

Let us explore a few specific examples of these social problems as they manifest themselves in America today. All are subject to export, and indeed some other countries have already received their shipment. Chief among these problems are severe damage to the institution of the family, the creation of a permanent underclass, and the sharp decline of education. These phenomena have contributed to an overall loss of social discipline, leading to broad confusion over values and goals. These negative developments are all taking place against a backdrop of a multiracial society that further complicates the national dilemma.

The Destruction of the Family

Modernization produced one early casualty: the institution of the family. The decline of the American family is perhaps the greatest single blow to the American social fabric. This decline did not occur overnight: the family as an institution has been evolving—or deteriorating—for some time. Originally, of course, the term "family" really meant extended family, or even clan—a word quaintly preserved in the Sicilian culture of *The Godfather*. The family, after all, has been the primary social unit throughout the history of most cultures and the main source of support for the individual.

The extended family has always been the first refuge from the dangers of anarchic society and rapacious authority. Governance in the interests of the broader public, after all, is a relatively modern idea. Indeed, the history of government is the history of the gradual widening of the circle of those who benefit from the state. The idea of government as public servant would have seemed preposterous throughout most of history. Up until fairly modern times, the state has largely been an instrument to control society in the interests of various narrow, self-appointed groups; control of the state has signified the privilege to exploit, sometimes even loot, the land and its people in the name of one or another dominant group within society. "Let us enjoy the Papacy, since God has given it to us," as the Renaissance Pope Leo X put it. Although history has witnessed enlightened rulers with social conscience, or those who viewed the public as a flock to be preserved, throughout early stages of history no one in his right mind would have looked to local rulers for fulfillment of basic individual needs apart from broad public order and a certain justice, as long as the ruler's interests were not touched. The extended family was the main source of protection and the avenue of first resort to meet nearly all needs—economic, social, political, and reproductive.

It has only been in modern times that the state has begun to replace many of these basic familial functions. In many societies now, people do expect the government to meet needs; after all, today one expects relative fairness and justice from state institutions. We look to the state for health care, education, protection, family mediation, counseling, safety inspection, food purity, prevention of child abuse, provision of old-age care, abortion, etc. The truly extended family has virtually vanished from the scene, except among recent immigrants whose family structure remains intact—until it runs into the divisive character of American society. Even the three-generation family, complete with grandparents, is largely a thing of the past. Little wonder that the family, even as a two-generation structure, is an endangered species today. The assumption of a broad range of social responsibilities by the state—removing some of the practical needs for extended family—has thus posed one of the primary threats to the institution of family. And the process has yet to run its course.

The move toward the nuclear family was powerfully hastened by economic factors of the modern industrial age. First, demands for an increasingly mobile work force helped spread family members over broad distances. Americans now move all the time—at least 25 percent of the population moves every year. This development brought important—and negative—consequences emerging from the destruction of the three-generation family. Gone was the grandparent as social lubricant between intergenerational tensions; gone too was the ethical and moral influence of an older generation whose views were sometimes more acceptable to the youngest generation, since the grandparent was not in the direct line of fire of the parent-child generational struggle. The loss extended to the psychological realm; the opportunity to confide in or receive advice from grandparents or to find alternative haven when parent-child stress grew too intense disappeared.

But of course, the pressures of the economy gave no quarter, particularly with the reduction of the three-generation household to two. The family, in fact, was shortly to be reduced to less than the full interaction of even two generations in many cases. Two other factors brought this about: widespread divorce, and the emergence of the working wife.

The roots of American divorce are complex, but can be connected to at least several key developments. The first blow was struck by the growing freedoms and social laxities of the 1960s "cultural revolution," whereby self-fulfillment was elevated to a new pedestal and the pursuit of personal gratification became the new Grail. Marriage came to be seen by many as an outmoded and fettering institution ("If you want a glass of milk, you don't have to buy a cow"). Whatever we may think of the sixties—a mixed picture by any standard—they were not to be avoided; the sixties emerged almost inevitably out of the strictures of an earlier, more disciplined, and more hypocritical age. The values of the earlier period were under fundamental assault anyway: the Vietnam War merely hastened the pace and character of this revolutionary turning point.

Divorce was equally affected by women's lib, which rightfully demanded the freedom of a woman to back out of an unrewarding marriage as readily as the husband. Easy divorce is now a prominent feature of American life, with parental divorce patterns tending to be reflected in the next generation. Few would advocate the preservation of a destructive marriage. But the current assumption of society that a swift divorce is needed whenever one partner is "not absolutely satisfied" obviously has direct impact on the divorce rate. Casual divorce exacts considerable social cost upon the children, and upon children's ability to commit to marriage themselves as adults.

At the same time, women were acquiring new economic ability—and the legal support—to break away instead of remaining in thrall to their husbands. The more radical segments of women's lib also held the very roles of motherhood and the housewife in contempt as a remnant of an *ancien regime* of female bondage—although at least one of the movement's founders, Betty Friedan, still champions the full dignity of the mother and the housewife. Nothing more plainly documents the astonishing breakup of the family unit than the TV sitcoms that represent a parade of unmarried mothers, one-parent homes, and his-and-her children combined in new second marriages for both parties. The questionnaires schools now send to the parents *assume* that one or the other is not a biological parent of the child.

The move of married women into the marketplace had at least two key roots. First was the economic imperative to meet rising costs, and, indeed, rising economic expectations. Here one may rightly ask how much mass culture—an economy dedicated to consumerism, and its concomitant credit card bills—contributed to the economic need for the two-income family. Second, women's liberation had great impact on the legitimate aspiration of women to both choice and professional fulfillment. The entry of women into the work force in massive numbers meant the simultaneous absence of both parents from the home, and the creation of latchkey children and graduates of the uncertain environment of the day-care center. (The current national hysteria over child abuse in part reflects the anguish and guilt felt by parents who leave their children with strangers all day long.)

Hardly all of the problems of the family can be attributed to the two-income family. Children, after all, are not sent away from the home on a permanent basis: evenings and weekends remain. But it is commonly recognized that the strains on the family grow. "Quality time" has almost become a cynical synonym for longer-term deprivation of parental attention. Divorce only further attenuated parent-child ties.

There would seem to be little doubt that the sharp weakening of the family structure is a prime cause of contemporary social breakdown, of the weakening of most sources of societal discipline, and of the overall confusion of values that marks our society today.

The inculcation of values in the next generation is hard when parents have less time. As Christopher Lasch has pointed out, "quality time" within busy working families and divided homes—with its emphasis on the urgent need of "having a good time together"—makes parents increasingly loath to use that time for the less "feel-good" purposes of discipline or simple coexistence in the daily routine. Society conspires to separate the generations even further with the wealth of material produced for children's and teenagers' gratification: it is assumed that the interests of the generations must inevitably clash, that nothing could readily be shared by all, and that the young should never be "bored" by being expected to stretch into an appreciation of something outside kiddie culture.

It would be easy to blame all these dilemmas on a hedonistic society: parents lack interest, are preoccupied by their search for the good consumer life, are selfish and neglect their kids. The bad news, of course, is that many of these problems derive from developments that have been perceived as progressive and positive: economic "progress" and women's search for personal and professional fulfillment. We are just beginning to recognize the impact of these trends; the full consequences of this brave new world, in all their facets, are still coming.

The destruction of the family is probably most advanced in the United States, where we have pioneered the new economic and social institutions of the latter twentieth century. The only other society to have kept pace with America, if not surpassed it, is, ironically, Soviet society. In the USSR, the state has hastened—through the use of force—what are spontaneous trends in America toward the weakening of family. Marxism-Leninism set out early on to destroy the family, which was perceived as a bourgeois economic and social institution that weakened the hold of the state over the individual. All sources of morality were liquidated except for those perceived by the party to be in the interests of the revolution.

What the state did not destroy deliberately was destroyed by the pervasive cynicism and weakening of most moral values in the USSR and the destruction of religion, bringing about immense social and family tensions, rampant alcoholism, and the absence of civil institutions to ameliorate the harshness of the totalitarian order. Nearly all nationalities in the Soviet Union today speak of the urgent need for the reestablishment of values among youth.

The roots of the dilemma of the American family are growing clearer, but social policy has not kept pace with the problem. The independent American pioneering spirit, the distaste for Big Government and its dictates, and the desire for personal freedom and independence—all have conspired to delay government action to establish more progressive, and intrusive, social policies. Social policy has lagged in the United States relative to most of the advanced states of Western Europe—particularly as regards day care and family-leave policy. The healthy strain of American individualism has foundered when confronted with the heavy pressures of the new family work pattern.

If America has unwittingly pioneered in the destruction of the family, it has not yet found the remedy. The weak state of the family is an inevitable accompaniment of economic development, social freedoms in a liberal society, and a free-market economy. Perhaps the traditional level of commitment required to make marriage viable is no longer in keeping with contemporary values. Perhaps marriage may be perceived as increasingly "inconvenient." Although numerous suggestions that somehow "new forms" of social units be evolved have been offered, most involve yet further demands that the state stand *in loco parentis* by sponsoring programs of child care or even "communes" for children's upbringing. There is little to suggest that any of these communal formulas, with their *Brave New World* character, are at all promising either. Research into the communal child-rearing on kibbutzes in Israel has shown negative effects on children.

The preservation of the family as a unit must be the foundation of any new thinking about the roots of American social ills. It is a core value. Essential is an awareness that people can't "have it all"—neither men nor women. Like so many other critical issues, the preservation of the family involves hard trade-offs. The family will not be rescued unless society places new focus on social, structural, and economic incentives that will help preserve marriage and discourage casual divorce. Public articulation of these trade-offs is essential to an honest discussion of remedies. If social and economic programs—even "subsidies" of a kind—to strengthen the institution of marriage are not workable, we are left with the inescapable conclusion that the strengths of the traditional family structure are a thing of the past. The consequences for the overall health of American society are extremely serious—and perhaps crippling.

The New Underclass

The economic and social evolution of America has created another deeply disturbing phenomenon: the emergence of a semipermanent underclass. I say semipermanent, but the fear is that with the exception of a small proportion of transients who move into the underclass because of temporary hard luck, the underclass may be dangerously close to permanent.

The existence of an underclass is a product of both contemporary postindustrial American society and the free-enterprise market system, interacting with America's painful history of slavery and other forms of discrimination against various ethnic groups at various times, thereby preventing the benefits of society from being distributed with some degree of evenness among ethnic groups. Members of the underclass include a disturbingly disproportionate number of African-Americans, as well as members of various Hispanic groups and a varied mixture of Caucasians; a startlingly low proportion of East Asians are represented. The roots of the underclass problem are, of course, deep, and the problem has been resistant to a broad variety of approaches designed to alleviate it.

The origin of this class is itself a complex question, fraught with ideological intensity along all parts of the political spectrum. One can scarcely venture into it without raising specters of racism, social welfarism, social Darwinism, or laissez-faire liberalism. One offers opinions only at one's peril, and there are more than enough statistics to go around to support almost anyone's preferred conclusions, bolstered by a wealth of interest groups, massive bureaucracies, social activists, moralists on all sides, and acerbic guardians of the conservative verities.

It is important to define our terms. The concept of an underclass is not a euphemism for the black poor, although the black poor happen to make up a major element of this group in America. The term "underclass" as applied to any society should be not racial at all, but descriptive of those individuals of any race who are limited in their personal endowments and aptitudes, or otherwise so psychologically maladjusted to the demanding environment of contemporary society as to be unable to function or to break out of the underclass syndrome.

To describe the existence of an underclass as a "black problem" per se is to miss the main point. There are analytic conclusions to be reached about the mental, social, and psychological characteristics of every individual in the underclass that emphatically cannot be equated with statements about blacks as a whole—or any other group. Indeed, we often fear to characterize or draw conclusions about the underclass for fear that we will be perceived as racist. Races and ethnic groups other than black also inhabit the underclass. Nor is the underclass synonymous with the "poor" in general, for poverty alone is a more tractable problem if it is not attended by the destructive social environment of the underclass.

The most disturbing feature of the underclass in America is that it reflects not just individual weaknesses but rather a broad syndrome of problems that virtually doom its members from birth—or earlier—to a life within that underclass. The second disturbing feature is the disproportionate representation of blacks within that class.

Some of the problems of individuals in the underclass— any underclass—are attributable to limited personal aptitude, some are attributable to mental or psychological maladjustment, but a great many are attributable to the damaging social environment, including the home, in which these individuals begin life. These problems are often compounded by deep-set social patterns of welfare and welfarism, a kind of inherited social irresponsibility—a self-perpetuating syndrome that has drawn the attention of many black social commentators as well as white. In some cases it has become virtually a life-style of its own, based on a combination of welfare and crime; selling crack is vastly more rewarding financially than flipping hamburgers.

There has always been an underclass in the sense of a lower class—especially following the onset of the Industrial Revolution—but that lower class was largely employed and employable, even if miserably treated. The character of the underclass today—different from that of a working class—is that it is unemployed and often unemployable in terms of acquired skills or reliability. It cannot be defined in strictly economic terms. It bespeaks a condition that goes beyond "mere" poverty, suggesting an entrapment in a spiral of helplessness, social superfluity, alienation, crime, and unemployability in many cases. It suggests a semipermanent condition rather than a temporary one. It implies a set of problems that are increasingly exacerbated by modern society rather than alleviated by it. And it suggests intractability of the problem as well—at least to date. If the source of the problem were mainly traceable "only" to racism and racial victimization, the solutions might be more within reach—but patently much more is involved.

It is too early to speak of the underclass as an international problem, but time will surely demonstrate that nearly all modern industrialized countries suffer from the phenomenon to varying degrees. Usually immigrants and minorities make up the backbone of foreign underclasses, for these groups usually have lived under less promising social circumstances than the majority population. Unsuccessful or unendowed members of majority groups also can end up in the underclass. Our analytic task is to determine how modern societies, which place a high premium on free enterprise and individual self-initiative, contribute to the creation or perpetuation of the underclass. While a free-enterprise system undoubtedly exacerbates the problem by posing additional challenges to the less gifted, even Russia has its white underclass that seemingly has not made it even under socialism. The problems of the underclass in modern society demand comprehensive examination if our society is to be seen as any kind of model. What kind of changes might have to take place in society in order to make inroads against the underclass?

If we are to consider the problem in its full dimensions, it is imperative to isolate the underclass from race as much as possible. Blacks have made extraordinary gains in American society in the last three decades, and the rate of progress is accelerating. A strong and growing black middle class has emerged—one that has left the ghetto behind and unfortunately, but understandably, is not inclined to look back. Blacks are attaining increasingly prominent positions in all professional walks of life, from academia to business and the military. The problem is not how to improve the position of blacks in America per se, but how to alleviate the problems that typify an underclass, regardless of its ethnic makeup.

Yet one observation in principle seems to me almost ineluctable: as society grows more complex and the demands of the workplace ever more sophisticated, is there not always likely to be a small proportion of the population that is left behind, that just can't make it, at least as modern society is presently constituted?

In the past, small-town society and large families somehow found room for people whose insufficient aptitudes and skills, or social maladjustment, or perhaps psychological handicaps and inability to cope, prevented them from managing the demands of a normal job. Even if the support from those institutions was uneven, unpredictable, or absent, somebody was always ready to "help out." Society, especially rural society, was much more informal, the economic system looser, expectations lower, and the prospective candidates for the underclass could remain partially hidden. The problem, for better or for worse, was local. There was always a major job market for physical labor that required no literacy, few technical skills, little judgment. Contemporary, urban, postindustrial society, on the other hand, seems far less able to accommodate those with limited or no skills. Even McDonald's, that great ghetto employer and economic socializer, expects at least basic literacy of its employees.

In short, on the social pyramid of skills and ability, there will always be a bottom rung. By definition, there is no way the bottom rung can be eliminated. What is intolerable is that an individual be automatically condemned to the underclass simply by virtue of birth into that environment. It is intolerable that the sins of social history be automatically visited upon succeeding generations, regardless of individual endowment— that is, that minority status statistically condemns certain minorities to the underclass syndrome. What our society must do is to try to prevent any kind of generational permanence on the bottom rung, to improve opportunities for those who have the determination and skills to make it out of there. Failing that, society must also make life there less disastrous for those who occupy it, and hence also less dangerous for the rest of society, which is often the butt of underclass anger and depredations.

Education is another key factor. Some elements of the underclass resist—and sometimes even clog—the educational system, as the frustrated accounts of thousands of teachers testify. American education—discussed in greater detail at the end of the chapter—must also bear a great share of the responsibility for producing citizens who are educationally unready to face anything more challenging than dishing up Taco Belgrandes or engaging in other service jobs or menial labor. But the underclass syndrome acts viciously here as well. Many children of the underclass in schools pose special educational problems that are acutely demanding of any educational system. To spark curiosity, inquiry, and commitment in the indifferent student is a daunting and depressing task. Even more depressing are statistics that Head Start programs enable ghetto kids to perform well in the first three years of school, but that after three years the absence of any educational support from the home environment begins to erode the benefits of the head start. Little wonder that American industry itself is panicking. The *Los Angeles Times* reports that American industry spent $210 billion in 1989 to impart on-the-job remedial skills to workers.[1] The Project on Adult Literacy in Connecticut estimates that between twenty and thirty million Americans cannot "read, write, calculate, solve problems, or communicate well enough to function effectively on the job or in their everyday lives."[2]

As if insufficient education were not enough, the drug problem has moved the problem into a whole new arena: increasing numbers of the underclass are falling prey to drugs even while the middle class seems to be shaking some of the habit. There is an ugly cycle of failure: a class that is born into poverty and ignorance grows up with little or no chance to make the extraordinary effort of breaking out of the environment, where crime and crack are among the few passports to a good income, and where the failures of the parents (or parent, or no parent) are usually transmitted directly on to the children. The *Washington Post* has highlighted recent stories—reported by the black police officer corps of the city—about children of children—of young teen mothers—who now regularly and casually turn to murder to settle conflict, seemingly operating with almost no sense of compassion toward anyone. We are now producing more individuals prey to this no-exit nightmare as the phenomenon of alcohol and crack babies gains salience. These babies are almost guaranteed to be permanent wards of society. Indeed, initial reporting suggests that many crack babies seem to be doomed not from birth, but from conception. And the cost of raising and socializing them—if they are not so mentally damaged as to be unsocializable—is increasingly passed along to the state.

In this respect, the sins of the parents are visited upon the children. The problem grows even more frightening when we read that the underclass, with all its problems, is producing babies at a faster rate than almost any other class. These children inherit not only the more limited mental aptitudes that mark much of any underclass anywhere, but also the blighting cultural and social conditions of welfarism that make the breaking of the vicious circle nearly impossible even for those who have the skills and desire to make it out. It is for precisely this reason that the courts are debating the question of whether it is wrong to discourage documentably irresponsible and unsuitable mothers from having lots of children. Washington's former Mayor Barry himself suggested publicly to one welfare recipient that her problem was not just the city's but her own in having so many children. How strongly should they be discouraged? What does such a program say about individual rights in a democratic society? Here is part of the linkage between the underclass and the dilemmas of democracy.

America would thus seem to be the first major modern industrial state to create a permanent underclass, not hidden away in the nooks of traditional society, but out in the open and statistically analyzed. These tragic people are members of a system that can no longer physically or socially control the damage it wreaks on itself and the outside. England may not be far behind in the formation of this class. France, Germany, and Italy as well. How will we manage the problem? While we can hope to find new social programs that will enable larger numbers of disadvantaged people to function in life, a hard look at the realities of the modern postindustrial existence suggests that there may always remain a significant hard core who simply cannot make it in modern, complex societies—period. The presence of democracy and a free-market system in one sense only exacerbates the problem, for it places a premium on the ability of the individual to solve his or her own problems.

How does such a society manage when there are increasing numbers of individuals who perhaps will never escape from the poisonous embrace of the welfare system—residents of permanent child-care centers for adults who can't/won't make it? And what are the implications of free choice for documentably irresponsible individuals of the underclass when the social cost of their free options becomes ever greater? The question is unsettling; indeed, merely to describe it with any objectivity is harsh and depressing. But the problem is there. We may be on the edge of a new two-tiered society: a mainstream society that preserves competition and free enterprise for those who choose to compete and contribute creatively, and another society that is state-run and designed to take care of, and spare time from the mainstream economy, those who are tragically mired.

The underclass is a blight on all of us. It levies major humanitarian, psychological, and moral costs on all of society. It preys upon itself. And it disrupts the security, welfare, and even the budgets of a productive majority, especially in big cities. These problems are closely related to our system of government, economics, and society, and are inseparable from the general dilemmas of modern industrial democracy as a whole.

Empowerment?

While the benefits of welfare have been almost universally discredited—except to keep people alive—a new coalition of American white conservatives and black radicals are experimenting with innovative programs that attempt to enable those in the poverty zone—not necessarily the entire underclass—to choose their own housing and schooling. Such programs seem to recognize the critical importance of will and acceptance of personal responsibility to accomplish something with one's life. Any hint that this path might be productive raises the hope that it might have some application for the underclass as well. For surely there is no substitute for the exertion of private will to improve oneself and one's surroundings.

Looked at realistically, then, there are grounds for doubting that there is any way to eliminate the existence of an underclass. As long as there is not, society may simply have to learn to cope with the permanent existence of such a class, and to establish a separate state-run segment of the social system outside the mainstream economy, designed to take care of the underclass and recruit out of it those individuals who show the necessary talent and will. Such a program should involve work programs, perhaps some kind of industry or business not expected to be economically viable but of social value nonetheless, perhaps resembling FDR's old work programs from the Depression.

What is clear is that the free-enterprise system alone cannot solve this problem. It is unlikely to find a place for the mentally handicapped or the emotionally, psychologically, or socially blighted. The managerial skills of private enterprise could well be employed to make the program workable, but it would require considerable subsidization. Such a program should serve as a ticket out for those individuals who responded to it enough to move into the real economy.

It would be comforting to attribute the existence of the underclass "merely" to racism, poverty, lack of funding, or inadequate social programs. Those problems, severe in themselves, at least present an avenue for treatment. Indeed, some moralists like to attribute the problem simply to moral weakness on the part of the underclass. That view, of course, is absurd, for the comfortable and affluent also produce a regular stream of the morally culpable. We hear less about the well-heeled losers merely because their families' wealth can often shield them from becoming wards of society.

As noted above, the preponderance of African-Americans among the underclass is a deeply unsettling phenomenon. It is partly attributable to the continuing legacy of the moral ravages of American slavery. It is unacceptable that the underclass should include any particular ethnic group in highly disproportionate numbers. To the extent that such a significant overrepresentation of black Americans exists, special programs are needed to restore some ethnic balance. Programs not based on quotas but on special "head-start" advantages of all kinds, even at unusual cost, are called for until it is perceived that the American underclass is no longer marked by any special ethnic or geographical features. The ranks of black-middle-class America must swell.

But to describe the problem in bleak terms, to recognize the absence of any ready solution, is not to give up. Society can never give up. What is required is that the problem be looked at realistically. The problem goes well beyond victimization, but there indeed is victimization as well. Not all problems are susceptible to solution, but they must be addressed. Social planners should keep more radical plans in mind as they examine the future.

Foreign industrial democracies will surely encounter variations of this problem. For, at heart, the underclass is not a racial problem or a problem of racial capabilities. All societies have disadvantaged elements of the population, not all of it even minorities, stemming from the particular historic and social conditions of each country. Europe has growing numbers of Third World and even East European immigrants, some adapting and flourishing, but some not. The free-market system will exacerbate the problem because of the tendency of capitalism to intensify the polarities of the economic spectrum. State intervention is the most likely form of handling this dilemma, even where the state would not normally expect to intervene in other parts of the economy.

In the end, will a multiethnic underclass be a permanent feature of future societies that demand increasingly higher levels of skills and adaptability? Is America pioneering this problem too, without the solution? How will other free societies with free-market systems handle the problem?

The Collapse of Education

It is a depressing, but nearly inescapable, conclusion that the much-publicized faults of American education are also partially a direct function of American democracy and the contemporary social and economic values it spawns. In principle a free-enterprise system should produce the competitive spirit, the awareness among students that it takes education to get ahead, to get a good job, to acquire the necessary skills to make it. These values were largely prevalent among American youth in earlier decades. Something seems to have happened along the way.

First, the American cultural revolution of the sixties revolutionized educational values by stressing the voluntary—as opposed to compulsory—nature of student involvement in education, focusing on the necessary "relevance" of much educational material to students. If a student decided that his studies were "boring" or not "relevant" to his interests, then the curriculum was changed. The schoolroom was thrust into competition with the media; if classroom lessons were not as exciting to the student as prime-time TV, then something must be wrong with the teacher. Plain old hard work was viewed as just that—old-fashioned. Memorization was out, lest the "curse" of rote memory drive out student creativity. It was much more fun to talk about major issues than to have to study them in any depth. The fulfillment of student satisfaction with all facets of the classroom became a new educational value. Any sense of coercion—that the student "had" to do the work—was unwelcome. Multiplication tables boring? Sure, why not rely on calculators? History boring? Abandon it for contemporary studies. Like comic books? How about doing a history of Batman?

A second problem was the increasing tendency to view schools not as centers of learning, but as instruments of socialization, laboratories of social interaction. This was especially the goal set for minority students, although not just for them. In an interracial society it is deemed important that students "feel good about themselves." "Self-esteem" became the major buzzword. But self-esteem was all the harder to achieve when the new educational system virtually guaranteed that students would be very short on substantive knowledge. The legacy of this approach is now evident: today's American students possess the dual distinction of being both less educated than their peers in over a dozen countries yet enabled by their "self-esteem" to rate themselves at the top of the proficiency charts. Of course, schools do play important roles in socializing students and overcoming a variety of problems. But that function has now supplanted the more fundamental skills of being able to read, write, and think. What good are social skills without dreary old knowledge and an ability to think?

The technical age has also undoubtedly had its impact. Wave after wave of college students are told every year that they know more than any other generation of students in human history. No doubt, today's high school student has available more facts and data than any student in history. But that does not mean that today's student "knows more." It means even less that he or she knows how to think. For access to information is meaningless if an individual does not know how to think about information, how to analyze it, how to compartment it and relate it to a broader framework of knowledge. Indeed, the data glut of the contemporary era militates against the acquisition of analytic capabilities, judgment, and even wisdom, because it tends to crowd out the time available for reflection, for thinking.

Finally, American society with its consumerist and self-gratifying characteristics has simply weakened the work ethic. You can get along without a lot of education today—social safety nets abound. Everybody expects less. As Calvin, the little boy in the comic strip *Calvin and Hobbs*, remarks privately after a rare act of attention to household chores, "I like Mom to be impressed when I fulfill the least of my obligations."

Apathy toward accomplishment of goals is supposed to be a weakness of socialist societies; competence never matters in padded, state-supported systems that hire and maintain everyone. Yet free-enterprise America also seems drifting in that direction. Perhaps the safety nets are too great? Perhaps we need more draconian means of suggesting that only hard work and accomplishment will fill the dinner bucket? Perhaps we need less "get in touch with your feelings" education, need to start making underachieving students *not* feel good about themselves?

Recent immigrants to America still maintain the once-vaunted work ethic, and so usually do their kids. Asian students from Confucian cultures seem to have deeply ingrained work ethics, reinforced, no doubt, by pressure at home. I regularly have nagging feelings that my own teenage son, adopted from Korea as an infant, is actually underprivileged: he is growing up in an Anglo-American home that is "understanding" about the work ethic. If he had been brought up in a Korean home he would not have dared to conform to the current underachieving environment of America.

Education in America, then, is suffering from part of the same pathology that seems to afflict numerous other facets of American life. It is demonstrating confusion of values, diminished respect for authority, and absence of commitment in an increasingly open, democratic, and pluralistic society.

Japan, of course, is democratic, but much less open, and decidedly not pluralistic. Yet even in Japan there are inklings that the famed rigidity of discipline of the school system is beginning to show cracks. A newer generation is beginning to rebel, show some irreverence to elders, and question the automatonlike system of education and advancement. The Japanese film *The Family Game* is a savage and nihilistic satire of traditional Japanese education and the malaise that it is producing. Youth gangs are even beginning to turn up. While this should not be good news for anybody—social chaos is still too far down the Japanese road for Detroit to take comfort—it does provide tentative indicators that even Japan may be experiencing the longer-range effects of democracy and mass culture, the individualism that comes from affluence.

That the problem is not merely our own should give us no comfort anyway. The severe breakdown of a central pillar of American society should set off the alarm bell that a larger pathology is involved in this increasing failure of the American system—which has its roots in the culture spawned in part by democracy and the economic and social values that spring therefrom.

America the Pathbreaker

American mass culture thus finds a resonance in the cultures of most other peoples of the world. America, of course, discovered the chief characteristics of this mass culture in the roots of its own social and economic circumstances. These circumstances so far exist only in part in the rest of the world. That fact has not deterred other countries from embracing these American cultural innovations. A gradual process of evolution cannot be far behind; these societies will increasingly come to resemble American economic, and then social, models. International acceptance of American cultural modes does not therefore represent mere borrowing of certain superficial cultural characteristics of American life, but the yearning for, the anticipation of, newer social and economic institutions that characterize America. That is the importance of American culture: it is embryonic international culture.

Yet for all the desire that exists around the world to attain the consumerist values of modern society, the homogenization process is also proving profoundly disturbing. Global homogenization of culture, American-style or otherwise, poses profound threats to the existence of local cultures. These threats infect struggles over issues of national identity and ethnicity that will increasingly destabilize life in the twenty-first century.

As we applaud the emergence of Eastern Europe and Russia into the realm of democratic practice and consumer societies, won't they rapidly come to confront these same problems? Won't Africa, Asia, and Latin America as well? All these societies are in fact buying into a total package deal that includes increased political and economic freedom, individual fulfillment, social license, and consumerist orientation—and, almost invariably, the corresponding social evils. We have scarcely realized the problem ourselves. When do we market the antidote?

NOTES

1. See Jean Merl, "Corporations Find No Easy Cure for Education's Ills," *Los Angeles Times*, March 28, 1990.

2. Stanley Meister, "Reading the Signs of a Crisis," *Los Angeles Times*, May 11, 1990.

FOUR

Democracy and Warring Nations

The ghosts of global ideological war are now vanquished. Yet we stand on the threshold of a new era of global wars—small ones. The post–Cold War era, contrary to our present expectations and desires, will be marked by a significant increase in conflict and localized war around the world. Neonationalism and ethnic struggles, often attended by religious zeal, will lie at the heart of these conflicts. The spread of democracy will only be a complicating factor in dealing with these challenges, both for the warring countries involved and for the West. But how is it that the vanishing of superpower conflict and tensions evoke such contrary reactions in the rest of the world?

The Fading of Cold War Disciplines

The balance of nuclear terror—however hateful it was—has provided the underpinnings of the world order since World War II. The balance of terror has also imposed a certain discipline upon that world order: a general recognition that the world was an exceedingly dangerous place, that the possibility of nuclear war between the superpowers was ever present, and that it most likely would be sparked by some Third World conflict between superpower proxies.

And such superpower conflicts by proxy were indeed abundant throughout the Third World: we need only look at the East-West dimensions of the Korean conflict, the Vietnam War, several Arab-Israeli wars, Central American conflicts, and the African conflicts of Ethiopia, Angola, and Mozambique. The contest between the Brezhnev Doctrine and the Reagan Doctrine—an ideological struggle over whether Third World communist revolutions are reversible or not—was all about proxy wars. In most of these wars, the Soviet-American contest was not the source of regional conflict. Deep-seated local hostilities were long-standing, but they usually became quick grist for the East-West mill. The East-West struggle left no country, no player, however modest, out of its scope.

The USSR itself bore primary responsibility for world instability in the Cold War by providing military and political support to a whole range of radical Third World leaders with powerful ambitions: Muammar Qadhafi in Libya, Daniel Ortega in Nicaragua, Fidel Castro and Che Guevara in Cuba, Hafez al-Assad in Syria, Vietnamese expansionism under Ho Chi Minh in Indo-China, Saddam Hussein in Iraq, Kim Il-Sung in North Korea, and Mengistu Haile Mariam in Ethiopia, to name only a few. All of them were intent upon exporting regional instability, in the name of the revolution, but also in the name of aggrandizement. The Soviet Union profited from these actions because they led to the establishment of a global network of radical allies who were partially responsive to Moscow's own foreign policy agenda, posing constant challenges to the United States and preoccupying our foreign policy for decades.

Yet there were balancing factors. While the Cold War exacerbated regional conflict in one sense, it also set limits to those same conflicts. The superpowers were not bereft of any sense of caution or responsibility even while conducting the global struggle; both were attentive to the potentially cataclysmic consequences of regional conflicts—out of realization that many of their respective clients were quite capable of moving the world even toward nuclear war in pursuit of their own narrow goals. A Qadhafi lost no sleep over thoughts of potential East-West nuclear exchange stemming from his regional adventures. Conservative superpower politics thus tended to constrain the "normal" evolution of political and social development in many countries. Neither country could ever afford to be hostage to the reckless acts of local Caesars.

Now that kind of discipline is gone. Moscow has disengaged from its persistent efforts to implant little red flags all over the global map, thus liberating the United States from the pressure to implant countervailing blue flags. International conflict has now become just "normal regional conflict" instead of an upheaval in an interlocking global system of balance of power. An immense burden has been lifted off both former superpowers.

But with the disappearance of international discipline, states may now feel increasingly emboldened to act upon the international scene with impunity, unconstrained by old superpower interests. The attack by Iraq's Saddam Hussein upon Kuwait in August 1990 is just such a case: would Saddam have felt the freedom to move with such impunity in the course of the Cold War? Would Moscow have "let" him do so, knowing the East-West confrontation that would be unleashed? Almost certainly not.

Finally, with the death of global politics, small countries start to matter a great deal more. Regional politics become the primary vehicle of international politics. The local upstart can wield greater power and influence over the region, upsetting the balance in the area. In how many Third World conflicts will the United States now feel compelled to intervene militarily? Not very many, given the considerable domestic disquiet over any involvement—even for the sake of an oil-rich Kuwait at the very heart of the world's most strategic region. If Zambia goes to war with Zimbabwe, what countries will send troops? If India invades Sri Lanka, who will do anything? A UN force may be available, but there will be many fires to put out, all the time.

Neonationalism

Today there are yet other factors that will powerfully contribute to instability in the world order. At the top of the list is the dawn of a new wave of nationalism in the world. I call it neonationalism, for it will differ from previous expressions of Third World nationalism. Earlier stages of Third World nationalism tended to revolve around the national liberation experience, the zeal engendered by the throwing off of colonial ties, often supported by a healthy dollop of Maoist ideology and Communist support.

Neonationalism is the product of more recent decades, going beyond classical nationalism. Neonationalism includes separatist subnationalism, that is, the expression of communal/ethnic aspirations of groups *within* the nation-state that are unhappy with their lot: Shiites in Iraq, Sikhs in India, Uighur Turks in Chinese Turkestan. It involves strong new drives toward separatism and breakaway nationalism: Quebec in Canada, Biafra in Nigeria, the Moros in the Philippines, Georgians in the Soviet Union, Catholics in Northern Ireland, Hungarians in Romania. Nationalist feelings and aspirations will acquire a new assertiveness that springs from international relaxation of tensions and from rising expectations of national and communal fulfillment.

For other countries, the new era represents an opportunity to redefine their national and regional ambitions. Many states of the world have had little opportunity in the Cold War period to settle old scores or redraw national boundaries since independence. Their nationalism will no longer be directed against their former colonial rulers, but more against an "unjust international order" of winners and losers. But this will not be a Third World cabal. Given increasing diversity among Third World states themselves, there may not be a lot of solidarity over the way any new pie should be divided up.

Neonationalism will revolve around a new search for identity—the struggle to preserve the ethnic/religious community in the face of an increasingly homogenizing and homogenized world. The new nationalist movements will take aim at rival nations—or at other communal groups within the same nation.

The West will undoubtedly come in for its fair share of attack as the author of some of the inequities of past orders. The Ayatollah Khomeini and Saddam Hussein, while both identifying a number of legitimate regional grievances, made their anti-Western positions the centerpiece of their policies. The Third World will not run out of leaders who trace the roots of all sufferings to the West, partly because it makes for good rabble-rousing politics and partly because there is an element of truth to the region's grievances: a history of Western interventionism, colonialism, military occupation, manipulation or domination of rulers, economic exploitation, skewed economic development patterns under colonialism, vulnerability to Western-dominated commodity price structures, unfair tariff policies, foreign debt manipulation, and unequal treatment at the international level until recent times. The massive problems that spring from the region's own history, political culture, and economic and social underdevelopment also contribute mightily to the regional pathology.

Neonationalism and Democracy

Neonationalistic impulses cannot resist the impulses of democracy either. A wave of democratic aspirations is gradually spreading over much of the world—where power has historically remained in the hands of an authoritarian social or military elite ever since early independence movements. Today, slowly developing middle classes and technocrats increasingly demand a voice in the conduct of policy.

It would, of course, be naive to predict the dawn of a new age of universal democracy. Numerous societies lack many of the desirable prerequisites necessary to sustain democratic governance. But democracy is an instrument as much as a goal, the banner and mechanism by which frustrated elements—often a majority of society—will seek greater voice. The euphoria of Eastern Europe and the Berlin Wall has only heightened aspirations. And it's all on TV.

But euphoria will not be enough. When new groups come to power by democratic means—especially majorities previously excluded from the governing process—there is no guarantee at all that they will extend the same rights to former oppressors, minorities, or rival groups. Nor will democracy, once established, necessarily be sustained. Indeed, many Latin American countries have exhibited something like a "democracy cycle": periods of democracy alternate with periods of rule by a junta that eventually loses stomach for sustained military rule. But the expectation of democracy as an actual right is growing; increasingly informed and sophisticated publics press harder for its blessings. Democracy more than ever before is an idea whose time has come, bolstered by dramatic political upheaval around the world, and the impact of international media and communications that pose such a threat to authoritarian rule.

But the picture is not all rosy. Democracy and free expression will inevitably release new waves of populist feeling no longer constrained by traditional authoritarian rule, expressing itself in impulses of raw nationalism no longer held in check. The more alien the democratic tradition is to the state, the rawer the forms in which neonationalism will express itself. Newly liberated Eastern Europe is rapidly rediscovering its old ethnic causes, which now threaten the very unity of states like Czechoslovakia and Yugoslavia.

Democracy exacerbates nationalist impulses because it enfranchises broad elements of society previously deprived of an active voice in national politics, making them more vulnerable to demagogic siren songs. More significantly, whole new middle classes will demand the right to active participation in administering the state; autocracies cannot shut them out of the ruling process as in the past. New leaderships will prove highly responsive to the nationalist sensitivities of their constituents in the face of any seeming slights by great powers that dominate the international order.

Ironically, the United States is often seen as the first offender in this regard, as the policeman and primary architect of the Western world order—and as the cause of whatever iniquities it possesses. The Third World nations will grow more rather than less protective of their sovereignty, especially as the world aspires to a greater sense of equality among nations. Iraq is angered in negotiations with President Bush because the tone of correspondence does not treat Iraq "as an equal." These sentiments are not simply those of a megalomaniacal Saddam Hussein. They reflect rising expectations in the world, broadening education, greater public awareness, and widening sensitivity to past humiliations of national pride.

To be sure, democracy also can be a constraining force in international relations. "Democracies don't start wars" is a well-established thesis. But this observation was made primarily about seasoned Western democracies. Newer democracies, like newer nationalisms, will be rawer and more inclined to give vent to aggressive or chauvinistic feelings. India's raucous ethnic politics and Eastern Europe's rekindling nationalist resentments are cases in point. And fascistic figures can emerge out of this environment as easily as mushrooms in dark places, such as Serbia's Milosevic, who can win elections and lead the masses in chauvinistic directions. In the next decades, moderated fascism is a more likely alternative to democratic rule than is communism.

Already in Eastern Europe we see expressions of anti-Semitism and hatred toward other minorities—impulses that were suppressed during the decades of communist rule. The increasing enfranchisement of the masses can only assist in producing ethnic and national chauvinism that negatively affects state policies. Can this be avoided? Perhaps passing through a stage of nationalistic intolerance is part of the process of political coming of age. Democracy in the United States itself has passed through some rawer stages in the earlier part of its history, expressed in chauvinism, jingoism, public racial intolerance, and unprincipled electoral campaigns appealing to negative aspects of American society. Some would argue we have not yet passed completely out of that stage.

Nationalism and the Quest for Identity

But does neonationalism reflect only the politics of recent decades? Not at all. Its most characteristic features spring from far deeper roots: the search for meaningful identity in the modern world. Indeed, anomie—alienation and a sense of loss of self-identification—is a problem that affects the entire world, capitalist or socialist, advanced or undeveloped. It is a disease of the modern condition. How do we define ourselves? What is the social unit that we cling to in order to sustain our sense of identity—especially during the abrasive processes of modernization, and social and technological change? What are the associations or characteristics by which we identify ourselves? Are we Americans, engineers, Southerners, Christians, Minnesotans, females, North Americans, blacks, San Franciscans, workers, mountain bikers, or what?

We can belong to each of these different categories; some impulses are stronger than others in given societies and at given times. Today in the Soviet Union, it is no longer meaningful to be a "Soviet"; maybe it is more important that one is an Uzbek, or a Muslim. To be a Palestinian has new meaning now. To be a Kurd in Iraq poses serious problems of identity. What will be the social unit of membership that is most meaningful to us in times of travail?

Many political observers have marveled at the persistence—even the resuscitation—late in the twentieth century of feelings of localism and particularism, as among the Northern Irish, the Belgian Flemish, the Basques, the Quebecois, the Palestinians, the Kurds, the Azerbaijanis, the Sudanese Dinkas, the Native Americans, and dozens of other groupings—even resurgent ethnicity within America.

What is the reason for such a resurgence? The factors are many and complex.[1] But surely it is related in part to the broader process of rapid urbanization, the impersonalization and alienation that this modernization produces. The modern Third World state homogenizes, it permits massive influences from the developed world to squeeze traditional cultures to the point of endangering them. The modern Third World state is often in the hands of the most advanced—or powerful—ethnic/religious element within the state, such as the Christians in Lebanon or the Punjabis in Pakistan, and the dominant element threatens the way of life of the remaining majority or minority.

In the more advanced countries, the expanding bureaucratic state itself is busy supplanting the traditional community; it erases local culture even as it provides new social services that, since the dawn of time, were met by the extended family, the clan, the guild, or the community. However "efficient" the adoption of vast social roles by the state may be, it results in the increasing impersonalization of life. Much anxiety results that provides the grist for extremist nationalist or religious movements. Third World literature is rife with reactions to urban impersonalization, the anxiety of the villager come to the city.

A passage from Turkish novelist Orhan Kemal describes a young villager arriving in Istanbul on the basis of a letter from a relative several years earlier suggesting that he come. The villager is dismayed that the relative is not happy to see him:

—But, Gafur Agha, I came just because of you.
—Am I your mother or your father? What do you rely on me for?
—You said come, there's a lot of work, you sent a letter. . . .
—If I sent one, it was two years ago. Where were you for two years? There was work then. You think the work is going to wait for you that long? You think work is at your father's beck and call? If a Mehmed doesn't come there's an Ehmed, if it isn't an Ehmed, it's Hasan, if it's not Hasan, it's Hussein. Jobs aren't at your father's command. This is Istanbul. Here everybody tries to put something over on everybody else. Brothers become enemies. That's Istanbul. . . ."

Mehmed's moist eyes wandered over the surroundings. Was he going to stay in this big, this very big, this very crowded city which he didn't know at all, without friend, without a place or without a home? Was there really bad blood between brothers, did brothers become enemies? How could he stay in this city where brothers became enemies, how was he to protect himself from enemies? Why had he even come? . . .[2]

But we need not go so far as exotic Istanbul to find such sentiments. Indeed, in the United States itself, and in the rest of the industrialized world, the virtues and certitudes of identity in small-town life have given way to the city. People crave identity, but where are they to get it? In the Third World it is nationalism or subnationalism in its more extreme forms, or religious fundamentalism, that represents a reaction to this hunger for identity.

It is not just the city that weakens the sense of individual identity. In the Third World, the process of urbanization also involves processes of *Westernization*. America is obviously seen as a major vehicle of this process. The West comes to be deeply resented as the apparent instrument of the destruction of native culture and traditional mores. Indeed, these impulses are among the deepest wellsprings of Islamic fundamentalism in the Muslim world—the craving for firm values that are associated with traditional identity.

In the end, even nationalism will prove insufficient to satisfy cravings for a more precise, more manageable sense of identity. It is not enough to be one of many tens of millions of Nigerians, Bengalis, or Indonesians. People revert to smaller communal groupings, the tribe or the region, the dialect or the local language. These local nationalisms, regionalisms, and linguistic or religious minority identities can often be the vehicle against the more privileged regions, classes, ethnic groups, or religions within the same country. Poorly integrated multiethnic states are at major risk in the future as dissatisfaction grows under pressures of modernization and change.

We are thus faced with two phenomena related to nationalism, both certain to produce increasing conflict: communalism or subnationalism within the state, which threatens dozens of countries with debilitating separatist movements; and nationalism at the state level in conflict with nationalisms of other states. Neonationalism thus takes on great new strength in the struggle for identity and self-affirmation, and perhaps in the rectification of ethnic borders—all *within* the context of independence and modernization.

The Last Breakup of Empire

The long-delayed breakup of the Soviet Empire has provided the final impetus. By all natural rights, the huge Tsarist Empire should have collapsed of its own weight in 1917 with the fall of the tsar, when so many other empires disappeared. But the Tsarist Empire beat the odds; unexpectedly it did survive, transformed by Bolshevik force into the rigid, totalitarian structure of the Soviet Empire, which managed to sustain itself right down to the 1990s.

The breakup of empire is always destabilizing, for it throws new hunks of real estate onto the international market, charts new boundaries, and establishes new relationships. Even the end of the Portuguese colonial holdings with the liberation of Angola and Mozambique in the 1970s instantly dragged those countries deep into the East-West struggle, in which the Soviet Union won the race for influence, thereby beginning the process of long civil war and regional war around each of these states. If two small Portuguese colonies in Africa could affect the international system to that degree, how destabilizing will be the collapse of the Soviet Empire? What other processes might it unleash? What will separatism in the USSR mean for the rest of the world?

The Threat of Separatism

The world order since World War II has been extremely reluctant to admit the creation of new states. Separatism in very principle is viewed as a bane, and broadly resisted. Nigeria's bloody four-year war in the 1960s to prevent the separation of the large region of Biafra was generally upheld by the world, despite its one million casualties. Africa in particular has been viewed with the greatest trepidation, out of recognition that nearly all of Africa has been carved out along arbitrary colonial lines; redrawing borders or unifying divided peoples would begin a disastrous chain of interminable African wars in a process of total, continentwide national redefinition.

How can the breakup of the Soviet Union fail to bring major problems in its wake? The phenomenon produces at least two major difficulties. First, it opens the door once again to the formation of new nations—with perhaps fifteen different republics attaining some kind of independence, at least half of which have never really had any history of genuine independence as nation-states.

Second, the independence of the Muslim republics of the Soviet Union will involve serious border problems among themselves that could well spill over into states over the border.

- If six million Azerbaijanis live in Soviet Azerbaijan, at least ten million live in Iranian Azerbaijan, all speaking the same Turkic language. An independent Soviet Azerbaijan will threaten the territorial integrity of Iran.
- If three million Tajiks live in Soviet Tajikistan, at least four million live over the border in northern Afghanistan.
- Over a million and a half Uzbeks live across the border from Soviet Uzbekistan in northern Afghanistan.

• Over a million and a half Kazakhs live in China, over the border from Soviet Kazakhstan.

• Over a half million Uighur Turks live in the Soviet Union, over the border from twelve million Uighurs in China—who are already restive against Chinese chauvinism and imperialism.

• Four and a half million Moldavians (who are really Romanians) live in the Soviet Union just over the border from Romania.

These demographic realities suggest that the Muslim regions of the Soviet Union may be strongly tempted to redraw their own borders along more ethnic lines. How will Iran react if its own Azerbaijani population should be tempted to join with a newly independent Soviet Azerbaijan in the north? And what of northern Afghanistan, lying north of the formidable barrier of the Hindu Kush? The population there is largely Uzbek and Tajik, and long unhappy with the dominant role of the Pashtun population of Afghanistan. Will they find some attraction in joining with their newly independent ethnic brothers to the north?

The danger, of course, is in the "demonstration effect," the contagious spread of the separatist concept by example from one people to another. If Iran should suffer a breakaway of its important Azerbaijani population, Iran's Kurds who adjoin Azerbaijan will likely be impelled to seek long-awaited autonomy or even independence. Tibetans are interested in any progress by the Uighur Turks or the Mongols toward genuine autonomy in China. Separatism begets separatism. Any successful move of the Iranian Kurds toward independence will have immediate and direct impact upon the Kurds in Iraq, and those in Turkey. Nor are the Kurds a tiny, obscure people: they are the fourth-biggest ethnic group in the Middle East, numbering over twenty million all told, divided up between Iran, Iraq, and Turkey. A concerted move on their part toward unity and independence would devastate Turkey and Iraq. The unity of the Pashtuns in Afghanistan and Pakistan would tear both of those countries asunder.

Much better publicized in the West, the Palestinian problem remains one of the most volatile of issues as Israel remains intent on keeping nearly two million Palestinians captive on the West Bank and in Gaza. In other parts of the Middle East, Berber nationalism in Algeria and Morocco and the Polisario Liberation Front in Morocco have been active. In Lebanon, of course, ethnic and sectarian hostility and civil war have destroyed half the country—involving at least six major religious groups that contest power and territoriality in regular convulsions of terror and bloodletting. Syria, controlled by the small Alawite religious minority, seems destined for explosion at some point in the future. So does Iraq, where a Shiite majority is denied major voice in the state.

The Middle East is hardly the only region vulnerable to the redrawing of maps along ethnic lines. The Indian subcontinent is a patchwork quilt of ethnic groups. Pakistan broke away from India in 1947. East Pakistan, now Bangladesh, then broke away from Pakistan in 1971. All three of Pakistan's minority provinces, Sind, Baluchistan, and the Pashtun Northwest Frontier, have also seen separatist movements burst out from time to time.

India itself is potentially even more vulnerable, with its massive multiethnic state of over fifty distinct ethnic groupings. The Sikhs to date have been the most dangerous breakaway element, threatening to take the critically important province of Punjab with them. A large Muslim Kashmiri independence movement is currently conducting a jihad for its freedom and independence from Hindu domination—even calling themselves mujahidin. Hindu fundamentalism is rising dangerously, supposedly in response to Islamic fundamentalism (even though Muslims are not more than about 11 percent of the population), threatening major civil conflict. Other smaller nationalities have also had separatist guerrilla movements. India is the closest remaining thing to an empire in this world, without actually being one. In a world convulsed by separatist impulses, India needs to tend to its patchwork quilt of ethnic states and languages very carefully indeed if it is not to fall victim to dozens of separatist movements or even wars.

Elsewhere in Asia, serious breakaway and separatist movements of one kind or another exist in northwest China, Tibet, Thailand, the Philippines, Burma, and Sri Lanka.

In Africa, of course, the grist for separatism and war could not be greater: the highly tribalized structure of most African states and the arbitrary, nonorganic delineation of state borders by colonial powers are a certain recipe for conflict. Major civil war, or cross-border war, has already been a critical problem in Nigeria, Ethiopia, Sudan, Chad, South Africa, Zaire, Namibia, Angola, Mozambique, Somalia, Rwanda-Burundi, and Uganda. The relatively limited separatism on the African continent to date is not at all necessarily good news: it suggests that this movement has not yet arrived at full fruition in African politics.

Lest Europeans look smugly upon the ethnic bloodletting in the Third World, Europe itself is still the scene of breakaway struggles. While the Walloons in Belgium have largely limited themselves to language riots, the Basques, the Catholics in Northern Ireland, and the Turkish Cypriots have engaged in full-scale guerrilla warfare and even serious terrorism. Under the strictures of communist rule in Eastern Europe, history stopped for forty years; now it is just coming out of the deep freeze and is entering a new phase of potentially violent nationalism and chauvinism. Yugoslavia ("South Slavia"), earlier in the century viewed as a "success story" in its efforts to unite much of the warring Balkans, is once again facing collapse and dismemberment as the five constituent republics seek liberation from the heavyhanded central control of the unified state. Romanian oppression of some two million Hungarians in Transylvania could yet become grounds for war between the two countries. Bulgarian authorities have tried to forcibly assimilate a sizable Turkish minority. Greece, Yugoslavia, and Bulgaria all quarrel over the Macedonians living in Yugoslavia. Greece and Turkey quarrel over the ethnically divided population of Cyprus.

Ethnic and religious hostility, of course, does not necessarily spell war. Nor can separatism be a viable solution to the grievances of every small group that feels itself culturally, religiously, or ethnically oppressed: a large proportion of these groups are simply too small to exist separately. But they are capable of violent domestic disruption, terrorism, and civil war, seriously affecting the stability of the world.

The Democracy Trap: Self-Determination and Human Rights

The American tradition is deeply steeped in the concept of self-determination; Woodrow Wilson tried to enshrine the principle at Versailles in an attempt to build a new world after World War I. Indeed, Armenians, Kurds, and Arabs, among others, felt they had a Western commitment at that time to independent states.

How will America now confront the aspirations of large ethnic groups that seek self-determination in the new world order? Did the gates clang down on the creation of new states in the years after World War II? Who are we to say that the door is now closed to such aspirations, especially if they are expressed by democratic choice? By what reasoning can we deny the Palestinians an independent state on the West Bank? By what rationale can we tell the Kurds to forget about it? What if the huge Zulu population—eight million—wants its own state? Is there some law of economics that says that a state must have so many people or so much resources to be viable? Or does it suffice to say, "Tough luck, your aspirations simply harm the interests of already existing states—especially ones we like"?

As we move into a new era of democratic procedures and international rule of law, it will be extremely difficult for the UN to refuse to conduct plebiscites among significant peoples of the world on such basic issues as who they are to be ruled by and whether they have the right to cultural and political self-fulfillment. Yet the free and democratic expression of such aspirations will prove to be deeply destabilizing to many currently existing multireligious, multiethnic states. Indeed, democracy may stand or fall in many states depending on how the rulers believe it would change the domestic power structure. Do the Iraqi Sunnis, who monopolize power, wish to enfranchise Shiites, who are a majority of the population? Will the minority ruling Alawite (heterodox Islamic) clan in Syria allow itself to be dislodged by majority Sunnis? Clearly democratization unleashes instability in areas of long-suppressed, festering problems. But are stability and preservation of the status quo to be America's guiding principles, to be defended against destabilizing democratic inroads in the world?

The problem becomes even more intense when we consider the deep American commitment to human rights in the last three decades. When large national groups with aspirations for self-determination attempt to fulfill those aspirations— only to be brutally put down by existing national authorities— what does America do? Can we sit by and watch Palestinians, Kurds, Tibetans, Sikhs, Kashmiris, Eritreans, and others be beaten, imprisoned, and shot? For America simply to urge restraint is just a cop-out; it is no answer. In some cases, suggestions of permitting greater cultural autonomy might solve the issue, but not necessarily, especially if the aspiring nationality is clear about its aspirations. The United States will not, in good conscience, be able to back foreign governments that fail to respond to such legitimate aspirations.

"Legitimate," of course, is the sticking point. How is "legitimacy" determined? Precedents for recent American policy are not encouraging. We have interpreted legitimacy to a great extent in accordance with our own Cold War interests. We tended to be sympathetic to movements that would weaken the USSR and its allies, but to oppose movements that threatened our own allies. Latvians are fine, but not Palestinians. Tibetans thumbs up, but Kurds thumbs down. We were not entirely cynical, of course. We declined to support the Eritrean Liberation Front in Ethiopia—even when that front was waging war against the Marxist-Leninist regime of Mengistu Haile Mariam's Ethiopia. Our rationale was that separatist movements in Africa were uniquely dangerous, given the overall problems of tribalism and borders there.

And yet, we betray certain cultural prejudices and predispositions as well. It seemed fine to support Lithuania—and there are a lot of Lithuanians in the American electorate to hold President Bush's feet to the fire. But when it came to the Turkic Muslim Azerbaijanis, we were unmoved—a fact that did not escape attention in either Turkey or Iran.

Whatever the virtues of historical distinctions between the Baltic and the Azerbaijani cases, the United States has no firm principles or policies by which to judge these issues. Most cases will probably be decided only when they have to be, and in accordance with the existing balance of interests. But a constant domestic tug-of-war will remain over the kind of principles by which American foreign policy should be guided.

Is Appomattox Still a Viable Solution?

Foreign civil war scenarios will be marginally easier to deal with than international conflict. As Americans we have been particularly susceptible to the argument—Gorbachev used it with Bush—that, after all, America had its own Civil War; Abraham Lincoln went to war specifically to preserve the Union. How can we deny the unionist aspirations of other states to maintain their own integrity?

But what about our Union? Washington indeed fought four bloody years in order to attain a settlement at Appomattox that preserved the Union. And scars of that conflict are still not gone in the harshly vanquished American South even today. Is Appomattox still a viable solution for American problems? Could George Bush today call in federal troops and go to war against our own population if, say, the South decided that economically and culturally it no longer wished to remain in the Union? If it undertook a referendum and freely voted for independence? Or if the Spanish-speaking parts of the United States voted for autonomy or separation? Can anyone imagine American troops today killing tens of thousands of Americans—in front of TV cameras—in order to prevent regional separation? I submit that the Appomattox solution—the use of military force to preserve the Union—is no longer tenable. Should a new attempt at regional autonomy or separation ever emerge in America—supported by a local referendum—it could no longer be stopped by force from Washington. American and world values have changed too much for that kind of violence to be wreaked ever again— at least in America—simply in the name of preserving the Union.

Ironically, we conveniently forget that it was Gorbachev's USSR that passed legislation mandating the terms under which subdivisions and peoples can secede. We in America have no such provisions. We fortunately have no regional "homelands" in this country that are capable of expressing autonomous aspirations, with the possible exception of our Southwestern Mexican-American regions. We can argue, therefore, that secession in America is not "thinkable." But why should it not still be thinkable, however improbable? By what criterion will we judge that separatism and regional/ethnic self-determination, freely voted on, is a valid principle elsewhere in the world but impermissible here? And how will we stand if Canada, on our very doorstep, should decide to use force—which it surely knows it cannot do—to prevent the coming separation of Quebec?

America's faith in democratic principles and procedures will be sorely tested in the next decades as we confront problems of growing neonationalism. We had better be clear about it: democracy *will* produce both the desire for greater cultural and ethnic self-expression and the electoral vehicles by which to express separatist ambitions. Increasing worldwide acceptance of human rights will make repression and suppression of these aspirations all the more unconscionable. And the end of global ideological struggle will limit American ability to reject nationalist movements on grounds of American national security. More than ever before, each case will have to be judged on its own merits, and there will be fewer grounds on which to dismiss it.

What Is the "Highest Form" of Government?

As America and the world enter a new phase of political development with more powerful expressions of ethnicity, what will be the guiding principle? Is national self-determination on an ethnic base to be the wave of the future? Or multiethnic states and federations?

We have long accepted the idea of the nation-state as the backbone of the modern international order. Yet, is fulfillment of ethnic aspirations for self-determination really the highest political goal toward which we should aspire? It is, after all, a relatively new concept on the world stage. With the emergence of eighteenth-century English nationalism, the concept of nationalism moved into the political vocabulary of the Western world. It was a gradual but revolutionary development, coming on the heels of centuries of multiethnic states that had never even thought of themselves in those terms. Universal empires based on the Roman model had long been the guiding structures, fusing broad regions, religions, and monarchs. In the course of European wars before the eighteenth century, few thought anything of the fact that people of similar languages might be divided, and might even fight against each other in support of a regional prince or ruler.

The age of nationalism inspired heady research into a nation's own ethnic roots, creating the cultural excitement of ethnic fulfillment. Nationalism was intended to provide a mystical, almost spiritual quality to the individual's life in the nation-state; the citizen was part of a greater ethnic community—at once more concrete, specific, and immediate than any concept of empire or monarch. In an age of new awakenings, ethnic nationalism powerfully formed the individual's sense of identity.

But intolerance was the flip side of the coin of ethnic fulfillment. Nationalist movements were not necessarily "progressive" at all in terms of international harmony. They were, in fact, often retrogressive in their promotion of intolerance and prejudice against those outside the ethnic structure. It was just such narrow nationalism that contributed directly to World War I, and, in a different sense, that was the driving ideology of Hitler's Third Reich. The purer the ethnicity of the state, the more intolerant it could be. It is probably no accident that on the eve of World War II, both Germany and Japan stood out as preeminent examples of ethnically highly homogeneous populations—states that literally worshiped the principle of ethnicity. Japan's ethnic intolerance today stems primarily from its own continuing remarkable ethnic homogeneity.

Today, we Americans are inclined to believe that perhaps in fact the multiethnic state is more inclined to produce tolerance and understanding than is the ethnically homogeneous state. Even more to the point, is not the multiethnic state most representative of what is to come in the world, given the immense fluidity and mobility of modern population movement? The Third World is migrating heavily into the Western world in search of education, jobs, and freedom. Once relatively homogeneous ethnic states such as England,

France, Germany, Holland, and Italy now find their character transformed by new waves from abroad, producing new domestic intolerance that takes direct political expression. Even Japan is not fully able to resist the inflow of East Asian immigrants in search of work in a Japanese economy increasingly short of labor.

One wonders, in fact, whether Europe is going to make it in this respect. There is no question that it will be forced increasingly to absorb other nationalities in large quantities, from Eastern Europe, the Mediterranean, and the Third World. Yet Europe is not ready for this. Nothing in the European countries' cultures prepares them for either internal ethnic pluralism or the weakening of national culture. Over the longer run, ethnic hostilities could cripple hopes for an increasingly integrated political union. The Europeans are not ready to give up, or even heavily dilute their national cultures. France is deeply disturbed at the prognosis for French cultural distinctiveness and the preservation of unique French traditions in the new Europe. In this respect Europe is in far worse shape than America, where we already have a well-developed ideology of ethnic and cultural pluralism, even if there are occasional problems in fully implementing it.

Do we believe that the multiethnic state should be encouraged as we move into the next century? Does the diversity of such a state produce a greater richness of life, a greater tolerance and awareness of other cultures, religions, and lifestyles? One can argue that in America, at least, it does, as we will examine in a subsequent chapter. While a melting pot may not be in the cards for most countries for a long time to come, is not at least a federated or confederated structure a higher form of political entity to which the world should aspire? Should this ideal be the guiding feature of American policy abroad in situations of ethnic conflict? Is it not better to remain together than to separate? As Lord Acton wrote in 1862, it is not the one-nationality state but the ethnically pluralistic state that

> tends to diversity and not to uniformity, to harmony and not to unity; because it aims not at an arbitrary change, but at careful respect for the existing conditions of political life. . . . It provides against the servility which flourishes under the

shadow of a single authority, by balancing interests, multiplying associations. . . . A State which is incompetent to satisfy different races condemns itself; a State which labours to neutralise, to absorb, or to expel them destroys its own vitality; a State which does not include them is destitute of the chief basis of self-government.[3]

But, let's face it, nationalist impulses may have to run their full—often ugly—course before they can be contained. Realization of full-blown ethnic self-determination—in the shape of an independent nation-state—may be a necessary stage of development, especially for those groups that have felt historically oppressed. Perhaps only after living through such a "cooling-off period" can they comfortably acquiesce to some limitation of cultural and political sovereignty within the framework of a larger political association. Such voluntary federation does not come easily if an ethnic group has previously been forcibly contained within a broader multiethnic state dominated by another ethnic group. Thus the Soviet Union may have to break up entirely before any of its component parts can eventually come back together under some mutually advantageous, voluntary form of association.

In short, federalism most likely represents the "wave of the future," but this form cannot be force-fed or hastened; indeed, any attempt to do so is likely to be counterproductive. And memories of a hierarchical relationship of "superior" and "inferior" elements in such previous entities must be largely erased before the new association can begin to work.

The Choices Ahead

The next century thus offers the prospect of newly invigorated nationalism, and a demand for equality of relationship among the nations of the world. There will be less tolerance now for external intervention and great powers' use of *force majeure*. These resentments lay barely beneath the surface in the Iraqi-Kuwaiti crisis of 1990.

Indeed, the modern international state structure is still very new; most independent states have been on the world stage only a short time. They have not had a chance to shake down completely and to think about reordering relationships. They have so far had very little chance to demonstrate what their natural interrelationships—their patterns of actions, of friends and enemies—will be in a loosely organized world. The world has almost no precedent, no experience to go by.

Even Western Europe itself has had little experience at long periods of coexistence in a relaxed world order. We're not just talking about the Third World: Germany and Italy came into existence only late in the last century; the very concept of "Italy" seemed artificial to its founders scarcely a century ago. England and France both had empires and an imperial rivalry around the world. Russia ran an empire; Eastern Europe bore no resemblance to today's borders; the Balkans were barely coming out from Ottoman and Hapsburg control. Most of the Third World was under the control of some European colonial power. The interwar period was stormy, and the Cold War again froze the world order significantly after World War II, highly distorting political relationships around the globe. What experience, then, do world populations have for living together as peaceable, independent states under "normal" circumstances? The reality is that we simply don't know how it should work—the world has never been there before.

Africa is in many ways the worst off—and the best off. Because ethnicity has played such a minimal role in shaping the borders of African states, reordering the borders of African nation-states along more ethnic lines is almost impossible, and a threat to all that region. Ironically, therefore, the African state could have the best shot of all at a full acceptance of the idea of the multiethnic state—given the drastic absence of viable alternatives. But what if Africa really hasn't even *started* to explore the concept of ethnically determined boundaries? That, unfortunately, may be the greater likelihood, and a surefire recipe for massive disorder.

Much of the world now may well decide against direct intervention in many future regional struggles; "just let 'em fight it out on their own." The Iraqi-Kuwaiti crisis was not quite typical of future regional conflicts, since any crisis in the oil-rich Persian Gulf automatically seizes world attention. In less critical areas of the globe, international peacekeeping mechanisms under UN auspices may be gratefully welcomed by

Western publics less willing to send their own troops abroad in large quantities. If these mechanisms can be developed in the new international order, it is just possible that international conflict might actually lessen. If swift, unanimous international multilateral action can be anticipated, future Saddam Husseins may think twice about quick territorial grabs.

If the world wearies of constant struggle, however, the richer states of the world may then simply sit by and watch the rest of the world kill one another until the poor, too, simply tire of it. Even if the developed states of the world have acquired some misgivings about massive arms sales to poorer states, there will always be a thriving arms market for up-and-coming arms producers in more advanced Third World states.

As a new era of nationalist, religious, and democratic trends opens up, the United States will find itself caught between the role of guardian of order and stability and passive witness to the roller-coaster effect of nations exercising newfound freedoms of nationalist expression. How will we look out over this world? We may avoid involvement, and for good reason. America may be the least desirable instrument for international police action, simply because we carry too much political baggage to be the interventionary state of choice. We have a long history of unilateral intervention that most nations do not appreciate, however grateful we believe they should be. And we have a population that is increasingly less willing to run the risk of dying for anything. That, too, is one major effect of democracy.

NOTES

1. For a good general overview of this issue, see Ted Robert Gurr, "Ethnic Warfare and the Changing Priorities of Global Security," *Mediterranean Quarterly*, Winter 1990.

2. Orhan Kemal, *Birds of Exile* (Istanbul, 1962); passage translated by Graham E. Fuller.

3. Lord Acton, "On Nationality."

FIVE

Democracy and Ecology: Ideals in Contradiction?

The Plague of Numbers

The shattering revelation seems to have come only late in the twentieth century: the earth and its capacities, far from being infinite, are distinctly finite and are visibly shrinking in our own lifetimes. Mankind is already pressing against the limits of the ecosphere, as in other areas of our existence. Thinkers like Malthus had enunciated for us the grim prophecy in the previous century that there might soon be more mouths to feed than food to feed them.

But Malthus was dead wrong. And that is probably the bad news. Our ecological problems would take care of themselves if food were a limited resource, automatically limiting population growth. But there is plenty of food to go around; we are poised to feed ourselves to death in an ever spiraling orgy of growth that ultimately overcomes the planet's ability to absorb not people per se, but the population's agro-industrial excrement. Vast crowds beget the destructive psychology of the rabbit warren and produce the anomie of the urban masses dissatisfied with their existence. Cities seem to grow more unmanageable, but we seem to have no clear alternative but to abandon them to the underclass in a flight to the suburbs.

We have too many people—not because we can't feed

them, but because they are destroying the quality of life. Sheer human masses ever distance us from the primordial, physical roots of life—Nature. The urban existence becomes a human anthill as the human race no longer inhabits but infests the planet. People demand ever greater production, ever more energy to produce it, and ever more space to dispose of it. Yet most of the suggestions on how to cope with these predicaments are palliatives that fail to come to terms with the basic issues—and there may be no way that our society can cope with the basic issues.

An examination of the underpinnings of the ecological dilemma inevitably confronts one with the possibility of an actual incompatibility between democracy and free enterprise on the one hand and the ecological salvation of the planet on the other. Can such an incompatibility be managed? The ability of democracy to persuade Western—and Third World—populations to accept greater sacrifices for the long-range sake of the planet—indeed, possibly to change their very consciousness—is questionable. If this judgment is perhaps too stark, society should at least keep it in mind as it grapples with the fundamental flaws of our own political and economic systems.

In the decades ahead, consciousness of our ecological dilemma will develop unevenly over the globe, as the ecological issue moves onto collision course with many of the aspirations of the Third World. Conflict may well develop. Democracy and infinite freedom of choice will affect, and be deeply affected by, the ecological movement.

The New Ideology

Ecology as a vision only slowly and only recently moved into the focus of public concerns—within the last two or three decades at most. While the concept at first seemingly struck the public as dealing "only with Nature," its implications have come to gain worldwide attention. People instinctively felt that something indeed did seem wrong with our environment, even when they lacked hard scientific data on tonnages of effluence or the levels of mercury in the water table. Today, the Green movement most likely contains the seeds of the dominant political struggle of the next century.

Green has now replaced Red as the focus of concern. Conjuring with far more than "mere" politics and military power, ecology can claim to invoke nothing less than the future of the Earth itself. While public awareness has now grown dramatically, the actual politics of ecology have only begun to penetrate into daily political discourse. Far harsher battles than that over the safety of the spotted owl in the California redwood forests will be shaping up in the years to come.

Originally a subdiscipline of biology, ecology historically dealt with questions of relationships between organisms and their environment. The scope of meaning of "ecology" has expanded vastly beyond its original focus to denote concern for understanding and protecting the environment, and even for philosophically establishing man's proper relationship with it. The discipline has burgeoned in scope to contain a multiplicity of new subdisciplines in their own right. Ecology is no longer "just" a science: any body of thought that deals with such cosmic issues as the shared destiny of Humanity and the Earth will naturally take on the dimensions of an ideology.

Indeed, with such pretensions, how could ecology not become the new battleground for a whole range of contending political and ideological interests of the world today? It is now possible to speak of dozens of "ecological ideologies" or "ecoisms" that increasingly impose themselves upon the debate. We have eco-capitalism and eco-socialism, eco-fascism, eco-feminism, eco-anarchism, and even eco-terrorism. Nearly every political trend has carved out for itself a place on the political spectrum of the ecological movement. Serious ecological thinking goes vastly beyond the technical and biological spheres to talk of theological and even teleological issues such as Humanity's philosophical relationship to the Earth, the ultimate purpose of our life on Earth, and the prospects of the end of life on the planet. The most "theological" aspect of ecology, known as "Deep Ecology," is concerned with relationships among humans, other forms of life on Earth, and the Earth itself, as the starting point for a broad plan of action for saving the planet and all its beings.

The Dimensions of Ecology

"Simple" ecology—that discipline which most directly affects our politics today—deals with straightforward questions of increasing environmental consciousness and the need for industry, communities, and individuals to reorder their habits to preserve the environment. This level of ecology seeks to better manage the world's resources in order to use them more rationally and to preserve them longer. Its imperative is to make Humanity's life on the planet safer and healthier, and to preserve the natural balance of all species and their ecosystems.

These concerns all fall within the confines of ecologically sound management of growth. Indeed, the program is designed to permit growth tempered by ecological consciousness. How can we combine increased lumber yields and still maintain forests? How can we meet our rising energy needs without polluting the air and the environment any more—indeed, polluting it less than before? How can we recycle consumer items to avoid littering the earth and the beauty of Nature?

The Deep Ecologists

More radical ecologists are scornful of this "mainstream" approach to ecological problems. In their view it begs the fundamental question and constitutes no more than an ecological bandage on a festering existential cancer. Expressing themselves in more drastic terms, these ecologists, like the German Rudolf Bahro, speak of the need for "industrial disarmament," seeking not to temper future growth, but actually to reverse the entire Western cycle of exploitation of nature, consumption, and pollution. They will be happy with nothing less than reducing growth, reversing the process outright. The need is not to manage resource consumption more gently and efficiently but to limit consumption absolutely.

Indeed, in some of ecology's most radical manifestations, these thinkers call for a radical reorientation of the very philosophical foundations by which Humanity deals with Nature. They argue that domination of Nature by Humanity is fundamental to Western philosophy, starting with the Old Testament:

> God said unto [Adam and Eve], "Be fruitful, and multiply, and replenish the earth, and subdue it: and have dominion over the fish of the sea and over the fowl of the air, and over every living thing that moveth upon the earth."

The idea of dominating and subduing Nature was also implicit in the Greek scientific approach; the secrets of Nature were viewed no longer as mysteries to be contemplated or forces to be propitiated, but as objects and laws to be uncovered and revealed, and eventually mastered. This attitude is fundamental to the scientific/materialist bases of Marxism as well; Stalin and his successors spoke repeatedly of socialism "conquering Nature." The American spirit in the pioneers' long move westward was implicitly concerned with "taming Nature" as they went.

To Deep Ecologists, of course, this entire philosophical basis is anathema. Not only is Nature not to be subdued as some final victory by Humanity, but Humanity is an integral part of Nature and not dominant over it. Ecologists like Joanna Macy emphasize that people must conduct their lives on the planet in a nonintrusive fashion, for Humanity is not the center of existence, but only one of its elements.[1] Rudolf Bahro sharply criticizes "mainstream" ecological concerns as merely an attempt to shift Humanity's own crisis of being onto the environment; in his view it is not the *environment* that is in crisis but Humanity itself. This vision of ecology calls for nothing less than a wholesale reordering of the very character of Humanity and of attitudes that have persisted for millennia.

The First Seed That Plunders the Earth

Yet there is a dilemma in the Deep Ecological approach. While nearly everyone would applaud the idea that all mankind could benefit from a more reverential approach to Nature and the world in which we live, the roots of Humanity's exploitation of Nature lie very deep. It can be argued that only the hunters, fishers, and gatherers of prehistoric times lived in a full rhythm with their environment, taking no more than they required. Native Americans indeed did evolve deeply spiritual attitudes to the forces and bounties around them. But the first seeds of exploitation were sowed, so to speak, even in the early settled agricultural communities of prehistoric people. With the planting of that first seed, people sought to gain something extra out of the earth, to "push" the process, to multiply their holdings. The planting and harvesting of seeds rapidly led to production in excess of the individual's needs—the first step, in a sense, toward a plunder of the earth.

The very development of ancient civilization rests on the concept of *surplus* production of agricultural goods, to meet the needs of others. More seeds were planted in the earth than were required to meet the personal needs of the planter and his family, for the planter could use this surplus produce to acquire other goods in exchange. The very concept of specialization of profession rests upon excess production of all goods, so that they serve as instruments of barter for other goods that the individual farmer or craftsman cannot make for himself. Already in ancient times there was theoretically "no limit" to the amount of resources that people could require for commerce and for the creation of rich and variegated urban culture. It was excess production that fed, clothed, and housed the talents of Homer, Socrates, and Euripides, hewed the stones for the Parthenon, and took Sparta to war with Athens.

Indeed, the process went far beyond the avarice of the individual. Implicit in anything but the most basic subsistence economy is the thought that the production of wealth is the chief economic goal of the state. The production of wealth by definition requires production in excess of personal need, for this is the economic margin by which yet greater wealth can be produced to meet needs and goals as yet unarticulated. And the state, producing no wealth on its own, derives all its power from excess production of its citizens. In short, the problem seems almost endemic to the very concept of civilization.

Deep Ecology calls upon us to abandon this exploitive and plundering approach toward the planet and urges a sense of sufficiency, of "enoughness," upon the collective culture of

Humanity. The Native Americans, long viewed as a savage and primitive barrier to the spread of American civilization, have now come into their own as a philosophical model for all Americans. In a culture where "growth" was entirely absent as an idea, sufficiency was a living concept for the Native American for centuries.

But Native American philosophies in part sprang from centuries of limited technological capabilities—whether limited by choice or by circumstance. People can live more in harmony with Nature when they are either unable to understand its operation fully or feel subordinate to a power that they cannot change and that must be propitiated. This Native American philosophical coexistence with Nature is rendered no less admirable if much of it is attributed to an elementary stage of technological and scientific development, typified largely by intellectual (but certainly not spiritual) stasis in terms of mastering the environment. An understanding of Native American reverence toward our environment can only benefit us deeply today, for it suggests something of the attitudes that we must now adopt—this time by moral choice and conviction, rather than from necessity because of an absence of alternative technological approaches.

But even the Native American was not immune to blandishments of technological advancement when it became available—this time from the outside. Once the Spanish introduced something even as simple as the horse (theretofore absent), Native American culture was revolutionized: longer distances could be traversed, greater resources garnered; contact and conflict with other tribes increased; a rudimentary market economy was stimulated. A market economy automatically triggers the creation and accumulation of excess wealth in order to extend the range of possibilities for the individual and the tribe. A process of "corruption" of a purer state had begun.

Yet it would be erroneous to consider reverential or religious attitudes simply a mark of primitive culture. The scientific spirit as evolved from the Greeks indeed did begin the long process of erasure of mystery from the physical workings of all aspects of science. Today virtually no mystery remains chaste as we observe actual photographs of the most infinitesimal pieces of physical matter and the most hidden recesses of human biological processes. This is entirely appropriate as our knowledge of the physical world advances. The "fault" thus lies not with efforts of the ancients to explain the workings of the physical world, but with ourselves; we have assumed that understanding must inevitably lead to domination; understanding has produced the hubristic belief that we are fully masters of our destiny.

It is perhaps only the retention of some sense of "mystery" that permits an attitude of reverence toward one's surroundings—an attitude that is not necessarily incompatible with the scientific spirit of inquiry. After all, it is not inquiry that is the problem, but the loss of respect for resources, Nature, and the environment that often flows from "understanding" and "mastery."

In the end, no electron microscope can ever tell us what the purpose of these physical constructs is, nor what our relationship to it all should be. Herein lies the "mystery." These judgments must fall to the individual himself, but they still remain profound "mysteries" for which science cannot ever provide answers. Science can only tell us what is, not what it should mean to us. These are essentially ethical, moral, or even theological issues—as some ecologists will tell us.

None of this means that we must abjure further investigation into the nature of the atom or the gene, or into new plastics whose properties will better serve human life. The heart of the problem lies in the attitude toward these endeavors. If we feel that sheer scientific advancement and the inexorable development of new products are part of a predestined march toward Betterment, then we will perhaps be espousing ideas as primitive in the moral sphere as we regarded the views of primitive man to be in the scientific sphere. For primitive man regarded Nature uncritically and hence made no progress. Our own culture seems so seduced by the constant penetration of new scientific barriers and by our scientific "advances" as to lose all measure of a moral dimension. Indeed, many will feel that there is no such thing as a moral dimension to science. That is precisely why we are headed toward some kind of ecological catastrophe if the moral questions of "why?" and "how much?" and "to what end?" are not pondered on a regular basis.

But the Deep Ecologists can only entreat and raise consciousness. Heightened consciousness is fine, but who will take the decision not to pursue a scientific lead out of respect for a mystery? Scientific inquiry is usually quite amoral in its approaches. It is the applications that induce more severe questions of ethics and morality. The Deep Ecologists cannot make society freeze further economic, scientific, and technical advances. If Deep Ecology has an effect on society, it will most likely come—as the influence of religion does as well—through its impact on the private individual. We must feel compelled to constantly ask ourselves what the issues in balance are—must not only avoid further violating a now vulnerable planet and biosphere, but develop a truly enlightened understanding of our relationship as individuals and as a society to that environment. It will be social policy as derived from the public, and as it affects the courts, that will influence the way in which science and technology are applied.

Ecology and Walt Disney

Not all is well among the ecological activists. It turns out that one of the growing clashes within the movement itself is the struggle between the animal rights activists and the traditional conservationsts.[2] Mark you, this is no struggle over political turf, but actually a yawning philosophical gulf that characterizes much of the dilemma of contemporary mass culture. The clash reveals much about the Walt Disney moral vision with which we sometimes perceive contemporary American social problems.

The animal rights activists are concerned with animal life and the lives of individual animals. There is much that is admirable and important about this. By demeaning life through the casual destruction of its "lower orders," we are also diminishing ourselves. If we are to reach an accommodation with the biosphere we must distance ourselves from the sense of Humanity as Dominant and develop reverence for all life. People are not at the top of a pyramid of life, but part of a circle of life.

Yet there is also a Walt Disney streak to this line of thinking, at least as it is translated into broader public sentiment. There tends to be a correlation between a creature's fuzziness, the size of its eyes, and the degree to which we respond to calls for its preservation. Photographs of ruthless seal hunters clubbing furry white baby seals to death so as to preserve the hide for the fur boutiques on Rodeo Drive move me too to write letters of moral protest to the governments involved. Endangered species of slugs or snakes stir hardly a twitch of remorse in anyone. Mountain lions in the Santa Monica Mountains are threatened, but the ecological ardor of a sympathetic public reportedly cooled when it was revealed that mountain lions kill deer.[3] Deer have big eyes.

The Nature of Nature

A lot of feel-good-about-Nature ecological populism commits the profound heresy of misplaced sentimentality—a sentimentality that denies the vital force of Nature. Nature is a system of coexistence and balance, but it is also a system of predation, one species feeding off another. The rhythm and balance of life includes a "food chain," the interrelationship of species that feed on one another and that also keep the proportion of species in balance, one with the other. While we may feel existential sympathy for the prey rather than the predator—especially if it is fuzzy—we cannot deny this function of Nature. None of this means that Humanity, popularly regarded as residing at the "top of the food chain," therefore has greater rights to exploit Nature than any other species. Because of our ability to reason, we have an obligation not to behave toward the food chain, or Nature, in an "animal" way.

Life is not always pretty, even in Nature; how far do we intervene to *overturn* the natural order when it is less aesthetically pleasing? Forest fires in beautiful places are part of the natural rhythm and cycle of vegetation. Groups of animals often do starve as part of Nature's way of natural limitation. Species do perish naturally. We cannot apply these draconian laws to our own society, but we cannot act as if these laws did not exist either. To do so is to perpetuate the idea that all misfortune stems from accident or malice or neglect—from what "should not have been."

Public disquiet over the harsh, predatory side of Nature raises a broader issue, a basic theme of this book: liberal society's preference to ignore or deny the darker and crueler aspects of Humanity and Nature. The danger is that we have come to romanticize away the harsher facets of the inequalities of Nature, rejecting all aspects of Darwinism or heredity out of fear of its implications for our own society. Heredity is a disturbingly powerful force in human life. Conception, with bold strokes of DNA, denies at the very outset a great deal of what we are, what we can be, and what we will die from. Heredity perpetuates inequalities among Nature and among individuals. Liberal thinkers feel distress at these darker, deterministic aspects of Nature because they suggest that human beings and society are not infinitely malleable to the will of the social engineer. Nature, Humanity's nature, and heredity—all posit finite limits to what we can do to improve Humanity, society, and the lot of the individual within that society.

None of this means that we do not try to improve society and ameliorate undesirable conditions. Genuine progress can be made, indeed is made, as the history of the human race demonstrates. Social organization can be improved, or can deteriorate. Each individual's raw material can be artfully used, or wasted and abused. But it all has its finite limits. A reasonably just order should strive to compensate for inequalities, but it should not pretend that they do not exist.

We must keep sight of the nature of Nature, and the nature of Humanity's finite limitations, as we seek to improve society and Humanity's relationship with Nature and the planet. If we are to come to terms with the planet, our relationship must not be distorted by romanticism or unreal, sentimental perceptions. The absence of a broader sense of the roots of Humanity's problems can lead us to the dangerously simplistic belief that mere manipulation of political structures and programs is all that is required to overcome fundamental human difficulties, including our relationship with the planet.

Democracy and Ecology

The Deep Ecologists, of course, are not out of the Disney mold. They are ruthless in denying to Humanity any special place in the chain of existence, and certainly disavow any whiff of the Humanity-at-the-top-of-the-pyramid idea. We are all in this together. They urge a long-term educational campaign designed to teach human society its place in the larger order, in which Humanity's salvation can only come through intimacy and self-identification with other facets of Nature. (Indeed, the key to better racial relations as well demands that we learn to *identify* with other races and groups before we can demonstrate true tolerance—extending the perimeters of our sense of self-identification in ever broadening concentric circles, a process of increasing enlightenment.)

How politically realistic are the Deep Ecologists, who challenge society to a set of extremely ambitious—almost utopian—economic, social, and spiritual goals entailing a complete turnaround of all the old concepts of limitless growth? People are not likely to embrace difficult courses of action in the absence of strong and palpable reasons to do so. More to the point, democracy does not present the most efficient means of attaining sweeping ecological reform. The public is likely to recoil from an environmentally based economic reorientation that sharply affects jobs and living standards. (A 1990 radical California Proposition 105—the Big Green—that called for sweeping ecological measures throughout the state was strongly rejected by the public. Rejection may not have been entirely the result of selfishness, however; critics claim the proposition was badly conceived.) While environmental education starting with kindergarten coupled with broad public education campaigns and efforts to raise consciousness can make a significant dent in public perceptions, exhortation alone will not suffice. Most popular ecological concern in America right now tends to point the finger at the industrial heavies, at the other guy, especially the institutional polluters, such as smokestack industry, nuclear energy plants, weapons plants, chemical plants, and the oil industry.

But when it comes to personal sacrifice, there is much less willingness to act. Indeed, most Americans tend to fall into the classic NIMBY mode; they will recognize the need for many things, but Not in My Back Yard. We all agree we need to cut back on dependence on foreign oil. We also don't want drilling for oil off our beautiful Pacific coastline. And we want to preserve the Alaskan wilderness from the ecological damage of a pipeline. We want to keep giant oil tankers away from our coasts. We also want to end the blight of coal strip mining. Indeed, fossil fuels in general are undesirable for the atmosphere. But we don't want nuclear plants either because of the potential of a *China Syndrome* meltdown. If we do have nuclear plants, make sure to put that nuclear waste in Wyoming where "nobody" will have to worry about it. And it is outrageous that the price of gas should go up—never mind that we have the cheapest gas in the world. And electric cars just won't have the convenience and power of gas engines. Besides, we all have a "constitutional right" to use of our cars. And, by the way, why isn't government doing more to help us meet our growing energy needs?

Is this moving toward some kind of consensus on environmental policy? Indeed, how can a meaningful consensus be reached until the threat is immediate and palpable? Even where the public is coming around, "special interest groups" (i.e., the people who will pay the price as against those people who will not have to pay the price) will complicate any congressional resolutions on the issue.

Then too, ecological concerns must be balanced against jobs, the economy, and regional politics. Los Angeles must have its water, and it has the political and economic clout to get it—over the objections of the rest of California and several neighboring states. The public can be persuaded to pay a small price on occasion to make certain improvements, but they are palliative rather than systemic in nature. Californians will vote for a mild gasoline tax to help keep the freeway system in repair, but they are unlikely to vote for a limitation on personal cars, or for compulsory public transportation.

With considerable effort, the public can be persuaded to make the sacrifice of dividing its trash into separate barrels for recycling. But no one has yet seriously proposed that throwaway containers should be outlawed. The most the California legislature is willing to do on millions of tons of disposable diapers every year is to put a notice on the package stating that they are harmful to the environment. It's like the cartoon of a crestfallen Moses on a mountaintop holding a tablet, newly acquired from on high, that reads "Thank you for not sinning." There's no teeth there.

In short, politicians are likely to find it easier to temporize and ameliorate, to seek palliatives, than to turn to the hard questions. They fear the hard answers. The Bush administration takes an agnostic attitude on the question of global warming, wanting more convincing proof that the phenomenon is truly upon us before taking any concerted action. Perhaps with our ingrained American sense of the wide spaces we feel somewhat safer than European politicians, whose eco-home is smaller and more vulnerable. But one wonders whether in the end the democracies are going to be able to make the hard judgments that will be politically and economically unpopular. Can twenty million Southern Californians be deprived of charcoal starter for their backyard barbecues—which combined produce more pollution than Southern California's oil refineries? A little sacrifice is one thing, but barbecued ribs are another. The barbecue controversy, of course, is as literal as NIMBY gets here.

Conscience can work at the margins of the problem, but it can't bring about systemic reform. Nathan Gardels observes in the *New Perspectives Quarterly*:

> The striking thing about our capacity for eco-cide is that it does not issue from some dark and demonic force; it resides in the way we live and in the ordinary habits we keep. The evil is not extraordinary, it is banal. Our main enemy is not some bushy-browed Russian tank commander poised for invasion at the Fulda gap, it is the Los Angeles commuter driving to work. The chemical warfare that threatens us comes not so much from a sinister madman on the other side of the globe as from Alar in apples at the local supermarket.[4]

Ecology Wars

Ecological concern could well be the ground for future conflict. After all, we were ready to go to war in order to preserve Western liberal democracy against the Soviet totalitarian challenge. What greater justification could exist than going to war to save the planet itself?

Military conflict may well arise as nations compete for a greater share of the Western El Dorado, as developing nations flail at the consumerist piñata, all flaunting the health of the environment in the process. Who will be there to say no, to say the world can no longer afford such antienvironmental indulgence? The United States, after all, has already attained the pinnacles of the consumer society, establishing one of the world's highest standards of living for most of its society. We have already derived major economic advantage through damaging the environment—long before anyone realized that there was an environmental problem to be concerned about. Pollution, after all, was more seen as a question of aesthetics than a biological challenge to the ecosphere. We were able to pass through the smokestack phase of industrialization while no one was watching. By now we have either cleaned up our steel act or we import our steel from Korea and let the Koreans worry about their own air quality. We were able to spend half a century producing the chlorofluorocarbons (CFCs) to saturate our population's need for refrigerators and air conditioners, conveniently in advance of learning about the potentially serious damage CFCs have on the ozone layer.

While many other nations were patiently waiting in line for their turn to enter the consumerist Eden, we have suddenly switched rules on them, potentially denying them admission to the ranks of the consumerist elite. China, for example, is finishing the construction of twelve CFC plants that will gain entry into the refrigeration era for its one billion plus citizens, already long exhausted by the austere deprivations of Chairman Mao. Substitutes for CFCs are much more expensive, require new technology, and are less efficient. Why should the Chinese pass up being able to keep that leftover mu shu pork until the next day? Indeed, who will force them to stop their CFC production—especially when the post-Deng regime will be anxious to meet the long-suppressed desires of the public? As Gro Harlem Brundtland of Norway has observed, our spy satellites may now stop counting missiles and start counting the refrigerators, air conditioners, and cars that threaten the world's environment.[5] Do we just make the Chinese buy our expensive new replacement for CFCs? Or might it come to declaring an embargo against China for environmental aggression?

The rain forests of Brazil present at least as volatile a prospect. Having chopped down most of our own forests in America and Europe, we now adjudge that the destruction of the Amazonian rain forest is intolerable; the carbon-dioxide-absorption capacity of those forests is essential to diminishing the worldwide carbon dioxide surplus that is responsible for global warming. Even though it makes little sense economically, the poor farmers of the Amazon region are slashing and burning the forest in order to grow crops there—in what is clearly substandard soil. Who will take action to prevent this? Will populist governments of Brazil be gutsy enough to take action when the results of rain-forest destruction are only a scientific abstraction to most of the population, and the political costs high? And when the warnings issue from the *yanquis*? The Brazilians may *vote* not to curtail the "harvesting" of the forest in their quest for faster development—possibly hastened by new roads into the interior courtesy of Japan. Is the vote inconsequential in American eyes? Would we send troops to Brazil to stop the process? Would we send troops to Brasília to force the Brazilian president to cease and desist? Liberal-minded Americans, otherwise dead set against American military intervention overseas, might readily be brought to cheer such a military crusade to save the earth.

And how about Mexico, on our doorstep? Mexico City is now the foulest city on earth, as is so well documented in Carlos Fuentes's novel *Christopher Unborn*. Can we, should we, force Mexico to limit its contribution to world pollution? Or do *we* pay for it? Mexico City may be far enough away that we can afford to let its citizens asphyxiate in their own industrial effluence. But what of Canada? Could we witness a replay of the War of 1812, with troops coming down from Canada to seize Washington, because of our unwillingness to put a prompt end to acid rain that is destroying the Canadian wilderness?

Eastern Europe and the Soviet Union are societies emerging from long-term stark economic deprivation. While these populations are well aware of the ecological catastrophe that communism has visited upon their lands, will they now be in any mood for self-sacrifice in the name of ecology and the environment, for denying themselves their first enjoyment of a consumer economy?

While the industrialized minority of the world produces the

greatest share of environmental pollutants, the Third World is the locale for some of most egregious and flagrant single cases of gross pollution of rivers, water supply, and air. More to the point, the Third World is becoming ever less able to develop the kind of modern postindustrial information-based civilization required in the changing world.[6] In short, it will be ever harder for the Third World to come up with the resources either to clean up the mess or to switch to a newer economic base of production that will be less environmentally damaging.

Eco-Totalitarianism or Eco-Fundamentalism?

It is hard to imagine that any other issue will challenge the world on a global scale in the next few decades as much as the saving of the environment. It will most likely carry overtones of the North vs. South struggle. The Northern Hemisphere will be more concerned about the environment than the Southern—mainly because it has already attained its high standard of living and, through literacy, has developed a greater awareness of ecological concepts. After all, a well-fed conscience can be more resolute than a deprived one. Some action will have to be taken.

But what if most of the advanced industrialized and democratic societies aren't up to the challenge? What if negative information about the state of the environment continues to flow in while few states seem to be able to get their acts together? Is there not a cause here that will generate a man-on-horseback? The world may well witness the emergence of an eco-fundamentalism that takes upon itself a holy mission, a Green jihad, to save the earth.

While states with firm democratic institutions and a deep belief in the workings of the market might limit action against egregious polluter states to economic sanctions, other states with passionate ideological outlooks and less firm democratic traditions could move into the breach. The Green Movement has been very strong in Germany; ecologists like former East German Rudolf Bahro speak of "theology, not ecology" as lying at the heart of the problem—they believe that we must reform the very nature of human thinking, not just tinker at the technological edges. Deep Ecology could grow into an even more passionate cause in a country like Germany with a romantic and activist radical tradition, a country that might seek to impose its views upon Europe—at least to compel acquiescence to an austere, global ecological mission. Such movements might even be replete with latter-day ecological Baader-Meinhofs carrying out Gaia's retribution against key ecological offenders in their BMWs. Russia, too, could possibly play such a role, given its long history of messianic outlook reinforced by nearly a century of its "global mission" under communism—and a deep sense of shame about communism's rape of Mother Russia. A green Solzhenitsyn has not yet emerged, but may be in the wings.

Harnessing the Engine of Greed

Capitalism, or free enterprise, has been so spectacularly successful in raising standards of living that there can be little challenge to its fundamental strengths. For the system harnesses the engine of greed, by far the most potent motive force there is to drive human society to productive labor. We in the West know that any constructive energy source—like fire or nuclear energy—is a powerful force that must be carefully contained and channeled if it is not to threaten its custodians. But any political system that does not draw strongly upon such energy sources is not likely to succeed. You can't eat ideology, as Russia has learned to its grief.

But in the end we must ask the same question: what is the purpose of all these human endeavors? What is the good life? Is it defined in material terms? Certainly it must be defined minimally in material terms. And the old question still persists: what role should the state play in the process? Is it simply to provide a minimum standard of living so that everyone can then choose his or her own higher goals and personal fulfillments in life?

At what point can we determine that "enough is enough" when it comes to material advances and continuing growth? There may be a "spiritual cycle" in man that emerges from the polarities of material wealth and consumption. Humans deprived of nearly everything have historically turned to religious and spiritual concepts for succor and strength in facing adversity. But when the wherewithal for vastly improved material life hoves into view, material concerns have a way of squeezing out the spiritual as the dominant thought in people's minds. Then, as material needs are increasingly satiated, perhaps our attentions return to more spiritual dimensions as we realize that man does not live by bread alone.

Don't we perhaps have to have the bread—and maybe the VCR and the medical care—before we can again focus on the spiritual quality of life? India has produced much glorious spiritual and metaphysical thinking in its concepts of Buddhism and later Hinduism, very likely stemming right out of the harshness of life. But India today is much too busy ameliorating those harshnesses of life to devote as much time to contemplation. That will come later. Perhaps spirituality can come only before and after material satiation, not during.

If there is such a "cycle of spirituality" it would hold meaning for our own considerations of the problems addressed by Deep Ecology. The Deep Ecologists insist that we are facing a basic fundamental crunch-point at which the endless quest for material improvement will destroy the earth's capacity to endlessly produce—and destroy us too. They have not yet been able to prove this point. But it does not take too much imagination to recognize that everything on earth is in fact finite, especially as populations spin out of control. If there is a practical end to growth, if material life doesn't just keep on getting better and better as our linear Western thinking loves to have it, then indeed only the kind of intellectual revolution that the Deep Ecologists talk about will save us. At that point the spiritual stage of the cycle must indeed kick in if we are to understand why we are suddenly no longer chasing more goods with more money.

The process of spiritualization is basically an individual experience. The state cannot spiritualize society. The issue of ecology is thus deeply related to the fuzzier disciplines of spirituality, human purpose, and the role of the state in that process—if any. But how much can we leave it to the free individual if the existence of the planet is at stake?

Ecology, Democracy, and Totalitarianism

Will politics in the next few decades have shifted out of the Marxist struggle and into the Green struggle? Who will be on which sides of the barricades? Will the lines of conflict in the Green struggle coincide with the lines of a North-South Conflict? How can democratic forces take the lead in the struggle?

One could even imagine a few idealistic North societies joining the South in prosecuting a moral struggle against the polluting "haves"—never mind that the "have-nots" are also polluting. Nothing could be a more potent combination: the environmental demands of saving the planet coupled with the problem of equitable distribution of the world's bounties. This explosive mix could bring forth a new messianism, potentially quite ugly. The warning is clear: democracy and free enterprise must never become synonymous with a helpless hedonism, global neglect, and isolation from the needs of the growing have-nots of the world. It is both an irony and a tribute to democratic/capitalist economies—powered by greed—that they have a better record than the Marxist states—created in the name of the "people's interests"—of avoiding gross ecological vandalism. It may be that democracy and civil society at least keep people honest. These advanced societies must remain vigilant and sensitive enough to avoid inadvertently falling onto the "wrong side" of all these issues—ecology, the have-nots, and material deprivation—that will be so fatefully interlinked in the new era.

Or is an "idealistic" and demanding ecological agenda altogether too threatening to the bourgeois comforts of advanced societies? Indeed, are democracies and the free-enterprise system capable of spearheading the move toward a new world vision on issues such as limited growth and a new view of consumerism? Or will it take heavier doses of state intervention—more socialism—to bring about the necessary revolution in the philosophy of growth and consumerism?

Capitalism admittedly would not at first blush seem to provide the ideal renunciative spirit for the new age. For we would be asking it to do what it is not designed to do. Yet much of the genius of capitalism—as Marx totally failed to grasp—is in its infinite flexibility to channel forces of greed in desired directions. Will we have to accept the commissar to save our country? Or can capitalism be creatively redesigned to provide incentives to achieve our own ecological goals? Must we forgo our economic and political freedoms to meet Gaia's plight? Or can we use the powers of taxation, tax incentives, and assorted economic instruments to herd the world's public toward a more altruistic attitude about the environment? This is the ultimate test of the next century, for both democracy and its corollary, free enterprise. The cost of failing is high, invoking overtones of the failure of democracy itself.

NOTES

1. See John Seed, Joanna Macy, et al., *Thinking Like a Mountain* (Philadelphia: New Society Publishers, 1988).

2. See Maura Dolan, "Unlikely Foes Clash over the Protection of Animals," *Los Angeles Times*, December 16, 1990.

3. *Ibid.*

4. Nathan Gardels, in "A New Ecological Ethos," *New Perspectives Quarterly*, Spring 1989, p. 2.

5. Gro Harlem Brundtland, in "The Test of Our Civilization," *New Perspectives Quarterly*, Spring 1989, p. 5.

6. Wolfgang Sachs, "The Third World: A Technophagic Majority?" *New Perspectives Quarterly*, Spring 1990.

SIX

Democracy and the Perfectibility of American Life

Our society is growing increasingly schizophrenic over a classic dilemma of political philosophy: the tension between the individual and the state. On the one hand, we celebrate deeply held traditions of individualism and self-reliance—born of the experience of immigration and the frontier. At the same time, even as life grows materially better we seem increasingly troubled by any elements of insecurity in our lives and look ever more to the state for protection, demanding that the state make life safe from the uncertainties of life. As a result, our very concept of "rights" has undergone a dramatic change from its original meaning and today encompasses a vision increasingly paternalist in content. The traditional power of individualism is under assault in a society that gravitates increasingly toward state interventionism in the solution of problems. Today our society seems at loose ends about what the very purpose of our freedoms are.

Freedom vs. Rights

In our democratic tradition, freedom has historically been understood in affirmative, positive terms: freedom of speech, freedom of worship, the freedom to pursue happiness, etc.

127

We have believed that these "freedoms-to-do" liberate the individual to fulfill himself as he or she sees fit. It has only been in later years that the concept of "freedom to do" has evolved in the direction of implicit "rights to" certain things, or "freedom from" certain things. This concept was most notably articulated in FDR's "freedom from fear" and "freedom from want" as a distinct new addition to the American agenda. An overall climate of social legislation has come to include freedom from hunger, freedom from disease (or at least the absolute right to medical treatment), and, more recently, freedom from private discrimination. Freedom from unwanted pregnancy has arrived; freedom from lingering death (or the right to die) is now at the doorstep.

It was actually European socialism that first strongly pioneered the idea of "freedom from," or deliverance from, the inevitability of undergoing the ugly features of traditional human existence: disease, poverty, hunger, homelessness, unemployment. Indeed, communism carried this thought to its ultimate: the Soviet state trumpeted rights to freedom from hardships as the very essence of its own style of freedom—never mind that communism in practice failed to deliver even this freedom at a satisfactory level.

Traditional America: The Individual in Flight from the State

America, unlike European socialist models or the USSR, was by definition an antistate creation from the outset. Virtually every one of its immigrants was in some way escaping *from* the state, or at least from a repressive economic and social order. America was a refuge from the state, and on the way to becoming a bastion of individualism. The pioneer spirit of the West bolstered this powerful sense of individualism, instilling the character of the American people with nitty-gritty individualism, self-reliance, and independence of spirit. The so-called bounties of the paternalistic state were not to the taste of most early Americans. This spirit still lives on in a widespread bumper sticker in contemporary Montana that reads, "Thank God we're not getting all the government we're paying for."

American attitudes began to change subtly, however, as various elements of the population sought redress from the economic hardships of the late nineteenth century, and as the seemingly limitless prairies could no longer provide indefinite refuge from the growing power of organized government. Gradually government came to be seen as a potential ally capable of protecting people from Big Capital, the railroads, or other major threats. Urban life was quicker to see benefits in the state than rural life. The Great Depression and FDR's drastic remedies in the form of the New Deal marked a decisive turning point for the central role of the state in positively looking after the welfare of the people.

So what has been left of American individualism, born of immigration and the frontier? Psychologist Harry Triandis has suggested that affluence has historically been an additional factor that has helped to stimulate individualism,[1] that affluence can release the individual from dependence on the bonds of traditional collectivist society and allow him to pursue his own calling. That kind of financially supported individualism, too, has been a powerful part of American drive, creativity, and individual freedom. But some have suggested that as the state's function grows in the life of society, limiting the role and scope of the individual, these values are negatively transformed.[2] Individualism then tends to revert to a kind of every-man-for-himself attitude, a social selfishness that weakens community action and allows Americans to ignore the problems of others and the health of their society as a whole. Never having had a strong impulse to preserve traditional, collectively oriented society, Americans are poorly equipped to think in terms of the collective health of society. This negative transformation of one of America's best qualities will act deleteriously upon our future society.

An increasing acceptance of state intervention into society has thus come to dominate the American public over the last several decades. The state is now perceived as the first recourse for the treatment of nearly all ills. This pro-activist trend reached its most vivid expression under Lyndon Johnson, when the major experiment in welfare, the War on Poverty, and other sweeping entitlement programs came into being—despite the costs of the Vietnam War. As we know, it was the many failures of the War on Poverty and skyrocketing federal budgets that led to sharp public reaction—embodied in Ronald Reagan's formula that "government isn't the solution, it's the problem."

Reagan's political formulation established a philosophical watershed of major importance, laying down a conservative political marker at the popular national level where one had never seriously existed before. But Reagan's fulminations were much more important than his actions: his effect on the national debt was, of course, even more disastrous than that of his predecessors, and, in the end, he did not fundamentally tamper with the basic welfare features of government. Indeed, the public has shown no serious sign of wanting to dispose of most national programs under way—they just want them cheaper and better run. The transformation of our traditional suspicion toward the state seems now well advanced.

Socialism, the Refuge?

Democracy will eventually be the strongest impetus for the increasing role of the state and a continuing trend toward socialism in many walks of life. While residual individualism will occasionally resist this trend—in periodic throwbacks such as the Reagan phenomenon represented—social demands will increase the state's role. Democracy enables people to demand greater services from the state as they seek to improve the quality of their own lives. The decisions about what to improve and what to sacrifice will almost surely be selfishly drawn. In California an aging population demands greater medical coverage but will vote against money for schools every time.

Democratic society will demand that increasing shares of wealth be spent directly in the public interest rather than on foreign policy or defense. Few issues will be seen as worthy of diverting state funds the public seeks to earmark for treating the huge range of economic and social disorders and needs around us. These disorders and needs will grow rather than diminish. The budget will have to be quantitatively greater under the pressures and expectations of a modern society that demands ever greater sophistication from the citizen. Even where society's shortcomings are of long-standing character, over time they grow less acceptable. Each decade thus sets new thresholds of "unacceptability" in a modern, selfish, and occasionally compassionate society.

The concept of socialism, of course, has historically run strongly counter to American values of the eighteenth and nineteenth centuries. We will never like the word, especially because of its long use as a euphemism for communism. Yet with modernization, the increasing intrusion of the state, regulation of life, standards, safety, health, and now ecological demands, socialism is inevitably the future trend of America. While unfettered capitalism is too harsh for the social order, unfettered socialism too will destroy the American economic engine and its entrepreneurial creativity, and make it a bountiful (if not always equitable) society. One can only hope that as the state role continues to grow, the American form of socialism will still be American enough, limited enough, to preserve the vitality of individual and creative entrepreneurship.

The Ultimate Horizon: The Perfectibility of Life

But America's gradual turn to the paternalistic state, a turn much of the rest of the world has already made, is not the whole story. We have done more than slip under the thrall of Big Government and the welfare state. Something more powerful, yet unspoken, perhaps even unconscious, has been working all along to create new horizons of expectations in the American psyche: the American dream, the lurking conviction that people can master their environment and work toward the infinite perfectibility of life.

America in particular has historically possessed a powerful sense that it is in control of its destiny, that it can solve any problem no matter how great, given enough willpower and the resources. Indeed, until sometime before World War II most problems seemed to consist primarily of resources and their fair allocation. The size of the country, the endless availability of land, suggested that endless resources could be thrown at a great variety of problems, leading to great optimism about overcoming poverty and other deep social problems.

But the spirit of confidence in government, science, and progress has spread more deeply in America than in any other country in the world, for several reasons. America was the refuge, an escape from inequity; the horizons were unlimited. We rapidly achieved supremacy in technological progress; miracle after miracle came out of American engineering and medical labs. The quality of American life—overwhelmingly good for most Americans decade after decade—seemed to suggest that we were on the road to permanent improvement. Medicine was conquering one disease after another. Americans, originally brought up in the pioneering and frontier ethic, in a world of dangers, seemed to have forgotten the struggle of life. Suburban America erected a glass dome around its life, shielding it from the harder realities of the rest of the world. There was no reason to think that things should not keep on getting better and better. We had not yet even heard the cry of the ecological movement that resources *are* limited.

Without our realizing it, we had come to be hooked on the opiate of progress. In the order of things, life moves toward perfection. And indeed, life should be perfect. If something goes wrong, it is against the natural order of things; somebody somewhere is responsible and should be identified and punished. Disease means that medicine is not doing its job; an accident means negligence. Something must be done to ensure that these things never happen again. Even death comes to be regarded as the bitter result of a losing struggle by medical technology. Books rocket up the best-seller list trying to explain to people "why bad things happen to good people."

Fate as "Kismet"

The Western passenger on Saudi Airlines, a first-class airline in nearly all respects, makes his acquaintance with the nonperfectibility of the world almost with the first announcement to buckle up seat belts. In its flight announcements the Westerner is greeted early on—unreassuringly—with a nod to the Unknown: passengers are informed that "we will be flying at an altitude of thirty-five thousand feet; we will be arriving in Riyadh, *Insha'allah*"—God willing—"at five twenty-five P.M." It would seem the Muslim mind still has not lost the sense that fate can play a role in people's lives. Indeed, to the Muslim, it smacks of blasphemy to make a bold unqualified assertion about the certain fulfillment of human intentions. Human intentions alone do not determine absolutely whether one will arrive in Riyadh at 5:25 P.M.—or at all. The airline pilot's "God willing" is a statement not about his flying skills, but about the possible fickleness of life on this planet. (Lest the agnostic Westerner feel too smug about this outlook, we should remember that even the legal departments of airlines in the Western world still admit the possibility of "acts of God" in the fine print on the ticket about air crash liability.)

To an American, however, a plane crash is not just a plane crash: it should not have happened, someone is responsible, someone must pay, and it must never happen again. A disease should not occur; we have been "cheated" if we fall victim to some malady at any point in our life. We commonly hear people refer to the "tragedy" in someone's family when an eighty-five-year-old member finally passes from the scene. We are not quite yet saying that one should not die, but we are getting close. Cryonics is alive in California. American society undoubtedly has developed the unspoken expectation that somehow we should eventually be able to overcome death itself.

We demand that all accidents be banned. A fast-food chain quickly withdraws free plastic toy soldiers because a child might stab himself with the plastic bayonet. We put warning devices on everything to ensure that no accident can occur. It is astonishing that we do not yet stamp our yellow pencils with a warning label that the pencil can be dangerous if stuck in the ear or the eye; forks could carry warning labels that they should only be directed accurately and slowly into the open mouth lest one stab one's nose; cats should carry prominent warning labels on their collars lest children play with them and get scratched.

AIDS, of course, has been the ultimate cruelty after nearly two decades of the greatest sexual freedom the world has ever known. Here too, afflicted groups demand that a prevention of the AIDS virus be found immediately, though the disease stems primarily from life-style. Of course, medicine must find a cure for that appalling disease. But one senses that part of America's anger is that we are still vulnerable as a people to such an incurable disease; something is "wrong" that people are dying from it.

Our national passion for litigation now makes one hesitate to hold a dinner party without obtaining liability coverage for each guest before he or she steps into the house (but check your policy, because liability might actually begin at the driveway). We have just begun to explore the limits of warnings that need to accompany every daily act of life. For it is not just that Americans are greedy and want to sue for every problem that overtakes them. There is anger that things did go wrong, and someone must be punished, for things should not go wrong.

I am not suggesting that there are not myriad ways in which life can be improved, or that unnecessary threats and dangers should not be avoided. We do want safer aircraft, laboratory testing of electrical and other appliances, and better caps on medicine bottles so that small children cannot open them. The improvement of life and the elimination of gross dangers are major goals of the human odyssey.

But Americans by now have lost all sense of the concept of fate, and are outraged at the very idea of insecurity in life. People want a risk-free life. Our quest for perfect health has spawned an immense new industry of "pure foods" untainted by anything. The scare over the apple insecticide Alar in 1989 sparked a massive panic, leading to the withdrawal of apples and applesauce from all school lunches in California for several weeks. One woman, when told of tests indicating that the risk of cancer from Alar was minute, replied, "No risk is acceptable." We have indeed reached a point where we seek the "no-risk life." We want life shielded from life.

One of the cruel ironies of natural foods, of course, is that natural does not always mean good for you. Chemicals, too, are natural. Broccoli, a glorious vegetable, is a mainstay at our own family dinner table in dozens of interesting recipes. Our family happens to like it very much—President Bush and his childhood experiences with the vegetable notwithstanding. Aside from its great taste in American, Italian, Chinese, and

Indian recipes, it also happens to contain all sorts of stuff that is very good for you. Yet we are now told that broccoli, like many other vegetables, also contains some real, natural carcinogens. You just can't win—until biochemists can at some point develop the vegetable to the point of placing a seal on each cluster stating that we are about to consume "guaranteed risk-free broccoli."

Shit Happens

Given my own growing sense over the past decade of America's instinctive and growing fear of risk as an inherent element of the human condition, I have been fascinated to observe a lot of people wandering around in public places in recent years with T-shirts, baseball caps, and bumper stickers on their cars emblazoned with the bold message "Shit Happens." While the thought is not perhaps couched in the most elegant and felicitous language, this message nonetheless is actually an extremely profound one. I have not yet been able to determine whether the wearers are registering a cosmic complaint or simply proclaiming to the world their perceptive observer status—but either way it demonstrates a deeper sense of the character of life than many other popular slogans we see around us.

The baseball-cap crowd may indeed be partly charmed by simply flaunting a scatological word in public, but must also be expressing some kind of lurking awareness of the uncertainty of daily life. Owners of these T-shirts might in fact be surprised to learn that they are proclaiming one of the profoundest thoughts of the Buddha Sakyamuni, whose precept that "all life consists of suffering" was proclaimed many centuries before the Christian era as one of the Four Noble Truths of Buddhism. Indeed, shit does happen, all the time. Not all of human life consists solely of it, but a lot of it can. The wearers of these T-shirts may be unconsciously grasping at the Buddha's Noble Truth, the truth that there is no guarantee at all, anywhere—even in the American Constitution—that nasty things will not happen to us. Indeed, we can be sure that nasty things will happen to us in one way or another during our lives. We would do well to emblazon that message upon our minds, even if not on our T-shirts. Such a statement does not compel us to passively accept all flaws of our society, but it does suggest that we must understand that there is no such thing as a truly safe world, especially when passage through it in any case is fatal.

Indeed, it has been our very extraordinary human advances in medicine, technology, and social organization that have enabled us to limit some of the grimmer features of life that have plagued human existence since the dawn of human history. To be sure, it was perhaps easier in India of the fourth century B.C. to recognize the place of human suffering on earth, for there seemed to be little recourse or refuge, few apparent solutions. Buddhist thought sought to enrich the human being with a sense of his or her existential character and place in the natural order. It has been a central feature of Stoic philosophy and most religious thinking as well that adversity, while never welcomed, can enrich and ennoble. Conditions of life in the world have in fact been exceptionally precarious until relatively modern times. But the striking improvements in our human environment should not blind us to the fact that there is still no ultimate alleviation of the human existential dilemma. Whatever our philosophy or theology may be, it must include a humble sense that in the nature of things, shit happens.

Our Litigious Society

The idea that life should not entail risk has found its mightiest defenders among the legal profession. No one could accuse lawyers of commitment to perfection of the human order, but lawyers' eagerness at the prospect of burgeoning legal work in defense of Americans' right to freedom from disaster has helped multiply exponentially the grievances Americans take to court. Children's playgrounds are closed, riding stables turn away the casual weekend rider, the obstetrician becomes a dying breed, hiking trails are closed, and personal liability insurance suddenly becomes a fundamental act of self-defense in current society. The entire field of medicine has found costs spiraling out of sight as successful malpractice suits have doubled or tripled medical costs within a decade. Lifetime smokers struck with lung cancer now sue tobacco companies for compensation for their impending deaths. The emergence of new medicines into the marketplace are immensely delayed because of the staggering cost of possible future lawsuits over potential side effects. You're not even allowed to go out and do something foolish to yourself anymore.

To be sure, society should seek reasonable protection against the practice of gross negligence. Food, medicines, and products do need to be held to standards to ensure general public safety. Indeed, no one seeks to arrest progress toward the greater safety of the community. But can't some philosophical sense of reality be retained in the process?

The Fate of the Individual: The Highest Value?

It is a basic theme of this book that we are losing recognition of the classical vision of people's lives, in which danger, risk, grief, and death are an inevitable part of the human experience. The sense of the inherent weakness of humanity, its tragic character, has been a leitmotif of most philosophical visions of the human condition since time immemorial. An understanding of this condition sustains our course through life, provides the depth and richness of human experience, the humanizing element of an otherwise antiseptic, packaged existence.

It is the increasing emphasis on American individualism that causes the intense focus on self and obsessive concern for personal welfare. When the values of family, community, and collective society come to mean less, then the fate of the individual becomes supreme, and the individual supremely selfish. Thus death for us has become the ultimate obscenity, the unmentionable, the thing that shouldn't be, for it threatens the only thing we have—our own individualism. Life comes with no guarantees, yet our society obsessively seeks a warranty from some paternalistic Underwriters Laboratory up there in the sky. With no sense of the tragic, of the role of the individual in greater human society, all life becomes trivialized, shallow, and obsessed with the quest for absolute guarantees.

I am hardly urging that we all turn fatalist, that we should not bestir ourselves to improve our lot in life or prolong our time on earth. But we need some sense of proportion, some greater philosophical sense of what life is all about—the themes in the vision of the great writers. Nobody is arguing that society and the individual should not be protected, but these goals must be measured against three things: the freedom of the individual to sustain personal risk to himself; an admission by society that risk pervades life in many areas where no one, especially not the courts, can or should always protect the individual; and a recognition that the fate of the individual must be understood against the backdrop of our mortal character, which is what gives life its meaning.

In the end, what is worth living for? What is worth dying for? It seems the closer we get to perfection, to the better life, the more fearful we are of its disruption. America's vigor is likely to be sapped as philosophical boldness goes down the tubes. We are becoming a society wrapped in cotton batting, which tends to limit the vision.

Yet contemporary America seems to be forsaking philosophy in sweeping areas of our social and political existence. We are returning to the naive Rousseauean vision of Humanity's inherent goodness, corrupted only by corrupt social institutions. The centrality of this vision in American life helps explain some of the most troubling phenomena plaguing our society today. It infects our expectations, our assumptions, our approaches, and our reigning political philosophy.

The state cannot control or determine the philosophical outlook of its citizens, although our educational system could well incorporate a broader and deeper vision of human life than its current Pollyannaish feel-good-about-yourself approach to social problems. But democracy faces special problems here. For few politicians will find it congenial to preach harsher facts to the electorate about the deeper nature of our social problems. It is far easier to blame the system, or certain groups or classes, for existing problems, or to hold out hopes of alleviating what are problems of human failing through simplistic political formulas.

Problems vs. "Stress"

Our society lurches ever farther along in its quest for the perfectibility of life, affecting even the realms of psychotherapy, and its more practical offshoot of social counseling. Now, the importance of social counseling is beyond question. There is no one on the face of the earth who cannot profit from an examination of his or her problems in dealing with other people and life. We should never stop expanding our knowledge of ourselves, of our weaknesses and foibles, right up to the grave. When the family doctor, clergyman, rabbi, scoutmaster, and grandparent no longer serve their traditional function of providing sage advice on problems of life and coexistence, social counseling may be all that is left to fill a necessary gap. But as psychologist Carol Tavris points out in an attack on the "stress industry":

> If problems were called just that, and not some psychological term, the solutions would be clearer. The stress industry has wrestled most of us to the floor and is breaking our arm. "Are you tense, worried, overworked, fatigued, frustrated and hassled?" it asks. "That's stress!" My grandmother would have said, "That's life," but that was before psychology transmogrified everyday feeling and problems into disorders and pathologies. . . . [In fact,] stress is often good for us, it keeps us from degenerating into mindless blobs and it reminds us that bills are due. In fact, too little stress—prolonged boredom, stagnation and lack of stimulation—is more unhealthy for people than too much. . . . We should dump the word *stress* altogether, or at least give it a breather, and replace it with the word *problem*.[3]

Such counsel is wise in the face of a report in the *Los Angeles Times* that tells us that "stress-related complaints now are the fastest-rising type of job disability claim in the state and may be costing hundreds of millions of dollars annually."

> Despite the growing attention to job stress, there is little agreement on how to determine when workplace demands become mentally debilitating or on how to evaluate the merits of an individual complaint. . . . The issue is an extremely

touchy one for employers, who may recognize that stress is a fact of modern life but fear being exploited by opportunistic employees whose complaints are hard to disprove. . . . "There are legitimate stress cases, but there is also an opportunity—because it is so subjective—for a lot of abuse." . . . "Lawyers want to make money off of this."[4]

In the end, one is left with a sense of uncertainty about how stressful life is in these modern United States in the late twentieth century, in comparison with almost any other place or period. Surely life in medieval Europe must have featured acute "barbarian distress" as a countless parade of Goths, Visigoths, Vandals, and Huns swept through, looting with regularity. Life under Caligula in Rome must also have had its stresses. "Black Death Stress Syndrome" must have kept a whole lot of alchemists busy, as well as denting the social life of the late Middle Ages. American pioneers actually experienced a fair amount of stress as they moved along the North Platte River on up the Oregon Trail where Indians, floods, blizzards, and disease took their toll as part of the price of getting to the West. Native Americans know a little bit about stress themselves, as they have been placed under unceasing assault for over three hundred years. Standing in line for hours in hope of some sausage or toilet paper in Warsaw and Volgograd does not do a whole lot for the nerves either. Contemporary Palestinians suffer from severe "Intifada Stress," and rubber bullets tend to have more severe impact than migraine headaches. Indians growing coca plants in an Andean environment disturbed by American pesticide-spraying helicopters and Sendero Luminoso terrorists also suffer sleepless nights.

In most countries of the world there is barely one day off a week, no day-care centers, and unstable politics bolstered by local armies that are less than respectful of the right to free speech. Most countries of the world are filled with fear and suspicion about their own national groups in a constant atmosphere of ethnic hatred and rivalry—often acted upon violently. In short, it is difficult to make the case that the average American today faces greater problems than others in the world now or in the past. Sure, the Swiss and the Dutch may have withdrawn sufficiently from international politics to top the list of unstressed societies. By almost any broader measure of physical standards, however—security, food, housing, medicine, education, job security, working hours, recreational facilities and entertainment—America comes out near the top of the list.

Of course, to be fair, this is all a relative question. But the nagging question arises whether all these syndromes of anxiety may not be *increasing* as life gets materially better all around. We have more time to worry about the type of pesticide on our broccoli, the level of cholesterol in our frozen yogurt, the quality of our orgasms, the breathability of our air, and the possibility of an ethnic or gender slight at the workplace. I am not suggesting that we do not have genuine problems requiring deep examination today, but rather that we must maintain some sense of proportion about the gravity of these problems relative to the overall uncertainty of life on this planet. Otherwise, as things get better materially, how can we have a sense that life is getting worse and more insecure? What kind of vision do we possess about the art of the possible? What are we getting out of all of this if greater stress seems to be the result of our progress and growing security? The cheerier our slogans get (Hey, loosen up, chill out!), the more the society of *Angst* seems to be upon us.

The growth of the religious impulse around the world may provide another indicator of the problem, and of people's search for answers. Garry Wills reports, for example, that "nine Americans in ten say they have never doubted the existence of God."[5] Perhaps we are witnessing, then, some public awareness of a profound disconnection here: between societies whose implicit philosophical bases are the perfectibility of life and Humanity, and a disquieting sense that our actual lives do not reflect this process of perfectibility. Did humanity turn to religion as solace against crushing problems of daily existence that could not then be solved? Or is that to put the cart before the horse? Perhaps the religious/philosophical impulse actually results from an awareness of that permanent disconnection—contrary to what our feel-good democratic societies may instill in us? Indeed, if we do not have some kind of profound philosophical (some would say religious) grounding in the character of life and Humanity, then the contradictions between the uncertainties of life in a time of plenty and freedom and a belief in the perfectibility of life will surely drive us mad.

The Anxieties of Freedom

That freedom and choice can produce anxiety is well known. It has been the theme of countless writers. In Dostoyevsky's *The Brothers Karamazov*, "the Grand Inquisitor," a berobed church official, interrogates Christ about whether his mission to humanity to challenge the human soul will actually increase human happiness or diminish it. Today in America we face, more than almost any other country in the world, the crisis of freedom, well-being, and leisure.

As we noted above, the evolution of various types of freedoms in America introduced first the "freedom to do" concept, whereby we were guaranteed certain rights to freedom of speech, religion, assembly, etc. But these freedoms did not fill the belly. "Freedom from" constituted the next phase, in which social democracy sought to spare the public from want, hunger, disease, etc. But today we confront the issue of "freedom for"—freedom for what end? This is likely to be the most daunting challenge of all, for it strikes at the heart of the dilemma of our existence. In the end, what are we all here for?

In past eras we had less reason to worry over this issue. Thinking individuals, of course, have always pondered the purpose of our life on earth: this issue lies at the heart of ancient as well as modern philosophic thought. But the majority of people have perhaps been partly spared excessive anxiety over this problem because of the simple demands of trying to survive and make ends meet. Thanks to extraordinary advances of modern technology, we have by now been relieved of a great many of these most pressing anxieties through basic medical treatment, adequate food, and security from predatory rulers. We are increasingly left face to face with ourselves and our own goals.

These thoughts are not merely the domain of modern philosophers. Social psychologists themselves face the phenomenon in examining contemporary social discontents. Mihaly Csikszentmihalyi, a distinguished University of Chicago social psychologist—who must himself suffer stress at listening to people mispronounce his Hungarian name (cheek-sent-me-high-yee)—points out that (as summarized by a reporter for the *Los Angeles Times*) the pursuit of time-saving conveniences has taken on a life of its own and for many people has become self-defeating. . . . People too often rush through their daily activities to create more free time for themselves but then spend that extra time narcotized in front of their television sets or doing something else that is unchallenging and unrewarding. "Everybody wants more free time. The fact is, though, when they get it, they don't enjoy it," Csikszentmihalyi says.[6]

The Shrinking Nature of the Physical Challenge

In short, the American dilemma may increasingly be what to do with ourselves now that we have the time and money to do something. While myself suffering periodically from Los Angeles freeway stress and the problems of trying to keep the pH balance in my swimming pool just right, I am sobered by spending time with people from around the world whose political, social, and economic problems are truly daunting. The hardships of the Afghan mujahidin fighting for their country, the Uzbek nationalists seeking freedom and self-determination, the Russians struggling to create an entire new society, the Chinese struggling against the last vestiges of a tottering Maoist-Leninist regime, the Ethiopians fighting fearsome famine, the Sudanese racked by decades of decimating civil war, the Arab peoples seeking democratic expression, the poor in Brazilian slums seeking basic living conditions, and indeed the poor and the homeless of our own inner cities, whose stress syndrome is never measured against that of the suburban yuppie—all of these give pause for thought as we consider how relatively trivial the problems of the majority of Americans are. There are indeed unfortunate economic minorities in this country whose life by American standards is inadequate and must be improved. But I am referring to the malaise of the vast majority of Americans whose material lives are quite adequate—luxurious by world standards.

I do not mean to make light of the problems of anyone. Indeed, the existentialist dilemma is a very real one. Why are we here? What are our goals? These issues cut to the very heart of the human condition and, to many, can be deeply unsettling. The chances are that these issues now face us more squarely than ever before because we now have time to contemplate them more. That is the result of a high degree of social welfare and the freedom to articulate our concerns. For the basic dilemma of existence is not to be solved either in democracy, or in technology, or in higher standards of living. In one sense it is aggravated by those developments: we don't even have the galvanizing qualities of war or revolution that can draw heroics and sacrifice out of Americans. We have little need to sacrifice for much of anything at home. Is that our problem? Psychology and counseling can perhaps steer us toward the behavioral roots of some of our own personal shortcomings, but they cannot touch the heart of the existential dilemma.

The Growth of Interest in the Moral and Spiritual Challenge

It is perhaps for this reason that we see growing interest in various traditional and untraditional religious movements in America that address the existential problem. We witness a growth of both traditional Christianity and the newer evangelical churches. Asian thought—especially Buddhism—is beginning to attract numbers of Americans with its insights into problems of human existence. For these are not secular issues at all and cannot, will not, be dealt with by the secular state. While few of us in the West believe that the state can be anything but secular, even Gorbachev has come to recognize that the building of a new Russian society will require the participation of both traditional Russian Orthodox religion and the moral thinkers that were once deemed irrelevant, antediluvian, and subversive to the construction of the ideal humanist society. Gorbachev has suggested that the dilemma of values for Russia, with communism utterly compromised and collapsed, requires attention to moral values as the essential foundation for a sound society. The churches are reopening. Christmas has been reestablished. Inevitably these questions of values must drift toward the transcendental.

What greater modern philosophical and ethical *volte-face* could be imagined than this pronouncement from Moscow?

But it has been the problems of a social nature in the last three decades that have finally begun to shake the unshakable American faith in our ability to solve any problem. The simple application of ever greater resources has been perceived as insufficient to "solving" the problem of poverty, crime, drugs, violence, and the development of a permanent underclass. The Soviet Union has traversed a similar path; its leadership once believed resources and "rational" planning to be capable of solving all economic and social problems, and the country faces utter collapse.

Freedom for What?

America is thus caught up in its own material well-being, paradoxically accompanied by growing anxiety and stress. It is shallow and superficial to assume that "stress" is simply a function of faster pace and increased commitments. On the one hand, lacking the threat of a barbarian invasion or Black Death, we now have time to contemplate the gentler sources of anxiety such as air quality, pesticides, and the need for personal fulfillment. As children of the Age of Rationality and Technology we are stuck with a society that suggests that all problems can be solved if we simply approach them right. The politicians of democracy are inclined to further this approach as well: find those responsible if all things are not right. We are angered when they are not. We even sue. And yet, as social problems seem to grow more intractable—and less affected by application of simply money and goodwill—we are anguished by the thought that something deeper in fact may be wrong. We are returning to recognition that values, and a sense of the character of Humanity and its classical "tragic image," may be involved in our concerns. We have not, after all, been able to escape those classic human problems of existence that the great literature of all cultures has dealt with.

History is not over at all. In fact, it is in history that we trace the roots of our modern dilemmas. While technology has changed, our human character has not. It is only through recognition of these classic human dilemmas of character—giving rise to philosophical and religious understanding of life—that we will ever cope with the social problems of modernity. We need the moral courage to recognize that many problems ultimately must be lived with rather than solved. It is not feel-good sociology, but a good grounding in the lessons of human thought, the dilemmas of the human experience, wherein we might find the inner resources to cope without despair or panic. It is then that the problem of "freedom for what" may take on greater clarity as well.

This is the ultimate question that democracy cannot answer, of course—the purpose to which individual freedom should be put. For freedom cannot be understood as a goal of one's life. Freedom is invariably instrumental in its character, designed to facilitate the attainment of other, more concrete goals. Yet it has been observed that our society, with its technical facility, seems more comfortable with developing means than ends. The challenge of establishing ends may yet be the ultimate existential dilemma for the modern democratic society, which in many respects already seems to "have it all."

NOTES

1. Harry Triandis, discussed in Daniel Goleman, "The Group and the Self: New Focus on a Cultural Rift," *New York Times*, December 25, 1990.

2. Dr. Robert Bellah, a sociologist at Berkeley, quoted in ibid.

3. Carol Tavris, "In Other Words, That's Life," *Los Angeles Times*, June 2, 1990.

4. Jonathan Peterson, "'Job Stress Claims Increase Dramatically in California," *Los Angeles Times*, May 22, 1990.

5. Garry Wills, *Under God: Religion and American Politics* (New York: Simon & Schuster, 1990), p. 16.

6. "Time: Marketers Eager to Fill Needs of Harried Consumers for Products, Services," *Los Angeles Times*, April 30, 1990.

SEVEN

Democracy and Ethnicity: Ethnic Struggles, American and Soviet Style

The Character of American Ethnicity

Ethnic fires burn the world over. Even in America, the most celebrated multiethnic state in modern times, we seem to grow more uncomfortable with the growing implications and problems of ethnicity. The American media bombard us with problems of racism in America wherever we turn. We regularly hear from various radical groups within the country that we are "the most racist country in the world." Tulane University students are told that "we are all the progeny of a racist and sexist society."[1] White vs. black, white vs. Hispanic, black vs. Hispanic, Asian vs. black, Native Americans vs. white America—all these oppositions haunt the American conscience as we match reality against the ideals of equality upon which the country was founded.

In the meantime, the immigrants continue to pour in. We are now told that the white population will be a minority in the United States by the middle of the next century. California is already a state made up solely of ethnic minorities—including whites. Political tensions in many respects seem to rise as each of these ethnic mixtures jockeys for greater advantage and power for itself in American society. The traditional Anglo-Saxon and northern European white populations of America already feel a sense of displacement in what culturally used to be "their own country" as these European elements of the country give way to a much broader pluralism. Are we really racist at heart? Is racism getting worse? Or are we simply more sensitized to it?

The ethnic mixture becomes not only greater but more diverse all the time. Political oppression abroad has an immediate and direct affect not only on our population, but even on the culinary choices available in America: who had ever eaten in an Afghan, Vietnamese, Salvadoran, Iranian, or Cambodian restaurant in America fifteen years ago? But was democracy meant to be tested against such an incredible array of ethnic diversity? Are we now reproducing in an American laboratory the same ethnically fissionable material that threatens the rest of the world?

No other country has been so ethnically and culturally tested in the history of the modern world as has America. Britain, the cradle of modern democracy, produced the concept of government by the consent of the governed—but within the confines of a small and ethnically highly homogeneous island. De Tocqueville's nineteenth-century classic *Democracy in America* based its profound admiration for the American democratic system on what was a relatively homogeneous American population derived primarily from northern European populations heavily influenced by those same English concepts of law and democracy. Those conditions are now fast fading as American society absorbs virtually every ethnic element in the world at a dramatic pace, quickened additionally by illegal immigration. What will happen to democracy in America as a result?

It is the thesis of this chapter that the problems of American ethnicity result not from the numbers and variety of ethnic elements but from the shifting significance and political role of ethnicity in our society. The old ethnic melting pot—which largely ignored ethnicity in the creation of the homogenized new American—is giving way to a society more ethnically self-conscious than ever before. We have become more sensitive to individual ethnic groups, and more "numbers-conscious" about the distribution of America's bounties to its constituent ethnic elements. Nor are we immune to the worldwide quest for community identity in a rapidly homogenizing world. Ethnic groups are more interested now in preservation of ethnic communities and the political power that solidarity might give them. Most serious of all is a gradual, unspoken, but inexorable drift toward the concept of ethnic quotas as the most reliable means of establishing justice and equality.

The Multiethnic Legacy—Unique in Modern Times

Unlike most other countries of the world, America was founded on a multiethnic basis. The die was cast by the history of multifaceted European exploration of the New World: we have accepted, and then embraced, ethnic pluralism. Uniquely, American nationalism has almost never been expressed in ethnic or racial terms. It is expressed rather in terms of commitment to a new type of nation-state and to the ideals that it espouses: freedom and equality before the law.

The uniqueness of America is often not well understood even by its own citizens. One has to cast back to the great world empires starting with Rome to find states in which ethnicity was not a factor; and even the Romans ran much of the rest of the world as a colony. Ethnic elements were starkly present in the multiethnic Ottoman and Hapsburg empires, in which ethnicity was rarely "melted," regardless of citizenship.

Nor do most Americans recognize the unique ethnic modesty—or virtually nonethnic basis—that distinguishes the character of America as a nation from other nations. All you have to do is spend a little time in other countries of the world— especially the Third World—to be astonished at the unblushing racial centrality and unbounded self-glorification of the dominant ethnic group that in America would be instantly tagged as rampant jingoism. Few Turks or Indians believe that their race is not superior; Chinese and Japanese are utterly convinced of their own racial superiority. If Americans are proud, they are proud of the traditions and ideals that make up the country, not of any given race within it.

Granted, many nation-states are relatively new upon the face of the earth; their exclusivistic nationalisms have lost neither intensity nor harshness. We have remarkably little of that here in America, in a society almost obsessively given to self-criticism. Our very concern with racism at home distinguishes America from most other countries of the world. Far from being the most racist country in the world, we are almost without doubt the *least* racist of any country possessing significant ethnic mixture.

Yet we too seem to be entering a period of confusion and uncertainty about race and ethnicity. We are now engaged in a fundamental and bruising debate over the very character of the multiethnic nation: is its social order to be based on individual merit, or on a quota system based on racial statistics that will apportion the fruits of society equally? Multiple voices, from many communities, are now suggesting that the multiethnic society can only be vindicated through demonstrable egalitarianism in all respects.

The old American ideal of equality of opportunity is under assault as a fundamentally fallacious concept. True equality of opportunity can never exist, it is argued, since the playing field is not level from the outset—and never can be, given the permanent disparity of background of absolutely everyone, racially, socially, and financially. A Doonesbury cartoon sequence shows one couple asking another couple why their daughter does so well in school, since "it's not like she grew up in an Asian family." The second father replies that they have actually raised their daughter with Asian values of hard work, the importance of education, and respect for parents. The first couple replies, "But doesn't that give her an unfair advantage? After all, this is America."

Today a new coalition is emerging; those who perceive the goal of democracy to be the creation of a leveled, egalitarian society have joined hands with those whose agenda is unabashedly racial, and for whom the fruits of society are gained not by competition, but politically by proportional apportionment and entitlement. Make no mistake about it: the cause of just apportionment and quotas will move to center stage in the next decades of American life and will make deep inroads, even if it may not triumph. The handwriting is already on the wall. This nascent national debate challenges the very bases of traditional American democracy. It raises the specter that our democratic practice could eventually start to resemble the pattern of ethnic politics in Lebanon, India, or the Soviet Union. While this prospect is admittedly distant for now, the outcome of this ethnic debate will fundamentally reshape the character of American democracy and establish new precedents for multiethnic states elsewhere in the world.

Varieties of the Multiethnic Model

Of course, there is more than one way to structure a multi-ethnic society. We are not alone in the world in maintaining a broadly multinational society—even if our way of doing so is unique. America as a multiethnic state stands in stark juxta-position to the other great multiethnic experiment of the world—the Union of Soviet Socialist Republics. The Soviet model is an intriguing variant, since the USSR, like America, has long had ambitions of representing the wave of the future. It too is a state founded on "an idea," unlike most other states in the world. In past decades it has also boasted of creating a "New Soviet Man" who not only was to give up most of his ethnic identification in favor of the common char-acteristics of the new Soviet state, but was even supposed to shed his class loyalties and identifications. America's melting pot at its most ambitious never toyed with quite so massive a piece of social engineering. But that is not the whole story of the fascinating contrasts between Soviet and American multi-nationalism. The considerable differences shed light on the nature of our alternatives.

The Soviet Ethnic Experience—a Failed Model

Years before the Bolsheviks came to power in Russia, well over one hundred different nationalities had fallen under the Tsarist Empire's sway. While the Bolsheviks sought to exploit these ethnic differences before attaining power to weaken Tsarist rule, once in power they faced the problem of coping with massive ethnic discontent themselves. In part they came to be victimized by their own ideology: Marxist theory reas-suringly predicted that a new Bolshevik state could quickly cope with ethnic frictions; after all, the communist state would eliminate the patterns of exploitation characteristic of capitalist society—the very basis of most ethnic conflict. Ethnic self-identity was viewed by most socialists and communists in this period as a pernicious distraction from the true issue of class identity. Here Marxist theory postulated that socialist/communist society would bring about a new class solidarity and focus on universal class interest that would eliminate ethnic strife. Russia was to be a kind of Marxist melting pot.

Not surprisingly, ethnic strife and breakaway movements throughout the length and breadth of the Russian Empire did not end with Bolshevism and the brutal efforts at elimination of "classes." Any whiff of ethnic separatism, or even nationalistic pursuit of ethnic advantage, quickly became a counterrevolutionary crime. By the late 1930s, Stalin had physically liquidated virtually every nationalist leader and figure among all major and minor nationalities of the Soviet Union.

The Soviets had their own version of the melting pot, perhaps more closely resembling a pressure cooker. A process of "coming together" under Soviet communism was designed to bring all nationalities together, increasingly sharing common Soviet culture and eliminating conflict; a later process of "merging" or "assimilation" suggested the ultimate blending of Soviet peoples so that no significant differences would remain. The end product, the ideal, was the creation of the "New Soviet Man," whose identity would be linked to the Soviet state and not to any narrow ethnic grouping. This ideal bears some relationship to the melting-pot concept, but the conditions and methods were wildly different from the American experience.

Not surprisingly, Armenians, Ukrainians, Latvians, Georgians, Uzbeks, and others did not really find the idea of "merging" a happy one; nearly all nationalities intensely resisted the process. But Soviet policy was strangely dualistic. On a tactical basis the Bolsheviks gave a nod to ethnic differences: they decided that one means of ultimately eliminating meaningful ethnic differences lay in the creation of a multiplicity of ethnic republics and autonomous regions, each dedicated to a particular ethnic grouping. These ethnic regions were supposed to imbibe the ideological character of the Soviet state so that differences among republics would ultimately fade, leaving only charming folkloric differences. Ideally, even regional languages might eventually give way to Russian, much as English became the language of most discourse in America. Indeed, for years Russia propounded its "model" of ethnic autonomous regions as the solution to all ethnic problems in the world; Brezhnev even spoke of the need to establish a "black autonomous republic" in America. (Will the idea remain preposterous to radical black leaders of the future?)

But Soviet dreams for the future were not to become reality. Seventy years later, Soviet communism had accomplished nothing more than placing in deep freeze—through force and terror—the normal evolution of ethnic expression and practice. That is why Gorbachev's thaw has now released powerful nationalist impulses that come to the surface like spring viruses, infecting whole regions, often much stronger than they were before the years of ideological deep freeze began. "Assimilation" is farther away than it has ever been in Russian history; the rage of widespread anticommunist bitterness only increases the intensity of nationalist feelings. Talk of "assimilation" smacks of culturicide, if not genocide. Today ethnicity and local nationalism in the Soviet Empire grow by leaps and bounds, demonstrating a virulence in some areas never previously witnessed.

Soviet "Amalgamation" vs. the American Melting Pot

But if the concept of amalgamation and assimilation is so sinister under the Russian system, what of our own American "melting pot"? Indeed, that term suggests precisely the same thing; melting can only suggest loss of ethnic identity. Yet there are sharp differences between the American and the Soviet concepts that point up the uniqueness of our state.

First, nearly all of the non-Russian nationalities who became part of the Tsarist Russian Empire were incorporated through *conquest*. They did not choose to join the empire—indeed, most fought to avoid joining. Whatever benefits there were in partaking of the broader and more advanced international civilization of Russia, the choice was never free. Each nationality—Georgian, Kazakh, Ukrainian, and others—constantly attempted to assert greater use of its national language and to achieve full cultural autonomy.

America was an immigrant society. All those ethnic groups who arrived came *voluntarily, as individuals*, in flight from some other government or society perceived as oppressing them politically, racially, religiously, or economically. Only three nationalities in America never had a choice in becoming part of the great American experiment: the Native Americans, a large proportion of the Mexicans, and the blacks. The Native Americans were brutally expelled from one homeland to another, and were often the victims of nothing less than genocide at the hands of some local authorities. American blacks, of course, were brought forcibly as slaves and integrated into American society—at the bottom of the social order. Mexicans and Spanish were already part of the American Southwest when those regions were annexed by the United States in the second half of the nineteenth century, although vastly many more have since arrived voluntarily.

All other ethnic groups, however, had arrived here in the expectation that their lives would be bettered in some way. Indeed, there now demonstrably exists an unusual American gene pool of self-starters—self-selected aspirants for a better life who had the ambition and gumption to come all the way to America in order to do something about it. Blacks, Mexicans, and Native Americans in America did not represent a self-selected minority of ambitious immigrants but rather a broad cross section of their own societies forcibly incorporated. Only today do new Mexican and African immigrants too share in that process of self-selection by taking the bold step of immigration for greater self-fulfillment.

Such a historical analysis of the roots of American character is not fashionable today and is sometimes called "racist," but it most emphatically is not, for it deals with multiethnic *self*-selection and not the qualities of any given race. The overall restless, intense, individualistic, competitive character of American society is surely the product of a political and social culture created by those with strong aspirations to escape, resettle, and prosper. Those who were historically abused by that American culture, who did not volunteer to join it, or were not encouraged to join it—the blacks, Native Americans, and many Hispanics—constitute a different historical situation entirely.

Herein lies another critical distinction between American and Russian ethnicity; the American immigrants who make up our multiethnic society left a native country, their cultural homeland, behind them. Members of the Russian multiethnic state did not leave their cultural homeland—the empire visited them. Even more important, the American immigrants always knew that there was an ethnic homeland back there somewhere; by choosing assimilation in the new land they were in no way betraying the existence, the character, or even the vitality of the native homeland. Poland, its language and culture, is not threatened by an immigrant's choice to come to America and give up his or her language for the sake of integration into the new American society. Nor is China, Italy, or Hungary.

Contrast this with those ethnic groups in the Russian/Soviet Empire who were pressured to abandon their sense of national separateness and even their language, culture, and religion as they became part of a greater whole. Assimilation there ultimately meant destruction of the very ethnic nation and cultural homeland—a terrible concept. In America, no degree of assimilation implied any destruction whatsoever of the old motherland—except for Native Americans. Indeed, immigrants could revisit the old country to renew their roots for themselves and their children, often even benefiting it economically. This is why a multiethnic nation built of immigrants can never be a model for those multinational states that are composed precisely of the old cultural homelands—India being another dramatic case in point. That is also why European states, for example, will find it intensely difficult to cope with ethnicity because they are each the sole repositories of an ethnic culture that is threatened by new immigrants.

Lastly, of course, the immigrants to America did not settle in some special area: there are no ethnic Polish, Irish, or Chinese "autonomous regions." To be sure, there is ethnicity: Pennsylvania Dutch country, the Czech towns of Nebraska, the Cajun and black cultures of New Orleans, the Mexican character of the Southwest, the Scandinavian character of parts of Minnesota, the Poles of Michigan and the Hungarians of Indiana and Illinois, the Anglo-Saxon character of parts of old New England and the old cities of the South. Our great cities still offer enclaves of an even more intense sort. The Chinese, Japanese, Jewish, Korean, Italian, Armenian, Cuban, Puerto Rican, Russian, Iranian, and Polish sections of New York or Los Angeles—each presents its own particular charm and character. But these are enclaves of choice, and are constantly breaking down as ethnic elements assimilate and move out into the more general melting pot that has long given up specific ethnic character. And these few ethnic "towns" are the striking exception to the rule that Americans of a particular ethnic origin do not, in general, congregate in specific regions or areas—apart from the major cities—and the mix is getting greater all the time.

In the Soviet Union, on the contrary, the preference is generally to stay in one's own region and to discourage the arrival of outsiders into the region. Russian workers have been sent to the Baltic area both to increase the work force and to Russianize the region, just as Russian peasants have been sent to Kazakhstan to take over "Virgin Lands" agricultural regions at the Kazakhs' expense. In this era of rising ethnic sentiment in the Soviet Union, however, a reverse process is now under way, the de facto "purification" or ethnic homogenization of national republics as Russians and other minorities are being intimidated by native nationalists into departing for Russia proper. "Russians go home!" is now the cry across most of the ethnic regions of the Soviet Union. Yet such a cry of "Americans go home!" is inconceivable in the United States, except from the justifiably aggrieved Native Americans, or perhaps patrician Spanish/Mexican families resident for nearly four centuries in the American Southwest.

Melting Pot

America, then, has always been a unique model to the world, the unprecedented melting pot in which foreign identities and even languages dissolve in the common American culture embraced voluntarily by all. In almost every other country in the world you will find ethnic enclaves designed to preserve tradition. Go to Malaysia and find Chinese and Malay communities determined to maintain their distinctiveness, their separate communities and languages. In Argentina, Anglos, Italians, and Spanish speakers all maintain separate social enclaves. In Lebanon each community—ethnic or religious—maintains a separate communal life. India and Pakistan are literally made up of separate national states or provinces with different languages and cultures. They do not want to abandon those ethnic identities, even when they emigrate internally or to countries other than America.

Yet the United States is different. I am constantly astonished while walking through supermarkets in Washington, D.C., and Los Angeles to observe small children of obviously foreign parents speaking confidently in English among themselves, and responding to the parents in English even when addressed in their parents' language. The inherent power of assimilation of American culture seems to be overwhelming. Indeed, an editorial in the *Jerusalem Post* a few years ago suggested that America in some ways is more dangerous to Jews than Auschwitz, because only America is causing Jewish culture to drift voluntarily into cultural assimilation and loss of ethnic distinctiveness. And Rabbi Jacob Neusner at Brown University says that America, and not Israel, is the Promised Land for Jews.[2] That is one facet of the assimilative power of traditional American life.

The last key difference between the American and the Russian experience is that the democratic character of America has granted each ethnic group the freedom to seek its own degree of cultural solidarity and political aims, if any. In America, ethnic politics has emerged as a result of individual action to exercise some kind of consolidated political action. Indeed, most of these ethnic groups have not acted in any conscious sense as a bloc. To be sure, there is the "Hispanic vote," the "Jewish vote," and the "black vote," but these are not usually clear-cut national voting blocs; where voting solidarity exists, it is usually highly localized within urban politics. The Hispanic or Mexican vote with its concentration in the Southwest is probably the closest thing to a regionally distinct voting bloc, and even here Hispanics do not vote as a bloc. That is one of the distinct features indeed of American ethnic democracy. But new challenges to our practice of democracy could alter many of these established patterns in disturbing ways.

The Specter of Quotas: The "Lebanonization" of America

American society has been grounded in the ideal of equality of opportunity for all, reinforced by the practice of nondiscrimination. Yet we seem to have lost our bearings in recent decades, falling into a confusion between equality of opportunity and equality of status. In our desire to improve the lives of the less fortunate we create mechanisms that restore aspects of racial discrimination back into American life. Highly liberal American universities have been at the center of this experiment, re-creating de facto racially segregated dormitories, dining halls, clubs, and even graduation ceremonies for black students. Quota systems lurk beneath the surface in many hiring policies, particularly in federal, state, and municipal governments. We are, in fact, witnessing a premonition of what may in one sense be seen as the "Lebanonization" of America.

Lebanon in recent years, of course, has come to represent a guerrilla jungle, an anarchic killing ground. That is emphatically not what I have in mind. I am referring to the Lebanese model in the "good old days," when things were relatively quiet, but when some of the seeds of today's tragedy of religious and ethnic war were sown.

What is the Lebanese model? It is the official enshrining of quotas and entitlements based on the many and different communities of Lebanon, religious and ethnic. Lebanon, a historic mountainous refuge for many of the Middle East's sectarian minorities, had attempted for over half a century to maintain a system whereby each group, according to its weight of population, had claim to different aspects of the state structure. Thus the Maronite Christians, who once enjoyed a plurality in population, dominated the country and were entitled to the office of the presidency. The second-largest group historically, the Sunni Muslims, were automatically accorded the office of prime minister; the Shiite Muslims (who probably possessed an unacknowledged plurality all along) were accorded the office of speaker of parliament. Other cabinet posts were carefully reserved, one by one, for various ethnic or religious groups in the country—the Druze, the Greek Orthodox, the Armenians, etc. Parliamentary positions were similarly reserved with careful apportionment of seats—albeit based on spurious census figures—in accordance with ethnic and religious proportionality. Voters cast ballots only for candidates within their own religious/ethnic group.

Yet this system, which distributed "fairly" the trappings of power in Lebanon among various groups, was notorious for its incompetence, inefficiency, and cynicism. Its moribund character was propped up only by natural Lebanese entrepreneurial instincts and skills. The country's exquisite political balancing act ultimately collapsed entirely in 1975 when Lebanon was dragged into the struggle between other Arab states and Israel.

I certainly do not foresee ethnic or religious war in the United States. On the other hand, we are at risk of allowing our concern for equality in our society to push us into a quota system in which individual merit gives way to preordained preference systems, in which a system that strives to be colorblind in distributing its highest rewards suddenly becomes racially discriminatory in its implementation. Of course, the model of Lebanon is presently farfetched, but it suggests the logic of future direction if we are not careful. The 1990 Kennedy-Hawkins Bill in Congress has raised explicit concepts of quotas in public hiring. Dianne Feinstein, an otherwise thoughtful and sensible politician, ran (unsuccessfully) for governor in the state of California in 1990 on a platform openly calling for quotas, based explicitly on state population census figures, in accordance with which all state jobs were to be allocated. The millennium of ethnic quota was nigh, brought to you first, as always, by the state of California.

While both attempts were defeated, the issue is far from over; in fact, it is just beginning. Important precedents have been set, and attempts will be made again—repeatedly. Feinstein next time might run against a less skillful candidate; her call for quota hiring did not seem to be a major determinant in her defeat. Democracy is, after all, about dividing the pie, and no group will give up trying for a greater share, especially if it perceives that it has long had the least share.

Other new concepts are slipping into the national debate along with "creeping Lebanonization": a sense of entitlements and "rights" that far transcend what this country has historically viewed as "rights" before. As we have noted in an earlier chapter, latter-day revisionist understanding of "rights" to be vouchsafed by the state has helped confuse and then infect our entire national outlook as we seek to make our lives safe from life. But it has had profound and dangerous impact on our sense of democracy and ethnicity as well.

The cornerstone of American belief rests upon the ideal of equality of opportunity: all are allowed to compete for personal, social, professional, and economic fulfillment, without discrimination of color, sex, ethnicity, or religion. That America has failed in the complete fulfillment of the ideal does not diminish the ideal. There is probably less discrimination in American society today than in any other society in the world. Failure to implement the ideal fully does not mean the ideal must be altered, or our society condemned as racist.

The assault against these shortcomings of the American ideal—indeed, the condemnation of America by some as one of the most racist societies on earth—has been immeasurably strengthened by elements of academia. University professors should not make such extremist and unfounded charges about American racism; they are in fact fostering their own ideological agendas. The criticisms do not stop with American culture, but also assault its foundations: the entire corpus of Western civilization has come under attack by many university radicals who describe it as oppressive, irrelevant, and odious. One can accuse such academic assailants of total ignorance of the course of human cultural evolution for starters, but one senses that the attackers have motives that override their knowledge of history. They seek the denigration of Western civilization as a whole, out of sympathy and solidarity with the "wretched and oppressed of the earth."

Condemnations of ancient Greek culture—as has occurred at Stanford in the great debate over the course on Western Civilization, for example—on grounds that it lacked a broad dimension of civil or women's rights is simply inane. The precious quality of human intellectual and social accomplishment becomes clear only when judged against man's long historical odyssey out of the caves of Lascaux—the gradual growth of human ideals and the institutions to implement them. To criticize earlier societies, including our own, for falling short of today's ideals is to demonstrate utter ignorance of what the historical process is all about. Are Jefferson's brilliant writings on principles of democracy invalid because he held slaves? Is the first establishment of modern democracy in the world—in England—to be contemned because it had a class bias to its voting privileges and excluded women?

But the revisionist critics of American society go further yet. They seek to engage us in a total reevaluation of what the very concept of equality of opportunity means. Now, some of this is justified. American elimination of discriminatory legislation and commercial codes against blacks and other minorities was not enough. (Indeed, in many countries of the world, even this stage has not been reached.) By the sixties we had come to believe as a nation that the state must also ensure absence of de facto discrimination in both the public and the private sector—a far tougher task.

While these advances brought remarkable change in the rights of minorities, and especially blacks, that too was perceived as insufficient. For, it was argued, the overall system was skewed so that minorities never had an equal chance to take advantage of equal opportunity. When one is born in the ghetto, what good is it to speak of color-blind admissions officers at Princeton? Without some special head start, how can one speak of equality? Thus the birth of affirmative action.

To the true conservative, there is much that is philosophically disturbing about affirmative action. The very concept decrees that the goal of the state is to ensure not equality of opportunity for all, but equality of head start for all—a very different concept. To establish equality at the starting line presupposes the actual obliteration of deep differences in background: wealth, parental education and commitment, and native ability in each individual. While blacks and Hispanics were particularly singled out as a racial category statistically less well off than other ethnic groups, the principle really needs to apply to all individuals as well. Not all Caucasians, Jews, Asians, or others start from a level playing field either, yet society has not yet deemed it necessary to give individualized head starts to these individuals. There is clearly a racial—not to say racist—emphasis inherent in the head-start concept. But we can accept this too. There are important social imperatives served by such a racial program, grounded in statistics that demonstrate relative deprivation of certain ethnic groups proportional to others.

But the argument has not yet run its full course. Critics of the American ideal of equality can make a plausible, indeed consistent, case in arguing that the playing field can never be level, that true equality at the starting gate is unattainable. At this point the line of argument takes a quantum leap: when equality of opportunity at the starting gate itself is deemed unattainable, the concept of equality of opportunity in fact shades on into a quest for *equality of attainment*. The self-serving conclusion follows that unless one has demonstrably made it in life, one is a victim of discrimination. Since many ethnic groups to one extent or another have been victims of discrimination, it is easy to see how seductive this argument can be when minorities fall short of personal aspirations. This rationale is already alive and undergoing widespread propagation.

Race and the evils of discrimination have thus come to be subtly blended with the concept of social egalitarianism. The radical racial agenda merges with the radical political, social, and economic agenda. The ultimate establishment of a creeping quota system—"Lebanonization" in its supreme form—inexorably emerges from this new synthesis of egalitarian thinking.

Yet how far can the state go? Can it remake nature and fate and decree that the rewards of society must be equally distributed, regardless of performance? Such a philosophical concept begins to verge upon the all-powerful social engineering of communism, in which the state decrees all social values, including the guarantee in principle of equality of life—or else. The goal becomes the establishment by decree of the ultimate egalitarian society. Most moderates rightly feel that such a system perverts the nature of differences among individuals. Do we all have equal right to play shortstop for the Dodgers? Do we all have a right to inflict our playing of the violin on the public at Carnegie Hall? Or to perform brain surgery?

We recognize, in fact, that even equality of opportunity itself can never fully exist as long as people start life in vastly disparate circumstances. Society cannot fully make up for accidents of birth, the genetic strengths and weaknesses of the father and mother individually, the wealth, skills, and marital stability of the parents, or indeed the part of town in which one is born; this is part of the "tragedy of the human condition."

Yet the conservative philosophical objection that the state cannot play God—however sociologically compelling—falls short of reality as well. We cannot afford to shrug our shoulders and fatalistically attribute problems of the underclass or deprived ethnic groups to nature and fate. The crushing social problem of a permanent underclass is a burden that impinges upon us all. Its existence is corrosive to all of society, physically, spiritually, morally, and economically. We must come to terms with it, regardless of its origins and even its degree of tractability.

Society is thus amply justified in providing many programs such as Project Head Start, special scholarships, and special small-business loans designed to give those born into poverty or disadvantage—or those who fall into the underclass—an opportunity to work their way out. To break out truly does require special assistance in overcoming the ugly syndrome of entrapment; many, if not most, still will not make it at the first go-around.

But we must keep an eye on the principles involved that affect the roots of our democracy. Affirmative action programs in hiring and school admissions policies move yet closer to the critical philosophical watershed between legislating equality of opportunity and insisting upon equality of attainment to prove that there is equality of opportunity. Affirmative action in school admissions or professional job hiring does in fact violate the basic principle of equality of opportunity. It suggests that even when color- and race-blind hiring and admissions policies are in place, the arm of the state will intervene and—specifically on the basis of race—arbitrarily select certain less advantaged or professionally less capable individuals over other more advantaged, slightly more capable individuals. To do so is to violate equality of opportunity for others.

But there are also at least three grounds on which affirmative action in admissions and hiring can be reasonably justified. First, affirmative action basically tries to make up for lack of true equality of opportunity at the start (that is, for birth into a bad environment) by slight violation of equality of opportunity farther along in life. Second, it can be argued that affirmative action will make it harder for groups, businesses, and society to discriminate against the equally qualified minority candidate who might, in fact, be unfairly rejected on discriminatory grounds even when roughly equally qualified.

Third, it can be argued that giving selected minorities a slight advantage in gaining certain professional and social positions may in fact help to strengthen that minority group's overall position and opportunities. Working in the new environment will hasten that group's broad social acceptance; the minority will also come to accept more quickly as equitable those social values of a society once perceived as excluding them.

Such application of affirmative action must clearly be undertaken with at least three provisos. First, careful use of affirmative action must ensure that it does not put clearly unqualified individuals into positions where they should not professionally be—a deeply damaging and corrosive experience for all. Allen Bloom's *The Closing of the American Mind* has well documented the dangerous syndrome in which unqualified blacks have been promoted or leniently graded in university, creating false expectations on their part about entitlements, about how society is going to work, and damaging the credibility of qualified blacks whose own academic qualifications then fall into public question. Secondly, affirmative action by definition must prescribe affirmative race-based advantages only on a temporary basis. Without constant discretion and judgment in application, affirmative action will become permanent entitlement, which will damage the self-esteem and qualifications of blacks themselves over the longer run. Finally, there is no guarantee that these programs will eliminate the problem of an intractable core of underclass. However, the continued existence of that core cannot be taken as de facto proof of failure of the program or of the injustice or racist nature of the system.

The Democracy Trap: The Quest for Ultimate Equality

It is only democracy that can truly establish genuine equality of opportunity. While the totalitarian state is the only political system that has the power to impose its vision of an egalitarian state, by definition its ranks of leadership are highly politicized, based on loyalty, and closed to the public, and the mechanism of advancement is artificial. Its egalitarianism becomes only equality of misery and oppression. Democracy, on the other hand, creates groups of people at the very least able to strive for self-improvement, or greater advantage if they can attain it.

As American democracy has evolved, it has gravitated toward the ideal of true racial equality. American society has come to realize the enormity of the injustices that were inflicted upon blacks and Native Americans in particular, and to a lesser extent upon other minorities at later periods. Americans have shown an admirable broad desire to right certain outstanding wrongs, including those done the Japanese-Americans incarcerated during World War II. Few other societies with blood or injustice on their hands—i.e., most societies of the world—have done the same. Social evolution in America has meant the development of greater sensitivities to other peoples, and identification with an ever-widening circle of humanity.

As the liberal ideal of true equality of all peoples becomes ever more attractive, our vision of human character once again plays a key role. Will the quest for equality come to rest on mechanical means for its attainment? Lebanonization is one such means—reserving by decree specific positions for certain races and groups. Washington, D.C., now implicitly assumes that its mayor "must" be black. If a city is predominantly Hispanic, should its mayor be Hispanic? We are not yet at that stage, but it could well be a logical development down the road unless we keep a very clear eye on our basic principles.

When social programs of affirmative action fail to overcome the gap in income, life expectancy, social prominence, educational achievement, and so on of minority groups, who or what is at fault? Is the system "corrupt" or "racist" or a failure? How equal must equal be to be "fair"? And aren't those expectations of equality rising, in a society that also glorifies consumption? What further steps should be taken to ensure equality? Does profound alienation from the social order emerge when equality is absent? That is a profound social concern, regardless of the "legitimacy" of the alienation.

Will disadvantaged minorities increasingly seek to "wire in" certain advantages into the system to make up for their failure to attain full statistical equality with other groups? The chances are very good that they will. Much liberal public opinion is likely to support that kind of action as "only fair." The failure of disadvantaged minorities will be seen ipso facto as evidence of the "failure of the system."

The heartening move of large numbers of blacks into the middle class suggests that this group, at least, will believe that the system is working. But the pervasive existence of a permanent underclass may well outweigh the significance and power of blacks who have made it in the system as presently constituted. In all likelihood it will be the black middle class and black elite that will decisively determine the future handling of the underclass. The character of American democracy is at stake.

The ultimate transgression of the quota system, as opposed to affirmative action, is the permanent enshrinement into concrete numerical figures of opportunities that should be open to all on the basis of merit. Such a quota system will condemn America's struggle for personal excellence and allow each and every group to reach attainments by virtue of no virtue except race or gender. Affirmative action at least has the benefit of vagueness, is applied on a discretionary and temporary basis; quotas are not. Quotas are in concrete and forever.

And how shall we determine what jobs are open to quota? The House of Representatives is already designed to reflect the proportional interests of different regions, urban and rural. Should not the House of Representatives in Washington ultimately come to reflect the racial, gender, and religious diversity of America—by the numbers? That is only a short step away from the policy currently propounded by the University of California that the university student population should indeed proportionally reflect the ethnic makeup of California society as a whole. And what of the White House? Will it eventually go to a different ethnic group every four years on a rotating basis? We already hear talk that we "have not yet had" a Jewish, black, Hispanic, or female president. The logic of Lebanonization is not all that far a jump from some of the seeds of today's reality.

The most corrosive feature of a quota system is that it flies in the very face of the democratic ideal, the goal of racial tolerance, and the existence of common interests in a multiethnic society. It suggests that only a minority representative is capable of representing that minority, for it cannot be entrusted to others to do so fairly. Harvard Law School is currently facing a lawsuit which charges that Harvard Law students are illegally deprived of a broader political and social perspective by the absence of a sufficiently representative faculty—that is, blacks and women are insufficiently represented. It is, of course, disingenuous to talk of "deprivation" of the law school students; the deprivation is felt by the minorities who seek to wire the system by the numbers for a greater share of the spoils.

May not a Jew represent black interests in a state? May not a black represent white interests in a city? In fact, they already do. And a quota system suggests that there is no broader common good that a majority can agree upon, that ethnicity and gender are a zero-sum game in which the represented will invariably exploit the unrepresented. Such a system provides built-in incentive for the permanent propagation of the special interests of one group over another.

Academia Trashes Freedom of Speech for "Sensitivity"

Some still feel these concerns for the future of racial policies in American democracy may be exaggerated. It is sobering to examine the growing trend at universities across the nation on issues of race and minorities. "Politically correct" thinking—a term so commonplace in academia that it is now abbreviated in common parlance as "PC"—holds that all public expression in academia must now be constrained lest it offend or abuse minorities (sweepingly defined). The ultimate bastion has been broken: American universities, ready to fight to the last for freedom of speech (as long as it is PC), are now in the process of trashing that most holy of holies the First Amendment, in favor of minority sensitivity. The University of Michigan formally prohibits "any behavior, verbal or physical, that stigmatizes or victimizes an individual on the basis of race, ethnicity, religion, sex, sexual orientation, creed, national origin, ancestry, age, marital status, handicap, or Vietnam-era veteran status." Similarly, the University of Connecticut has prohibited "inappropriately directed laughter."[3]

These stunning gags on freedom of speech stand in stark contrast to the kinds of disruptive, radical, and racist language employed indiscriminately during the sixties, and even today, on university campuses against establishment figures, or white Anglo-Saxon culture. Actually one other grand refuge for the racist also survives: Arabs are still fair game in American culture for any kind of gross ethnic caricature, racial slur, or outrageous stereotype—they are the only major ethnic group left that can be treated prejudiciously with total impunity and "inappropriately directed laughter."

The danger here too, then, is that discussion of ethnic issues and problems can only take place within an exceptionally narrow framework that is politically correct. Efforts to discuss problems of minorities in terms that also include traditional political culture, or any theory that does not buy into "victimization theory," is not acceptable. Indeed, the latest "politically correct" thinking argues that whites are *by definition* racist since they control the power structure, whereas non-whites, because they do not control the power structure cannot, by definition, be racist. Shelby Steele's *The Content of Their Character*, an innovative book by a black writer, considers victimization theory to be one of the single most corrosive threats to the future development of black society.

The Distribution of Bounties

The ultimate question for democracy to answer is how far the state can and should go in attempting to right issues of unequal individual endowment or unequal background. Selection of those individuals to whom society will give special treatment is not a theoretical issue. It will be competitively adjudicated among different groups competing for a portion of the state's attention and funds. Should it be on the basis of race? Or individual IQ? Or individual income? The issue is not only about moral justice, but about who will get what, and on what basis. All groups will attempt to use state mechanisms to their own advantage.

But such competition need not mean that each national politician will possess a narrowly derived vision of the social problem at hand. Fortunately, the ranks of politicians, too, include those of genuine breadth of outlook who are eminently capable of representing the interests of a broad body of constituents as balanced against the national well-being. Such is the origin of most of the socially enlightened policies that the nation has already adopted. America must maintain some perspective on righting social and historical inequities in ways that do not destroy the emergence of excellence and quality wherever it may be found. The dual aspirations—for quality and for equality—must not be incompatible within democratic society.

But our society's quest for fairness and sensitivity has placed us in a situation of profound contradiction on race. We are intensely race-conscious as we start down the path of enshrining ethnicity in the grand sweepstakes of quota establishment. Each race and ethnic group understandably does not want to be left out of the distribution of advantages. A premium thus comes to be automatically placed on each group's ability to demonstrate historical discriminations and wrongs at the hands of American society. Maintenance of ethnic identity for political and economic reasons takes on increasingly greater value. Being Asian may make a big difference to one's chances of getting accepted at a state university where Asians are already "overrepresented."

On the other hand, we are asked to chastely shield our eyes from recognition of ethnicity in other circumstances. The university administration, which selects a minority student out of specific recognition of her race, then demands that the university social community be utterly "race-blind." Our determination that minorities receive full "'rights'" requires that we show absolute blindness to ethnicity on the social level—lest interest in ethnicity be taken as discrimination or even ethnic slur. It is increasingly poor social form now to register any awareness of someone's ethnic background. As a longtime student of foreign cultures, literatures, and languages, I find myself intensely interested in the origins of someone's family name, national origins, language, etc. But one must now be extremely circumspect in expressing such interest lest one be perceived as racist or bigoted.

In the social sciences it is politically quite incorrect to include essays on the political culture of other nations, or anything that borders on study of "national character." Hitler, of course, profaned the idea of "national culture" studies through his gross abuse of pseudoscience in Nazi studies of the "Jewish national character." Without doubt, ugly racism can be cloaked in pseudo-academic, pseudo-objective language, but today's political scientists are loath to touch any material that discusses political culture, or national political behavior, except in an almost purely anthropological sense. The observation that different races and nationalities tend to behave differently is an academic no-no.

But on the working level, if one is preparing to negotiate with Germans, Italians, British, Mexicans, Iranians, Indians, or Japanese, one has markedly different preconceptions about the nature of each of these exchanges. Out of fear of being "racist" we no longer feel comfortable thinking about the various strengths and weaknesses of various ethnic cultural traditions. Yet national cultures run an extraordinary gamut in this world, and there is nothing inappropriate in noting, or disputing, political and cultural qualities of each of them. Only in the United States these days has it become politically incorrect. It promises to be a grim nation when the traditional celebration of ethnicity is stifled. The great multiethnic state is becoming afraid of its own ethnic shadows.

Innocents Abroad in an Ethnic World

Americans, in fact, are in general grossly ignorant of the character and structure of foreign cultures and societies, the pattern of values which often differ sharply from American values, the types of political behavior, the psychological impact of history. While one can survive life in America under the Pollyannaish impression that all peoples are basically alike, any person or institution whose livelihood depends on dealing extensively with foreign cultures and governments requires some working concept of differences among ethnic groups and countries. Yet most American students, and even many young foreign policy analysts in government, betray deeply held, tacit, even unconscious assumptions that other cultures and countries will behave like Americans. Americans generally have little recognition of the extent to which the immigrant culture and society of America, and its deep-rooted Anglo-Saxon sense of rule of law, is absolutely unique in the world. We are therefore less intuitively equipped to understand foreign cultures than almost any other country on earth. Young Americans are generally shocked the first time they encounter in depth the attitudes, thinking and culture even of a European society, much less societies of the Third World. The person who grows up in Zaire is better equipped to understand the political and cultural motivations of an Egyptian, a Brazilian, or an Indian than is an American.

We can only go on for so long in the belief that not to recognize ethnic differences represents some kind of "sensitivity." We likewise cannot readily maintain such sensitivity and ethnic blindness on the social and professional level when so much of our academic, local and national politics are fought out precisely on explicit recognition of ethnicity in the distribution of bounties. Like the chameleon placed on plaid cloth, our "color blind" society is headed for an explosion.

Parlez-Vous Esperanto? Bilingualism in America

A second assault against the American idea and its values lies in the misguided ideals of bilingual education now being so zealously foisted upon the nation. The roots of the bilingual fiasco are many: First, increased concern that ethnic minorities not fall into the permanent underclass, hence the idea to help them get educated in their own language. Second, a concern for insufficient knowledge of foreign languages in America, suggesting that bilingual education might assist in the process. Third, there is an unspoken agenda that in the developing "quota sweepstakes" of the future, ethnic power will count for a lot, hence the desire to preserve ethnic blocs in which bilingual educational programs are a powerful symbol. Bilingualism is thus a political program. Already there is a huge bureaucracy of masses of teachers and translators employed in bilingual education who have vested bureaucratic interests in perpetuating the program.

The issue is at heart simple. The language of America is English. It most likely always will be, for there is no other language to challenge it domestically; English is now the world's most prevalent international language as well. Anything that hinders an immigrant's practical mastery of English, especially in primary school, represents damage to that person's future economic and professional viability in America. Bilingual education, the provision of education to a child in her native language, only delays the day when she will master the use of English—if she ever does.

Instead of the counterproductive and costly process of elementary (and sometimes even secondary) education in a foreign language, those monies should be lavished on the provision of special classes for the instruction of English as a foreign language.

To those who speak of the value of foreign languages in American life and education, I am a true believer: I am the author of the book *How to Learn a Foreign Language*. We must increase the level of language capabilities in America if we are not to grow out of touch with the world, culturally and psychologically. Children who are immigrants, or whose parents are immigrants, should be given every opportunity in school to pursue those languages, whatever they are. School districts that have a sizable number of Vietnamese children should be encouraged to have a course on the Vietnamese language and culture as a special course for anyone interested. But basic education must be solely in English and the acquisition of English mastery established as a prime goal for the immigrant. To do otherwise is to condemn him to a permanent second-class status in American society, a prospective new recruit for the underclass.

The alternatives are daunting. Can, will or should the United States continually expand the numbers and types of schools designed to teach in several dozen foreign languages when the level of instruction in public schools is already criticized as abysmally low? Imagine what becomes of those educated in Vietnamese when they leave high school with some knowledge, all in a language not functionally usable. Will the administrative business of local, state, and federal governments be increasingly conducted in a growing variety of foreign languages? What degree of true interest exists in acquiring United States citizenship if immigrants, or worse, a second generation, are unwilling to qualify in English as a basic prerequisite of citizenship?

The problem of Spanish is the most disturbing of all. For there is no other language in this country in which one can meaningfully live a life outside of a small ghetto without knowledge of English. Then why are many Spanish speakers insisting on bilingual education, especially in the American Southwest and Southern California? Do they believe that they do not need a mastery of English to live successfully in America? Surely their goal for themselves is not to remain a second-class minority unable to function in the mainstream. Do they believe that they are hastening the day when Spanish must become the second official language of the United States? If they are right, and are pursuing this goal, we are then moving toward a separatist Quebec scenario, with all the linguistic ugliness that that situation creates.

Imitating the USSR: Territorial Ethnicity

Ethnicity has never been related to territoriality in America. Ethnic groups are scattered all over the country, despite a few folkoric pockets of them here and there. Even the originally "captive nations" have spread out: blacks are everywhere, as are Native Americans. We cannot truly associate any one state or part of the country with any particular ethnic group. But there is one major exception: the Hispanic population. While Hispanic immigrants (themselves from an astonishing variety of countries including Spain, Cuba, Puerto Rico, Central America, South America, and especially Mexico) have in fact moved to many parts of the country, there is a growing concentration of the Spanish-speaking population—mainly Mexican—in the Southwest, especially in Southern California and Texas.

This ethnic concentration is not surprising: those states represent virtually our only land-border with another language, hence immigrants come over and settle in the border regions.

This phenomenon will grow. The object of concern is not the growth of immigrants in the U.S., for we have already recognized this to be a dynamic factor in American life, whatever its temporary problems are. What is disturbing is the unique coincidence of Hispanic ethnicity with specific regional territoriality. We may be building toward the one thing that will choke the melting pot: an ethnic area and grouping so concentrated that it will not wish, or need, to undergo assimilation into the mainstream of American multiethnic English-speaking life.

Such a situation has grave repercussions both for the population as well as the region. If we are not careful we may be in the long-term process of building a "Mexican Autonomous Republic"—Soviet style. Putting aside the most serious long-term threat—possible regional separatism—as not terribly likely, the presence of a minority that has less and less incentive to assimilate into broader American life will have deleterious effect upon the character of American ethnicity as a whole. It might increase the willingness of other ethnic groups to seek official use of their languages too, as a sign of pride and self-identity.

But we're talking about more than pride here. Bilingualism also speaks the language of political clout. The creation and perpetuation of a permanent, undissolved, Hispanic bloc establishes a base of political power, a bargaining chip with Washington. And as a blow against the cultural threat of the melting-pot concept, it is not in the interest of American society to encourage this process—another instance of Lebanonization.

Multilingualism in America—the knowledge of many different foreign languages, especially at a level of native fluency— is extremely desirable. So is instruction in the cultures of foreign countries, for which we have so much potential raw material in our immigrants here. But we do not wish to encourage concepts of either separatism, nonassimilation, special status for regions of the country, special status for any other language in the country on a formal basis, the assumption of cultural privilege by any one group over that of another, or quota rights based on numbers—as distinct from electoral clout. For historical and geographical reasons, the Spanish-speaking minority is the only group at the present time that presents this potential danger.

Monterey Park's Chinese Book Caper

The influx of ever greater numbers of immigrants, from an ever greater variety of countries around the world, has rekindled a debate about what are the linguistic rights of immigrants who seek to retain some linguistic ties to the old country. Monterey Park, a small city in greater Los Angeles, has come to exemplify the issue with the national attention its public library program achieved over the issue of Chinese books. Monterey Park is the only city in the U.S. where the Chinese now represent the majority of the city's population. Controversy arose over the amount of the library's budget which should be spent on the purchase of books in Chinese—a debate intensified by Taiwan's gift of many thousands of dollars worth of Chinese books to the library, requiring extensive cataloging costs. Other cities report other ethnic groups calling for more public library books in their native languages, for example, Russian in Pittsburgh. Other public libraries in the nation are responding to similar demands.

Do these trends suggest a new challenge to the use of English as the basic medium of communication in America? Do new immigrants have "rights" to ask for a portion of a public library budget to be spent on materials of benefit only to them? More interestingly, are we talking of a serious long-term trend or simply a transitory phenomenon? At a national convention of librarians in 1990 I asked a librarian from Pittsburgh about the large Italian community in that city: How many requests are there for books in Italian and how many are purchased? The answer was that no books in Italian are purchased nor are any requested. It would seem that the wave of Italian immigration as a self-conscious movement has long since crested. Italian-Americans read books in English. Will this not be the case in Monterey Park within one generation? Or will the Chinese community of Monterey Park seek to ensure that further assimilation does not occur if it threatens the political clout of the unified community?

It is at least heartening that the issue at stake involves literate, educated immigrant communities. When size of library book purchases is the center of debate, the problem can't be all bad. It becomes more distressing when we are talking about the provision of social services in foreign languages to an immigrant underclass scarcely literate in any language.

The American Ethnic Experience: What Does It Mean?

The critical imponderable for the future of American ethnicity is the degree to which we will move toward a "Lebanese," or even a "Soviet" model of potential territorial ethnicity. Is the melting pot process still alive and well? or will immigrants join with their co-ethnics in America to try to create or revitalize a separate cultural entity that will make demands on society and the government for the benefit of their own ethnic communities?

How will these ethnic demands be made? We are beginning to see a trend where ethnic communities, even scattered over the country, seek ethnic "rights" from the government inasmuch as it has deemed the black community deserving of them. Surely, a new emphasis on ethnicity will create a profusion of special interests and a trend toward ethnic consolidation and even cultural separatism—though to what extent isn't clear.

We may be on the threshold of a new phase of ethnicity in America. Where will Americans draw their sense of identification from in the decades ahead? If the modern era is characterized by a growing search for identity in an increasingly large, impersonal, homogenized world, ethnicity will continue to rise in America too. Local community identity is fading in an America that is increasingly on the move. Government social services are rapidly replacing the community, and sometimes even the family, in treating certain social needs. Anomie develops. People need to feel a sense of community and belonging more than ever before. Will they turn to their own ethnic reservoirs for that sustenance, that sense of identity and well-being? or will some other unit of identification successfully replace earlier ethnic identities so that people will feel a part of some neighborhood?

In short, we in America need to be exceptionally mindful

of these current trends in ethnicity and the dangers of creating new ethnic—or worse, regional—enclaves. That will spell the end of a melting pot that is unique in the world, and perhaps already losing steam. It will mark the distortion of democracy into entirely new channels of sharply competing ethnic interests. While it will not mean the end of democracy per se, it will foreshadow the end of democracy as it has historically existed in America, and with it, the end of an all-critical national consensus, our gyroscope of secure national existence for several centuries.

Immigration as the Traditional Source of American Strength

Yet it is hard to imagine that America will be unable to rise to the occasion over the longer run. Increasing immigration into the country will continue to provide a wealth of much of the world's best talent. Even where we see ourselves in decline, much of the rest of the world does not, in comparative terms. Where will the restless, the ambitious, and the talented go if not to America? Surely Japan, with all its skills, does not beckon: Japan is incapable of absorbing vast foreign cultures and providing the framework of freedom, opportunity, and social fluidity to enable outsiders to succeed. It is questionable whether its rich but rigid culture can continue to grow without severe trauma under the buffeting of international cultural change.

The new Europe offers only small opportunity; their societies are small, crowded, and still very ethnocentric, not necessarily welcoming an influx of foreign talent. And there is no guarantee that Europe can ever overcome its Gaullist vision of a future "Europe des patries," still hooked on kinds of national particularism and local culture. European cultures are not truly international in character like the American. The melting pot does not seem to be what the average Englishman, Frenchman or German has on his mind as the model of the ideal society.

It is America, with all its faults, that is better equipped than any other country in the world to provide the ultimate multi-ethnic model for the world. America has already written the book on the multiethnic state in its first phase. It will literally be centuries before other states just entering the phase of multi-ethnicity under democracy, can begin to adopt the pattern of multi-ethnic life we have pioneered. But we too are entering a new phase, one seemingly of far more resistance to the historic process of ethnic amalgamation than before. Can we remain a model, or will we too succumb to the ethnic whirlwinds of the future, sacrificing the traditional freedom and vitality of our culture for the rigidities of quota and strict apportionment of bounties in the new egalitarian state run by the numbers?

NOTES

1. Charles Bremner, "Thought Police Closing off the American Mind," *The London Times*, December 19, 1990.

2. Rabbi Jacob Neusner, "America Is the Promised Land," *Washington Post*, March 8, 1987.

3. Bremner, *op. cit.*

EIGHT

Democracy and the Moral Dilemma: America, the Islamic Republic?

The Islamic Republic of America? Give me a break! Yet that mind-boggling idea was proposed to me a few years ago in all good faith by a Muslim, an Afghan freedom fighter, who was spending some time in the States along with a number of fellow mujahidin. For many of these mujahidin, Afghanistan and Pakistan were all they knew, yet here they were spending many months across the oceans pursuing administrative training in America. Few of them were university-educated; nearly all had been well disposed toward America long before arriving. But all of them were experiencing American life firsthand for the first time, in a Midwestern city—and also experiencing many hours of American TV.

Their reaction was not all positive. Apart from being touched by the outpouring of traditional American hospitality and impressed by the development and technology of American cities, many of them were concerned about the constant American spectacle on TV of major crime, murders, rampant drug trade, teenage pregnancies, unsafe schools, sexual permissiveness, AIDS, pornography, a high divorce rate, etc. At one point one of them said to me in all seriousness, "Look, America has fantastic potential. You have a huge country, amazing wealth, broad education, technical and scientific capabilities, good people—but your society is coming apart.

179

Have you ever thought about becoming an Islamic republic? Think what you could do in the world if you had all your material capabilities *and* the moral strength of Islam to go with it!"

I smiled indulgently and brushed off the remark as a touchingly naive if well-meaning comment. But the thought stuck with me late into the evening—and in later weeks. I began to recognize that this untraveled Afghan, well disposed toward the United States, had in fact grasped some sense of the decay of the social order in America, even if his remark was wildly unrealistic and his recommendation absurd. Of course, the United States couldn't conceivably become an Islamic society, even figuratively speaking; it is hardly in the character of American society and history to tolerate the concept of any state religion, especially an all-intrusive one like Islam. Above all, for quite specific historical reasons, Americans are already deeply committed to the separation of church and state. An Islamic republic—or any other religious equivalent—would be an unthinkable proposition.

Yet consider the Afghan's viewpoint. Here he was, flushed with the mujahidin's incredible victory, the victory of a small underdeveloped Islamic country over a ruthless, occupying communist superpower. In the eyes of most mujahidin, it was indeed Islam that had won the war: "Islam is a superpower"— a refrain heard frequently from nearly all mujahidin. Of course, weapons and funds from the outside (especially from the United States) played a significant role in the defeat of the Red Army, but the victory essentially rode in on the Islamic spirit that sustained the Afghans during the cruel, harsh, decade-long struggle.

Islam is powerful indeed. The whole Islamic Middle East recognizes Moscow's enforced flight from Afghanistan as one of the greatest victories of Islam of the century. Nor does this put the mujahidin in bed with the ayatollah. In the eyes of the Sunni Afghans, Islam is under no obligation whatsoever to ape the Shiite Islamic Republic of Iran. Other forms of Islam are equally valid.

It is not surprising that the representatives of a society that has pulled off an amazing feat like this during its struggle for national liberation should currently be especially absorbed in questions of moral strength and commitment in Afghanistan and societies elsewhere. It was the fond desire of this particular Afghan to see America strengthened by what he believed the moral dictates of Islam could bring it. In his eyes, the United States was a nation that had lost its moral compass.

Islam is hardly the only religion that is concerned with problems of morality and society. Christian morality and ethics, as well as those of Judaism, speak out profoundly on these problems so central to the human condition. But it is instructive to look a little more deeply into the Islamic rationale. Its points of sharp departure from our own society's current sense of morals and ethics are striking—involving essential differences between the theocratic and the secular vision of government and morality.

We do indeed have a dilemma in American society. It is a fundamental dilemma of democracy: how to derive and establish moral values from secular sources. What are the sources of morality to be? Can a secular democratic society generate moral values to which society as a whole can subscribe? Can moral values really be derived from popular elections, Supreme Court appointments, or nebulous "community values"? Or are we forced to reach the conclusion that contemporary secular democracies find it increasingly difficult to establish firm moral values that the state can consistently implement?

It is a thesis of this book that these moral dilemmas profoundly threaten our social order. It is also a central thesis that there is no certainty that the workings of the democratic process will in fact be able to handle the problems of social decay. If it cannot, then society will demand some kind of reversion to a stricter order. In a historically stable state like America, any reversion to a more authoritarian order would come only through the pressures of widespread disorder and lawlessness, through conscious choice and calculated concessions by the electorate, backed by the Supreme Court. In states with less tradition of stability and democracy, the man on horseback is the more likely antidote to serious social decay. I do not advocate a reversion to greater authoritarianism in American life, but I fear that the current direction of social decay may lead inevitably in that direction unless society develops some greater sense of philosophical balance between unbridled further exploration of the freedom of the individual and the health of society as a whole.

Salman Rushdie and "God-Given" Values

Indeed, the Manichean struggle between Salman Rushdie and the Ayatollah Khomeini over the novel *The Satanic Verses* has starkly highlighted many of these moral differences between Islam and the secular West. Islamic society views its morality as God-given, immutable, and inherently nonnegotiable (although interpretable within certain bounds). Because it is God-given, its power and strength are not to be bargained away, nor its writ diminished, by the cleverness of lawyers and court findings, nor by popular referendum. Morality is conceived neither for the convenience of the community nor for its ease of conscience. Morality is sacred, hence nonnegotiable, and must be observed as a firmly fixed beacon for personal and social conduct.

Islam, of course, is hardly unique as a "God-given" faith. Both Judaism and Christianity also possess the concept of absolute values, expressed most simply in the Ten Commandments. And they are meant to be *commandments*, not optional activities. But of course we have drifted away from the idea of commandments in Western culture over the centuries; even something as laid-back as "God's Top Ten Tips" would surely ruffle feathers in contemporary American culture.

But although we now culturally flinch from any eternal dicta, we are kidding ourselves if we fail to recognize our own secular version of "God-given" dicta. If there is any "sacred" principle left in the West it is probably our absolute faith in freedom of speech. Freedom of speech has become such an article of secular faith that it is beyond any discussion or debate—an absolute above almost any other absolute in our society, not to be abridged or negotiated under any circumstances. Don't even think about it—it is the secular equivalent of the ayatollah's sense of blasphemy. It lies beyond question, as does the Muslim's belief in the need for a state and society with a vision of morality and a state commitment to the moral order. If we were aghast that Khomeini could condemn a novel as blasphemous, many Muslims were aghast that the West was seemingly willing to trample and demean the very heart of one billion Muslims' most revered moral traditions and sacred values—all in the name of one trendy writer's freedom of speech to write frivolously about cosmic issues. We are witnessing here a clash of the absolutes, an ultimate cultural confrontation that rouses equal and fervid passions on both sides.

The Death of the Absolute

Our American society is distinguished by a stunning, unrelenting march forward into new frontiers of human personal and social rights. Much of this experience has served to enrich the Western world. Concepts of the practice of democracy, freedom of expression, human rights, sensitivity to minorities, and the rule of law continue to wield profound influence even today, from Red Square to Tiananmen Square. At the same time we seem to have accepted the principle—as an unspoken article of faith—that freedom is an infinite good. It just goes on getting better. The freedom to filch and print government classified documents; to refuse to reveal that one has AIDS even though others' health might be affected by it; to advocate and practice virtually any kind of sexual behavior as equally valid with any other. The right to "libel" with relative impunity; the right to die, or even to assist in the death of another. Legal status for those living together unmarried, and for homosexual marriage. Exploration of new technologies in which sperm, ovum, and womb can all come from separate sources in the birth of a baby. The commonplace acceptance of birth out of wedlock. The granting of major legal rights and freedoms to noncitizens. Lack of particular personal respect for most kinds of authority, at least compared with most other countries of the world. The freedom to travel anywhere regardless of U.S. foreign policy goals, and to consort with and morally support foreign enemy governments in time of war. All these are trend-setting, bold new precedents in the rights of Americans. They are not even all entirely pernicious. But they have greatly contributed to an overall decline of the role of authority in America; they are also part of a broader process of the elevation of the individual's rights over society.

Yet an unsettling feeling insinuates itself into our American consciousness as we watch the present decay of our own society, starting with our big cities. New York is widely perceived as entering steep decline. What are the roots of this increasing social decay, which includes the decline of the family, the deterioration of education in a technical age, and the development of a permanent underclass? Why are socially menacing trends already high, or even rising: crime, divorce, drugs, failing education, burgeoning juvenile delinquency, pornography, sexual license, cheating, violence in the streets, increasingly graphic violence in our films, the decline of credible authority of almost any kind, a decline in the expression of "patriotism" relative to other countries, diminished idealism as a whole, a sense of alienation, the weakening of personal commitment to community, pollution, limited sense of personal social responsibility, the decline of organized religion, and finally, cynicism about politics and elections—the very instrument designed to address many of society's problems? No wonder that 71 percent of Americans in 1990 declared themselves dissatisfied with moral values in America.

These problems don't stem from some sudden spurt of evil in American character, but rather from the increasing relativism in our value structure. Of course, all values are relative to each other; we are constantly required to balance them off in our own daily lives and in our families. But the increasing relativism of values, the convenience of "situation ethics," cannot help but erode the strength of previous prohibitions of activities viewed as socially undesirable. The word "discipline" evokes largely negative vibes in American society; it is the stuff of satire about redneck military schools and Nazi generals, George C. Scott's *Patton* and English public school regimens. It is almost unthinkable to use it in reference to society.

It is also a fact that the concept of "moral" or "immoral" is by now almost quaint in character. Virtually nothing is seen as "immoral" in the personal life of Americans anymore except white chocolate truffles; or in the political language of the politically correct. "Obscene," too, is used today primarily as political hyperbole, not as a comment on art, film, or literature. To employ even such terms as "right" and "wrong" in any moral context is to reveal oneself at the minimum as hopelessly square, or more likely as socially insensitive and a bigot. "Chill out, man" is the usual response.

But can we blithely dismiss any connection between the

disappearance of the "God-given" values of a more structured society and the emergence of these negative trends that suggest the unraveling of society? "God-given" in the social culture of organized religion meant that certain values, however conservative, were posited as simply "right" and others "wrong." If these moral determinations are now archaic, they did at one time provide moral guideposts for society—but never without the continuing natural resistance and compromises sought by an evolving society. What established guideposts are still around today that we could even resist? We may well wonder whether *any* appropriate moral limitations to the indefinite expansion of freedom need exist at all. True, something as extreme as murder is widely perceived as wrong, but it too is consistently on the rise, and is commonplace among the underclass, and the grounds for defense of murder in the courts grow ever more creative. Stealing is on the rise, especially shoplifting among all classes, right to the top of Wall Street. When murder and theft are in transition from being absolute wrongs to being only relative wrongs, subject to more casual condemnation and judgment, what of the many other wrongdoings and acts of social corrosion that we cannot effectively deal with?

This is the ultimate dilemma of a contemporary, advanced democracy in a disintegrating social structure: when and how do limits ever need to be set on certain freedoms at certain times? The dilemma is old, but its contemporary forms are new and unprecedented. Humanity has always struggled with problems of freedom, but they have never been so fraught with implications and impact as now. This is the first time in history that a society has possessed such a unique combination of circumstances: greater freedom to express individual desires, greater options than ever before to fulfill them, greater financial resources to attain goals, greater time to do so, and greater mobility to multiply those options. All this contrasts sharply with societies in the past that had limited freedom, harsh laws, very little financial power (except among an upper class), limited options, limited information, limited mobility, and limited time. The moral dilemmas created by this quantitatively and qualitatively new society are unique and overwhelming to the traditional order.

Most of us have some atavistic recognition that people do

require some limits on freedom, since the propensity to do evil is always latent. Indeed, nearly every world religion contains a concept of people's nature that clearly includes the propensity to knowing choice of evil. Society was established in order to rein in people's impulses to do evil, in order to protect people from each other. This classic, restrictive concept of society was challenged most prominently by eighteenth-century Rousseauist Romanticism, which managed to turn the concept on its head by positing that it is society that brings out the evil in people. In this view, only radical change in the political system can redress the problems of society and evil. Indeed, the Soviet Union just spent nearly a century trying unsuccessfully to demonstrate precisely that proposition.

Two Sources for the Frailty of Humanity

Our society seems to have lost sight of its philosophical roots as we drift into happy historical amnesia. Not one but two of the basic precepts of the American philosophical heritage were in no doubt about the character of Humanity and its frailty. Both Christianity and the roots of American democracy are unsentimental about the problems of the human condition. In our modern era we find such austere views of society and man disquieting to the starry-eyed sense of life inculcated by rationalism and a healthy dollop of Rousseau. Even to mention the very concept of evil is in poor taste.

Christianity is quite clear that humanity's natural condition predisposes men and women to a frequent, knowing selection of evil over good during the exercise of free choice. In Christian terms this is called Original Sin, suggesting that people are born with this affliction. The church therefore tried to create structures and strictures designed to limit the damage from this dark streak and to enable the individual to handle his weaknesses as much as possible. Nor are these views of Humanity's nature unique to Christians. Both the Semitic religions, Judaism and Islam, are under no illusions about the character of Humanity and its propensity to stray consciously from the moral path; they posit the need, therefore, for institutions that help to avoid or minimize evildoing and apply sanctions where necessary to keep behavior within bounds.

Even nontheistic Buddhism states very clearly that a person is born "ignorant" and obsessed with the self; that only through awareness of the self and its natural character can one attain enlightenment and liberation from the natural condition of ignorance and its pain. Nontheistic Confucianism, too, is very clear about the weakness of people and the need for the arduous cultivation of the individual if he is to lead a correct and upright life.

The Founding Fathers represent the second major source in American thought of awareness of the weakness of Humanity. They may have been children of the Enlightenment, but they harbored no doubts that people had to be protected from people, and that the political order had to be structured so as to accomplish that goal. The American Constitution is a carefully crafted document, specifically designed to limit the damage people can do to each other by establishing elaborate checks and balances designed to mitigate their propensity for evil in the conduct of government. The same vision is explored in endless volumes of great literature, from Dostoyevsky to Faulkner.

Democracy, after all, by definition represents a deliberate limitation of freedom. If the human condition were ideal, the state of freedom would be sufficient; we would be able to appoint anyone to organize the administration of daily life without fear of abuse. But the American Constitution severely curtails freedom, while all the while granting certain basic rights within the restrictions. It is useful to remember that the Founding Fathers were neither starry-eyed naturalists nor anarchists.

Yet there exists massive confusion over the source of evil in human behavior today, and even a refusal to attribute any aspects of social evil directly to Humanity's own character. This confusion has released waves of ahistorical social engineers who see the source of evil as completely exogenous to Humanity's character. This philosophical approach is intimately related to our flirtation with the implicit perfectibility of life and Humanity—a problem discussed in earlier chapters. This philosophical and social romanticism courts real risks in the future evolution of our society: moral values must in some ultimate way be drawn from the foundations of absolute values if they are not to be bargained and chipped away. Hence the deep disquiet within our society today over the death of virtually every single moral absolute—except perhaps freedom itself, and the sanctity of life.

America's unceasing exploration of new frontiers of social freedoms stands counterpoised against religion's determination to preserve some immutable social and moral values. A Muslim friend once commented to me that the problem with America was that it didn't even have the decency to maintain hypocrisy. Hypocrisy, after all, by definition involves the act of at least paying lip service to society's values. If one transgresses values, one at least renders them the respect of flouting them only in private—and perhaps denying it, except to the priest-confessor. One does not revel in the flouting. But America, of course, does revel in the flouting, giving hypocrisy a bad name as ever newer frontiers of "honesty" and frankness are proclaimed by which the fulfillment of nearly every urge becomes licit.

The continuing extension of the limits of the licit is the main source of the problem, but not the only one. Administrative application of the law in America is a secondary but no less important problem. For much of society's increased acceptance of lowered moral standards results from the de facto inability—and eventual unwillingness—of the police and society to do anything about morality, until the public revolts. Legal statutes are littered with laws that are now considered functionally unenforceable, including laws prohibiting petty theft, breaches of public decorum, casual drug use, pornography that invariably now reaches subteens, etc. The police are overworked with more serious problems, the transgressions are widespread and so no one is willing to single out individual offenders, and moral decline is simply shrugged off as a sign of the times. Certainly old Sunday blue laws needed to go, as did other archaic laws from an earlier era. But there is a broader erosion of society's willingness and ability to do much about any violation of the law unless it is of a major order. Since the erosion takes place gradually and incrementally, we are sometimes scarcely aware of where society has slid to over a decade or two.

Other cultures tend to be more sensitive to these changes in America than we are. Hence the concern of the Muslim visitor to America or the Muslim community resident in the

United Kingdom about the moral values of the community. (Muslims in America will soon surpass Jews as the second-largest faith, perhaps challenging American moral perspectives in some respects—although most Muslims in America are hardly fundamentalist in outlook.) Muslims believe not so much that Islam alone can produce a superior civilization, but rather that society requires some unassailable moral principles that are not subject to adjudication. Both Islam and Judaism still view the preservation of the moral society as taking precedence over individual rights. Such views are perhaps no longer possible, or even desirable, in a Western civilization where the rights of the individual nearly always take precedence over society; where perception of the commonweal becomes increasingly complex as society itself grows ever more multifaceted, multiethnic, multicultural, multireligious (including nonreligious), and otherwise varied. Yet our society cannot afford to lose sight of the character of the dilemma involved. Otherwise, how can we make wise decisions when painful trade-offs are involved?

As citizens of a declining society, we cannot be unaware of what is happening around us. We even read in the *New York Times* that both liberals and conservatives are currently developing an interest in reintroducing education about religion into the classroom: not proselytization, but simply an awareness of the role that the sacred and "God-given" moral values have played in human society throughout history. There is a suggestion here that moral roots should run deeper than Supreme Court decisions about *United States* vs. *Challenger X*.

What might restore us to consideration of the origins of values? It doesn't take the church to remind us that killing and stealing and lying and adultery are wrong—are contrary to God-given values—yet even these moral prohibitions are weakening in all phases of society as they move into the more negotiable sphere of "secular values." From what legitimate sources will we drive immutable values in American life? What other source of morality has the ritualistic, ceremonial, awe-inspiring character of religion—has the authority to inculcate absolute moral values recognized by all, even in the breach? All societies have invested the moral code with awe-inspiring ceremonies. Native American society possessed a sense of natural law and the moral forces of nature; major ceremonies instilled these ideas. Today, except within formal religion, we have no such ceremonies for the inculcation of values almost anywhere, except perhaps in the Boy Scouts— itself a quaint museum piece from the days of "good old-fashioned values." A Boy Scout chapter recently had its funding from the United Way cut temporarily because of objections to the Boy Scout oath to serve "God and my country."[1]

We want no theocracy. The history of clerical authoritarianism is no happier than that of secular authoritarianism. It ran the full gamut of abuses in its own historical period, parallel to abuse of civil power in secular government. Nobody wants book-burnings, Iranian-style stonings, the veil, Torquemada's Spanish inquisitional techniques, colonial New England's obligatory Puritan society, Rome's Codex, Church supervision of the bedroom, or contemporary Israel's prohibition of selling pork or public transportation on the Sabbath. We are not seeking to impose creationism on the schools as an "equally valid" scientific view of the evolution of the planet and human life. But must all sense of the sacred be chucked out entirely with the burning stake, the whipping post, the scarlet letter, and compulsory church attendance? These harsh sanctions, after all, reflected the harsher values of those times, religious or secular. Have none of the great religions of the world anything left to say at all in the context of modern society and its values?

Indeed, what has gone so much awry today to produce such a profusion of social evils? What are the sources of the "wildings" in Central Park, rampant, uncontrollable drug use, a rising rate of crime and murder, plummeting educational accomplishment, and a nation slipping behind? Why has cheating in school measurably increased, with students finding little reason to condemn it? Why can Wall Street fat cats make their own rules, only occasionally offering up to the law its most egregious offenders? ("Taxes are for little people," as Leona Helmsley reminds us.) Can we really pretend that it all stems from "social deprivation"—a favorite phrase—in the least deprived nation in the world? Should we just look to developing greater "rationality" of mind, or more money for education as the means to bandage all our social wounds? The United States with its contemporary designer morality just might have something to gain from looking back to societies in which moral values are less subject to the tides of social preference or the interpretations and rationalizations of sociologists. That's where our own native Puritan tradition was coming from, and also our strong Catholic, Lutheran, Quaker, and other moral traditions. It has been the Baptist Church that has kept the American black community alive, dignified, and united for more than a century and has been the source of its finest leaders. If we don't like our historical moral roots, maybe only a moral lobotomy can completely liberate us from our history.

The Discomforts of Religion

The issue runs deeper. We as a society have been growing increasingly uncomfortable with religion, both at home and abroad, despite the continuing strength of private faith. While religion occupies a respected place in traditional American values, Americans generally become uncomfortable when it becomes too shrill, or inserts its values too sharply into our lives. Religion is quite acceptable as long as it is a private matter, an issue of personal faith. But when religious values begin to inform a political program or community action, then warning signals light up, for it then begins to intrude upon the life of others. Religion on TV has often been a particular desservice to the cause. Much of TV evangelism really seeks to exploit religion; its commercial hype leaves all but a minority discomfited by it. For many, religion has unfortunately come to invoke visions of unctuous evangelists, for some of whom, we learn, the therapeutic quality of going shopping apparently surpasses even the value of prayer.

But of course, in a sense religion has always meant to inform community life, and even political life when it comes to legislation on social issues. After all, religion is specifically intended to speak out on moral issues related not only to the individual but to the community at large. This point, of course, was repeatedly stressed by the Ayatollah Khomeini. He believed strongly that Islam is not merely limited to one's personal beliefs, or even to the relationship between the individual and God. Religion is political by definition. It is important for Muslims to go on the annual pilgrimage to Saudi

Arabia, the hajj, to partake specifically in political demonstrations there; in Khomeini's view, religion is in fact all about political values and the proper political structures designed to reflect the just order of God on earth. "We did not make a revolution over the price of watermelons," the ayatollah once remarked.

Closer to home, fundamentalist minister Pat Robertson threw his hat into the ring during the 1988 American presidential campaign with very much the same ideas in mind: religion is not just a matter of private conscience but of urgent political import. Ideas about morality and the place of morality in the state cannot be limited strictly to the private conscience but must inform the very political processes by which we live. To some, this is "politicizing religion." To others it is bringing religion precisely into those areas where it is most important; the purpose is not for the state to support religion, but for religion to exert influence on the political process—which is what society is all about.

Protestant and Catholic clergy often speak out on political issues, usually to the left on political issues as war and disarmament, usually more to the right on social issues. But it is getting harder for religion to enter into the political arena in America—for better and for worse—for several reasons. First is the increasing cultural diversity of our country; even the major Christian divisions, Protestant and Catholic, have developed incredible diversity within themselves. The current spectrum of outlook within Protestantism alone today is astonishing: there is no consensus, even among Protestants, as to what the relationship between private and social morality should be. The practice of religions other than Christianity makes national consensus on matters of religion increasingly problematic. Jews have every reason to be concerned with talk about strengthening the role of religion in society when they themselves are outside the dominant religion and therefore at possible risk of partial exclusion from the workings of society. In fact, any moral consensus within the United States is now largely shattered by an increasingly pluralistic society.

Second, with the "American cultural revolution" of the sixties and seventies, there is a greater sense of freedom—and social license—than ever before in nearly all areas of life, including ethics and morality. The public at large—whatever its particular set of values—would not be able to reach agreement on the character of any particular binding code of morality, or, indeed, on whether there should be one at all. The American attitude is also rooted profoundly in the lessons of our own historical experience. Persecution by organized religion has been a major historical impetus for immigration to America. But so has been the quest for freedom of religion, often denied to minority religious groups in other states. As a nation, therefore, we have special problems in coming to terms with any concept of state morality or any limits on freedom of speech.

It is hard to know whether organized religious institutions, most notably the church, will play stronger roles in shaping the future moral values of America. The church is likely to have only limited power as an institution per se on the political scene. Its main importance lies in forming the personal moral views of Americans who then participate in the shaping of our political system. A series of individually held values can have powerful collective impact on the attitudes of society. If the mechanisms of society, the courts, and the law move in increasingly relativist directions, the views of individuals can serve as correctives. This is where the church and other religious institutions will continue to play some role in a world where the religious impulse is hardly dead.

Alternative Sources of Moral Standards

If not religion, what sources are we then left with in the modern democratic secular society from which American morals and ethics can flow? The dilemma is more acute in America today precisely because democracy and freedom have tended to recode traditional sources of morality while failing to provide meaningful alternatives. Sources of American values and morality will be one of the grand dilemmas of the next century. It is one of the fundamental dilemmas of democracy, and if it is not addressed foursquare in debate, as Democratic gubernatorial candidate John Silber tried to do in a failed Massachusetts campaign, it can only spell trouble. But American society sometimes has a way of preferring not to articulate the really fundamental dilemmas because it is politically too risky. Jimmy Carter got trashed for what was called "blaming it on America."

Democracy, of course, originally evolved in states and times when secular authorities were not expected to be the source of moral values; the church in England and France still had major influence over these issues. Today, in a highly secular society, secular democratic institutions seem to have taken over the determination of moral values by default. Alternative moral sources currently would seem to be only two: the Supreme Court, and.the force of community moral consensus. Both avenues are important to consider. If traditional God-given morality is deeply problematic for us today in a practical sense, the other two approaches, too, are deeply flawed.

The Courts as Moral Source

Can the courts, or the Supreme Court, replace a fractured society's values as the source of moral legitimacy? Can they establish a viable secular basis for behavior? Are the virtues, then, by which parents bring up their children to be the latest deliberations of the current Supreme Court?

The strengths of the Supreme Court lie both in its function as the court of last resort and, even more important, in its reputed wisdom and balance. If state institutional wisdom resides anywhere in the United States, surely it must reside in the Court. But is it all just about wisdom? What is the role of community values in their decisions? The Court itself has debated whether it is the business of the courts to establish fundamentally new legal and moral positions when no consensus exists among the public. How "democratic" should the courts be? In their interpretations of the Constitution, do they also reflect broader contemporary American values, or the preferences and agenda of an educated elite—either liberal or conservative, depending on the pendulum swing? When a judgment on a moral issue is rendered by the Supreme Court in Washington, D.C., the judgment may well be less in touch with the "sense of society" than a court decision taken on the local level. Perhaps a state supreme court decision will also lie slightly closer to the "will of the people" than one of the national Supreme Court—which is why state laws differ in significant respects between Minnesota and California, Vermont and New Jersey, Alabama and Nevada. The state decision is inherently more "democratic," i.e., more reflective of local values, but lacks the authority of the Supreme Court decision. Indeed, a Supreme Court legal rendering in Washington perhaps comes closer to establishing a secular source of morality than anything else does these days.

The Supreme Court demonstrates recognition of the issue of "local values" in its tendency to split: on the left are the liberal justices with their individually derived moral views and support of social activism; on the right are the more conservative justices who prefer stricter constitutional interpretation or look to uphold state laws where possible as a better reflection of "contemporary community values." The abortion issue, for example, has partly involved this tension of approaches. The effort to define pornography entails much of the same clashes as well, as does debate over the "right to die."

But the option of relegating moral decisions to the court system is also highly unsatisfactory. The courts lack moral sanctity. On another level, the court system is increasingly viewed as an extension of the national political struggle. It has always been a highly politicized institution; battles royal are regularly fought over nominations to the Supreme Court, which are correctly understood to have immense impact on its final writ. So much for an "objective" source of morality. The community can hardly find solace and support within the court system. One popular public view of the Supreme Court's role on moral issues, reduced to its most vivid and simplistic formulation, is that "pornography is now legal but prayer in schools is illegal." A recent cartoon shows a roadside sign reading "School Zone—No Praying." The majority of the public at that point would probably prefer to leave behavior to individual conscience rather than to some politicized court's legalistic moral calls.

The "Community" as Arbiter

If we cannot look to the courts to establish moral standards, then what of the community and its locally derived sense of values? Surely the community itself has the right to determine its own standards. But this too is immediately susceptible to objection. A Florida court in 1990 bans the album "As Nasty as They Wanna Be" by 2 Live Crew for its reported obscenity, gross portrayal of women as sex objects, and sexual violence against women. The incident brought out a great wave of public defense for the group; learned professors analyzed the "literary content" of the music—you can always find some who will—and decried the suppression of freedom of speech in the county and outside. A higher state court struck down the decision.

But what right does Dade County really have to ban the music, however offensive it may be to most? In whose name does the county speak? Could the county sustain its decision in a countywide referendum? Almost surely not. Should citizens themselves articulate their own concerns, by objecting to what they deem to be morally objectionable?

The issue is complicated further by the fact that America is a *constitutional* democracy. The views of the majority of the public are in any case irrelevant to the court system if it determines that public action violates consitutional rights of free speech.

Some Christians were offended by the film version of a very serious novel by Nikos Kazantzakis, *The Last Temptation of Christ*, and proceeded to picket theaters showing it, successfully in a number of areas. Were my rights violated because I could not see an important film in my neighborhood? Were those picketers representative? Were they within their rights to intimidate theater owners who preferred to skip the hassle? And what of the small community of atheists who decided to take action to ban the Christmas nativity scenes on town-hall lawns? Was this representative of the community? Think of the risks taken by department stores at Christmastime that pipe any music into the elevators that goes beyond "Rudolph the Red-Nosed Reindeer," and ventures the dangerously litigious waters of "Baby Jesus." Do a tiny handful of activists possess the authority to impose their values on a broader community—separation of church and state or no? The biggest problem about community consensus is that there isn't one.

Democracy the Foul-Mouthed?

Another major company, Geffen Records, at roughly the same time as the 2 Live Crew case, declined to publish a record album on the grounds that it too was obscene and offensive in content. In this latter case, the charge of suppression of freedom of speech rang hollower; obviously it is within the right of any company to set its own standards of taste for publication. In the fall of 1990, Simon & Schuster, only months before distribution, at the last moment decided not to publish the novel *American Psycho* because of its reported gross and exceptionally graphic and vicious descriptions of sadistic sexual tortures and murders of women. An uproar ensued from certain quarters charging the publishers with "censorship." The author, of course, has no constitutional right whatsoever to be published, although any publisher has the right to publish him if it wants. In the event, greed seems to have won out over morality; Random House seems to have decided the profits are too attractive to ignore and will shortly publish it, especially after all that free publicity. It is comforting to know that "freedom of speech" has been upheld.

The principle is important. Private exercise of moral authority by the business community is one form of reflection of perceived community values, in the case of both Geffen Records and Simon & Schuster. Does this mean the marketplace might be able to do what the state is not really able to do? In both cases, of course, somebody else is publishing the offensive record and book. So much for community values in the marketplace. Furthermore, to abandon our values to the marketplace seems even scarier; as H. L. Mencken said, "Nobody ever lost any money underestimating the intelligence of the American public."

The divisive debate in Congress over the permissibility of funding by the National Endowment for the Arts of works judged to be pornographic by Supreme Court definition seemed to raise the issue of state censorship anew. Here too, however, the issue in reality was not about censorship of the arts, but about whether the public should be required to pay for offensive or potentially pornographic works through public funding.

The concerns far surpass the attitudes of little old ladies in tennis shoes. No less mainstream a publication than *Time* ran a cover article in 1990 on "America the Foul-Mouthed," taking note of the high degree of obscene language now common on the public scene. *Time* found *no* remedy other than living through what it felt was ultimately a passing phenomenon. If we really are talking of swings of the pendulum, then there is reason for encouragement. But if we are talking of ever braver horizons of boldness, then we are in trouble. This is particularly true in the area of increasingly graphic displays of raw violence and sadism on the screen—far more corrosive to society's health than any steamy sex scene.

Interestingly, the Federal Communications Commission in 1990 upheld a twenty-four-hour-a-day ban on "indecent" radio and television broadcasts. According to *Los Angeles Times* reporter Penny Pagano, Commissioner Duggan said that

> many parents today find their homes "alien territories" invaded by value systems and information that they find abhorrent. "Parents need the support of the society and culture. They are not enemies of the Constitution. They are people like you and me. We owe some decent concern to the upset and anguish they are expressing."[2]

America is hardly unique in its seizure with the problem. We read, for example, that Hungary, only recently liberated from Communism, is now a flourishing center for pornographic publications. According to the *New York Times*,

> the explosion of sexually explicit material has already produced a backlash. Parents, religious groups and feminists are recoiling from the shock of seeing photographs of nudes and graphic depictions of sexual acts on the covers of publications like *Sexexpress, Popo, Sexy Lady, Lesbi Girls, Apollo* and the other pornographic magazines . . . "Pornography is part of democracy, but human rights means taking the other side into consideration too" [says a spokesman of the Christian Democratic Party].

Feminism to the Rescue?

One of the more interesting developments is the emergence of increasingly outspoken women's and feminist groups expressing fundamental objections to the spread of pornography and violence in the public domain. While feminists have often been allied with more radical groups on issues of peace, the Third World, and minorities, they are increasingly de facto allies of citizens' groups concerned with pornography and violence. The feminists see women portrayed in graphic pornography as objects of lust, perversion, and violence; they furthermore suggest there is linkage to actual antifemale violence on the streets. Many have organized against pornographic publications. There was a feminist movement led by the National Organization of Women (NOW) to boycott Random House as a result of its decision to print *American Psycho*. Perhaps indeed women are quicker to reflect the "conscience of the community" than are men, and will bring about some fundamental reconsideration of the rampant growth of pornography and violence. Their methods so far seem to lean toward boycott. Boycotts might have greater teeth in the end than impotent and unenforceable court decisions; furthermore, they arise spontaneously from "community consensus," unlike court decisions.

Establishing some kind of moral standard for society that does not run afoul of the Constitution is the ultimate challenge. Perhaps the boycott of certain companies that produce offensive material is a start. It is important for society to be able to exact a higher cost from the purveyors of obscenity and violence in the future, in ways that cannot be challenged in the courts. The problem is that broad action is likely to be focused on a few egregious cases. Nonetheless, a useful "chilling effect" might emerge against casual profiteers in socially damaging material.

The state could take one step further by attempting to apply the principle of "sin taxes" to socially harmful material. If alcohol and cigarettes can be taxed heavily—in part to provide funds to pay to rectify the damage done—why not tax certain aspects of media? States could elect representatives to a review board for social values that would review all films, for example, much as the current rating system operates. An average of the negative points scored on graphic violence, obscenity, or romanticization of drug use, for example, would be translated directly into a variable percentage of surtax to be levied on the earnings of a given film. Ratings should not be mechanical; each reviewer should take into account the overall intent and caliber of the film in judging how gratuitous the violation of social standards are. Freedom of speech and art is maintained, but certain fringe materials would entail expense for their purveyors—and eventually for their consumers. Nothing can be readily banned, but some element of forethought and even self-censorship might result. Self-censorship already exists in most newspapers and magazines. Porno magazines would receive similar reviews, perhaps discouraging easy investment of money into this area. The price of such films and magazines would go up. Revenues would go for social projects. Such a proposal would need to be carefully developed, but society will probably need to create imaginative mechanisms to deal with problems of material felt by the community to be damaging to overall social health. Economic instruments are probably the best.

In the absence of more efficacious and meaningful controls, the continued deterioration of social values may also bring about more rapid rejection by the public of explicit pornography and violence. The American Civil Liberties Union predictably continues to share the same mentality as the National Rifle Association on these matters: just as abridgment today of the right to buy "Saturday night specials" leads inexorably to a ban on deer hunting tomorrow, the least abridgment by the state of the rights of the individual today leads inevitably down the slippery slope to fascism tomorrow.

But the burden of proof that these explicit materials are *not* harmful to society may come to rest increasingly upon the advocates of unfettered expression. As columnist Charles Krauthammer has pointed out in the *New Republic*, it is hard to argue on the one hand that the arts exert an uplifting effect on the community and society and should be encouraged, and on the other hand to deny that explicit pornography and violence have *any* effect on the community or teenagers. When answers are sought to crimes of sexuality and crimes on the street, some will indeed look to magazines and films. Rest assured some Ph.D. will always be able to "prove decisively" through research that the availability of such materials bears no relationship to crime and antisocial activity whatsoever; fortunately the public is smart enough to know better. Does it take a Jesse Helms to make the case when a more representative cross section of the public may share the same concerns? How American democracy handles these questions will affect the whole world.

Short of such government empowerment to concerted community action via the taxation instrument, the concept of "community values" doesn't seem to have much teeth. Ironically, it is the democratic process itself that has contributed to the moral immobilization of society; it is the democratic process that both *fosters* social diversity and *reflects* our society's diversity and inability to reach any community consensus. The courts are thus hard put to turn to community consensus on moral issues because there is none, on a great variety of controversial issues. Inevitably liberals tend to be happier with the Supreme Court than with state courts because they rightfully fear that the community or local consensus is less liberal than they would wish; conservatives feel that the Supreme Court's rulings are more liberal than the community consensus usually would wish.

The conflict between democracy and religiously derived morality, then, will persist long into the future. Most likely it will never be resolved—and maybe should not be resolved, for both reflect deep values worth retaining. We are in fact witnessing a natural tension, a natural dialectic of two virtues that spring from opposite ends of the spectrum. For religion is inherently authoritarian by nature, democracy inherently individualistic in its expression. The trade-offs will constantly need to be adjudicated by every society at differing times and under differing circumstances. The greatest danger emerges when any one group feels that only the courts, or only religious values and institutions, represent the right way to go, and then moves to permanently damage the power and voice of the other, or to cancel out half of the equation of values. Today it is the Church that is on the run—even if religion is not.

In the meantime, because there is such a tension between democracy and religiously based moral values, what is society to do about social and moral decay in areas that go beyond "simpler" questions of pornography and violence?

The Individual vs. Society

The heart of the dilemma of a deteriorating society may lie in the continuous affirmation of the freedom of the individual over the interests of "society." For it is only in the adjudication of each individual's rights in concrete cases that the granting of freedom takes on meaning. This is where "the rubber hits the road," where freedom is operationalized. If society is suffering from the continuing spillover of freedom into license, then the preservation of society perhaps can come only from a reversal of priorities—if some balance is to be restored. Perhaps the pendulum must now swing back to greater focus on the "rights of society."

How else is the process of social decline to be reversed? Voices inevitably rise against any weakening of the individual's position vis-à-vis society. Almost no one is comfortable with such a reversal, given the history of empowering the individual over the last century. But free speech is not an endangered species in America—despite the lunatic view of the absolute few who are still in the thrall of the romantic notion that establishing a society without rules is the true road to beauty and fulfillment. When the day comes when freedom of speech looks as if it might be threatened by more dangerous abridgment, then I for one will take to the barricades in defense of it. I do not see that danger on the horizon anywhere today. As it stands now, we are caught between the True Believers in the sanctity of the First Amendment over all else, and those whose fervent moral mission is to save society from itself. The rest of us are standing uncomfortably in the middle, exposed to much more heat than light on the issue. We should therefore welcome debate over such issues as the proper use of NEA funding, the propriety of the novel *American Psycho*, and the types of controls placed on obscene language in rock music—for it gets to the heart of the moral dilemma, however it may be resolved.

The ACLU absolutist treatment of freedom, like the ayatollah's absolutist view of the value of Islam, may be at least one of the very sources of our problem. Surely these two values, the individual and society, are also meant to be permanently in tension and ever shifting in their relative weight in accordance with circumstance and need.

Clint Eastwood and the New Authoritarianism?

Yet even if we acknowledge in the abstract that a greater balance must be struck between the interests of the individual and society, how is such an approach to be implemented? If we acknowledge that the authority and weight of religious institutions and their traditional God-given values have now been reduced to impotence in any executive sense, surely the law and its stricter or harsher application become the only viable alternative source of enforceable morality and social values. Should the power of the law and the state be strengthened by putting more teeth into them? Should the rules of evidence be relaxed in order to instill greater respect for the power of the police and the police's determination to maintain social order? Should divorces be harder to obtain? Shouldn't yuppies start bearing more of the brunt of white-collar crime, which is also destructive of the moral order and climate? Shouldn't the upper-middle-class recreational drug user start paying a far higher price? Why shouldn't the Coast Guard continue to impound yachts of those fat cats caught with only "personal usage" quantities of drugs if we are going for the fourteen-year-old pusher in the ghetto whom the yachtsman helps support? Shouldn't the FCC exercise stricter control over what is aired over the public airwaves? Shouldn't far stricter codes relating to movie violence be established that will complicate the showing of highly graphic films and financially penalize—through restricted markets or showing hours—of films considered socially undesirable?

One views these remedies with a sinking feeling, because they represent a reversal of a long trend toward ever greater freedoms and the weakening of authority in most respects that nearly all have enjoyed. Furthermore, it may simply be too late now to shut the barn door. It is one thing not to grant freedoms. It is another thing to take them back, to reestablish stricter social attitudes toward the preservation of society through more conservative means. But we are not really talking about the abrogation of constitutional rights so much as the "freedoms" that have come to be granted in an administrative sense by police and court procedure, or even police nonaction.

How might such a turnaround take place in our democratic

society? Regrettably, things might get worse before they get better. Perhaps the only thing that can turn social attitudes around will be the continuing and alarming decline of society and the social order. When New York is perceived to be truly unlivable, will a law-and-order approach win strong public support? Will Clint Eastwood win the day in the cities, or will the greater public simply abandon urban life to a state of rampant jungle?

Americans do not like to think of the rights of the individual and the welfare of society as trade-offs, as thesis and antithesis of the dialectic, as competing values that can only reach delicate compromise and never true coexistence. We like *both* individualism and society. American society at large seemingly has not yet reached philosophical recognition of the collision force of these two competing values. But already cracks are appearing, even in the liberal media. *The New Republic* has suggested that if our society is serious about the drug problem, then it must consider granting the private sector greater ability to "abridge" individual rights of the individual suspected of drug use: employers would be able to demand drug-free employees, and apartment-house committees—especially in all-black ghetto areas—could be empowered to reject rent applicants who are even thought to support drug use. Abuse might take place, but the message would get across fast as society sought to "liberate" drug areas from the overall contagion.

If we are unable to cope with the reality that trade-offs are involved, then continuing social decline is all but certain as our runaway democratic practice and helpless discipline structure both exacerbate the problem and limit our abilities to attain a solution.

If we are unable to take meaningful steps to reverse the drowning of society in the flood of statistically demonstrable decay, then grimmer prognoses loom. Under such circumstances, the future of Western democratic practice may be cyclical: absolute individual freedoms will infinitely expand until society reaches a breakdown point, only to pass into a phase of restorative authoritarianism until the demand slowly grows again for increases in individual freedoms. If, as argued earlier in this book, many of the new problems of society have spontaneously emerged from economic as well as political change in society—the decline of the family, the emergence of working couples, increased geographical mobility of the job market, casual marriage and easy divorce, teenagers as a new economic class—then it would seem very hard indeed to reverse a process of social decline through anything other than social cataclysm and true reversion to a period of authoritarianism of either a right- or left-wing sort.

These unattractive and depressing prognostications all flow from a belief that the traditional sources of moral values are mortally wounded, and probably cannot be resuscitated in contemporary, democratic, secular society. But not all segments of the public, in America or abroad, are willing to abandon the fight over religious vs. secular values—precisely because they view the latter as so weak. They are willing to do battle, in one form or another, worldwide. When the movement is purely moral, then democratic issues are not really affected. Where political action is under way, the practice of democracy is directly affected.

Backlash Against Secular Trends

Today we are witnessing a distinct backlash—worldwide—against secular trends. America itself is hardly immune to a similar reaction against the onslaught of secularization and its democratic consequences. As America moves ever farther from traditional "God-given" values and toward new court-imposed social and moral values, the trend will not readily be accepted by all. The backlash is particularly strong among those who feel directly helpless and threatened in the face of deteriorating social values around them, most typically lower middle classes and lower classes that lack the money to at least try to insulate themselves from the problems.

The coming decades, then, are hardly likely to find the forces of secular "rationality" automatically replacing all the wellsprings of traditional faith. On the contrary, religious faith is likely to grow. It will come in response to the moral and spiritual needs of the individual in times of continuing rapid transition and change in all societies, especially under circumstances of deteriorating community morality. It will also come in response to needs of various communities abroad to reas-

sert their identity against external cultural or ethnic challengers. Signs of social backlash can already be seen in several
areas, even where it does not automatically take religious
form per se.

• The death penalty may not be "rational," and perhaps
may not even produce the desired lowering of the murder
rate, but society is revolting nonetheless against what it considers to be the deterioration of the social and moral order
and seeks to preserve the safety of the community; hence
it strikes back.

• The widespread and sad community passivity to the
tragedy of AIDS also reflects a strong and harsh community
perception that it is the choice of irregular or immoral lifestyles that is the primary source of the disease.

• The American contemporary fixation on the ugly phenomenon of child abuse and rape has produced the first
efforts at a law that recognizes the possible incorrigibility
of some kinds of criminal and the need to suspend individual rights in the name of social protection. Washington state
has recently passed a "sexual predators" bill that calls for
indefinite incarceration of repeat offenders, *regardless of
jail sentence*, out of recognition that they will probably not
be "reformed."[3]

• Vigilantism against drug dealers in the ghettoes has
grown in proportion to police helplessness or impotence
because of process-related rules of evidence, etc. The
church has actually been a strong source of community
cohesion and of strength in the black community, and leaders like Martin Luther King and Jesse Jackson have sprung
from it. Black Muslims in the ghettoes have also been particularly effective in halting many kinds of neighborhood
crime, albeit through extralegal methods.

• American fundamentalism, voicing concerns astonishingly similar to many of those of Islamic societies, continues
to draw support. Even if the style, language, and remedies
of these preachers do not appeal to all, the moral dilemmas
they pose cannot be dismissed by anyone as meaningless.

In short, fundamentalist or traditional values—usually derived
in some way from the religious foundations of morality—are

still an active force in society and will "strike back," often sharply, when social norms are seen to be deeply threatened.

International Trends Away from Secularism

The most intriguing aspect of the resistance against modern secularism is its grass-roots nature. Modern secularism was not a sudden occurrence, or a one-time definitive blow against the forces of the church; it was an almost creeping accompaniment of political, social, and economic change. So too, the new antisecular trends hardly illustrate the resurgence of aggrieved church power triumphant. Quite the contrary, the powerful new countertrends against secularism are springing up in the form of popular rebellions from within society itself. Those spearheading the drive are not at all the traditional, formal, religious institutions of Islam or Christianity. These institutions are themselves driven along by believers who are dismayed at the acquiescence of traditional religious institutions to the weakening of religion in society. The new evangelical movements are actually rivals to the traditional church, and come almost as a rebuke to it. In Islam the fundamentalist movements have not been led by the clergy; they pose a threat to the formal clergy, which had long since reached accommodation with secular power.

Nor is the trend toward religious revival just a debate over theology. It stems from the very nature of the religious impulse and the profusion of forms that it assumes. Religion is often an integral part of the very national character and cultural heritage of a people, one of its identifying components vis-à-vis other cultures. Thus the role of Catholicism in Poland as a symbol of the anti-Russian, anticommunist impulse; the role of Islam in the Soviet Union, where it defines the differences between Azeri and Armenian, Uzbek and Russian, and in Israel, where it defines the Palestinian against the Jew; and the role of Hinduism in India, where it defines the majority against the Muslim minority; and in Sri Lanka, where it defines the Tamil minority against the Buddhist majority. Religion also serves to define community differences *between* states—the Iranian Shiite against the Saudi Sunni, the Irish Catholic against the British Protestant, the

Lebanese Shiite against the American Christian. As long as political, cultural, and economic rivalries exist, religious differences are pressed into service as powerful tools to define and strengthen the character of each contender.

Second, religion is a vehicle of political expression. In the Middle Ages the state employed the various forms of Christianity as the ideological vehicle by which to conduct their wars against other Christians and Muslims. Regional rivalry was cast in the more universal ideological terms of religious faith rather than local nationalism. The political and social character of the Reformation was expressed largely in a religious vocabulary. This is precisely the nature of Christianity in the Soviet Union today, where it served as a key form of antistate expression for anticommunist forces. In the Muslim world, Islam is still a key medium for many political drives, playing a role in international politics that largely came to an end in the international relations of Christian states several hundred years ago.

Because Islam, more than any other major world religion, has much to say about the formation and purpose of the state and society, it is a natural vehicle for movements against the state and serves as a highly legitimizing device for opposition against authoritarian state power. So too, Islam can be a protest vehicle against the corruption and maladministration of the state when such vices are cast as an offense against God's order. It also serves to justify the attack of one state on another, as in Iran's broadsides against Saudi Arabia. The use of religious doctrine lends legitimacy to antiestablishment political movements, making it much riskier and more difficult for an illegitimate state order to suppress those citizens who speak in the name of an Islamic movement.

Indeed, in times of stress it is normal for communities to turn to their basic root values—of which religion lies at the very core. Under pressure of the American cultural revolution in the sixties, Christian fundamentalist movements sprang up redoubled in America in order to correct what they saw as a growing confusion of values. The religious sense of the Jewish community was unquestionably strengthened by the pressures on the Jewish communities of Eastern Europe. Radical Islam has emerged in the Muslim world to protect itself against a perceived onslaught of negative Western values and seductive mass culture, of a kind of destructive "cultural imperialism" from the West—exacerbated by often heavy-handed U.S. policies that are perceived as "anti-Muslim." At the same time there is an unbridgeable psychological gap between American secular society and the impulses of Muslim fundamentalist movements, particularly when religion in politics—so basic to Islam—is anathema in "rational" American society. Indeed, we grow nervous at the sight of politicized Islam; it is outside our grasp why Iran should be in flames, or why Shiite terrorists launch suicide car-bomb attacks against our embassies.

Apart from these political roles, religion plays a key role in anchoring people in times of social, political, moral, and economic travail. Fundamentalist Islam has grown in the Middle East in part because of the overwhelming inundations of Western culture that are seen as undermining traditional moral and cultural values. Many Islamic women in the cities, even young female students at universities, find Islamic clothing a way to opt out of the more sexually challenging mores that exist in Westernized society. The very appeal of Western political and cultural values to some segments of Islamic society only heightens the vigilance of the traditional-minded. The urban sprawls of Cairo, Istanbul, and Tehran are drawing in peasants at a rapid rate, exposing them to corrosive and divisive pressures. Personal faith and traditional values are perhaps all individuals can hold on to as they experience the city's facelessness and dog-eat-dog morality. The loss of personal identity in the urban caldron is intensely threatening and regularly spawns a desire to turn to religion as solace and comfort, and as reassertion of personal identity. Such is a key source for the growth of personal piety in the Muslim world—even when it is not completely identical with the radical fundamentalist movements.

In America, too, interest in religion continues strong. Where traditional church institutions seem to have lost religious intensity, fundamentalist or evangelical movements have gained strength at their expense. The traditional church is often perceived as playing a comfortable social role instead of leading the battle on issues of concern to its congregations. Emphasis on issues like immigration and El Salvador is seen to dilute the powerful religious message of God in the lives of the congregation that so powerfully frames the appeal of the evangelical movements. Yet other Americans, dismayed by the loss of the mystical in life, have also turned to Asian religions, especially Buddhism, to find greater meaning and purpose amid the glitz of so much of contemporary life. These evangelical impulses have even spread to Britain, where the new archbishop of Canterbury, appointed in 1990, has rebuked the American Church for drifting away from mysticism and the fundamental theses of Christian faith in favor of watered-down ethical homilies.

For all these reasons, then, religion is not likely ever to fade as a phenomenon. The greater the social turmoil and the quest for personal and national identity, the more religion will serve as an important vehicle of expression. While nationalism and religion in theory represent competing ideologies, in fact they are in many cases mutually reinforcing. Lastly, the overwhelming personal impact on those who feel their lives powerfully changed by religion cannot be explained away in mere psychological or sociological terms. Our secular democracies—almost surely representing the best way for human societies to govern themselves in the future—will coexist in a state of almost permanent tension with the religious element within all societies.

Managing Conflicts Between Religion and the Democratic Secular State

But the battle for secularist values within the democratic context is not all lost. Interestingly enough, even in strongly Islamic countries like Pakistan the problem of reaching consensus on issues of religion and democracy is still great. Benazir Bhutto, who in 1988 became the first female prime minister in any Muslim country, relaxed some of the stricter controls of her more fundamentalist-oriented predecessor, President Zia ul-Haq. Pornography promptly began to appear in Pakistan under the relaxed rules of a more secular government.

At the same time, Pakistan's Shiite minority, with its own distinct vision of what religious, social, and moral practice should be, actually prefers Pakistan to be a secular state rather than the strongly religious Sunni Muslim state that it is; at least in a secular state the Sunni majority would not be able to impose its own religious views on everyone in the state. Thus even in Muslim states we find that democracy and the "religious neutrality" of the secular state are often perceived as more reliable safeguards of religious freedom—as well as nonreligious freedom—than any other system of government including the Islamic government itself.

The Soviets do not fare much better in terms of understanding the phenomenon of rising interests. In Marxism, of course, all religion is representative of primitive stages of development, and has dogmatically been treated as the "opiate of the people." According to the "scientific" laws of Marxism there should be no place for religion in socialist (i.e., communist) societies because exploitation—the source of despair for which religion is the opiate—will have disappeared. Moscow has been hard put to explain why vibrant and vital Islamic faith has remained among its own Muslim populations. Even more, the stubborn intensity of Christian belief in Russia itself throughout the worst years of communist oppression continually plagued communist authorities. Its resurgence today is impressive. The Marxist is more deeply panicked by the thought of powerful or militant religious belief than is the Western agnostic or even atheist; scientifically, according to Marx, it just "should not be so."

The tension between democratic secular institutions and religious faith is normal, and almost certainly desirable as representing complementary facets and needs of the human society. If neither element can coexist with the other—if the state tries to destroy the church, or the church tries to take over the state—there will be trouble. This confrontation could become one of the enduring features of the next age, demonstrating that even on the philosophical plane, history is anything but "over." The historical dialectic of grand ideas has hardly played itself out with opposing forces of religion and democratic secularism still at odds in many parts of the world—and unlikely ever to be resolved.

Christianity and Social Change

The fundamentalist phenomenon is hardly limited to Islam. Evangelical Protestantism has begun to pose an extraordinary challenge to Catholicism in Latin America—a major new phenomenon. In this fascinating shift we see again many of the same crises of identity and modern development. Richard Rodriguez, a San Francisco journalist, writes of the sweeping number of conversions to "fundamentalist"—i.e., evangelical—Protestantism by Catholics all over Latin America. He describes Protestantism in Europe as the faith that sustained the new arrivals in medieval cities—the world of strangers; it was Protestantism that taught them to stand up for themselves, to pray directly to God, and to resist authority, which no longer could tell them what to think. Rodriguez sees Catholicism in Latin America as representing the old order, the paternalistic society in which the faithful are treated indulgently as children who err and will be forgiven, as part of an immutable lifelong relationship. Evangelical Protestantism, on the other hand, involves a decisive act of personal assertion, the act and declaration of faith that, on the spot, transforms the convert by an act of will into a different person, looking at the world with new eyes, confidently empowered by God at that moment and from then on to take personal responsibility for his or her own life, instead of trusting in the paternalistic/maternalistic embrace of the protective Catholic Church. Concludes Rodriguez,

> What the secular American should realize is that evangelical Christianity is spreading precisely in relation to an international secularism within cities. Worldwide secularism is giving rise to its own antidote, a form of fundamentalism, whether in Iran or Bolivia. Implicit in evangelical Christianity is a criticism of the modern, of Los Angeles, of Lima.[4]

Rodriguez's discussion describes precisely those elements touched on earlier—Islamic fundamentalism in the great urban cities of the Middle East, the cry against anomie, and an act of will against the helplessness of living under modern, incompetent, and uncaring bureaucracies.

America Pioneers in Discovering New Ethical Dilemmas

It's not all just about community values vs. freedom of speech and individual rights. Modern society is busy throwing up new moral problems that emerge out of the rule of law, modern economies and society, and new scientific discoveries. The incredible growth of medical technology has raised dauntingly complex issues, creating moral dilemmas almost beyond the traditional moral sensitivities of the average citizen. Abortion debate has been infinitely complicated by new scientific information—and startling new photography—that emphasizes the human character of a fetus from the initial months of pregnancy. Judgment on women's rights vs. fetus rights has so far come down on the side of the freedom to abort. But where do ethics and the law now stand on issues of damage to a fetus through the mother's use of alcohol, tobacco, and drugs during pregnancy? Are not society's rights also affected here? *In vitro* pregnancies and surrogate mothers raise ever more complex moral questions. Cruel decisions will multiply that unfortunately place greater burdens on women than men.

We now frequently read that physiological and psychological problems may be the source of much of what we have historically been inclined to attribute to moral irresponsibility, weakness, and moral failing. Alcoholism may now be a "disease," a medical predisposition stronger in some individuals than others. Fetal brain damage in the criminal stemming from a mother's use of alcohol or drugs is increasingly being used as a point of legal defense in capital cases. In short, what was previously in the realm of ethics is now transformed into a medical issue, ultimately denying the concept of freedom of choice or any moral responsibility for conduct. All becomes forgivable—even if society will still not permit such damaged individuals to roam at large. Moral problems suddenly become accessible to treatment by the high priests of the pill and the syringe, rather than by the father confessor. The particular twists of the DNA strand begin to transcend the importance of moral training in the family.

The Return of the Sacred and the Mysterious

In the end, we discover that the sense of the unknown, the mysterious, the mystical, the sacred, takes on even more powerful appeal as the advances of science relentlessly roll back the terrain of what we previously viewed with awe and mystery. This has been true, of course, since the first empirical scientific discoveries of the laws of nature were made by ancient Egyptians and Greeks; but the electron microscope has now rendered the pace of acceleration extraordinary. The old existential questions return with new force, especially as modern society has given us ever greater freedom to "live" instead of just "cope." Questions of existential purpose arise—perhaps even more readily under the laid back and forever perfect weather of California than in those states and climes in which life can still present some challenges.

The attraction of religion and mysticism would seem to reflect a basic human need that will not be denied. There is in fact nothing in democracy that inherently places it at odds with these issues of transcendental values and mysteries. But in reality, it is democracy that permits the existence and expression of social and personal diversity, diversity that is exploding like a galaxy, rushing apart in all directions under the centrifugal forces of individualism, and the freedom and wherewithal to express it. Do we "blame" democracy and its tolerance for the phenomenon of growing social breakdown?

Abroad America will take a lot more flak if it is seen as the wellspring of a democracy that introduces this moral confusion and ethical uncertainty into rapidly developing societies. These societies, too, need every anchor they can find in their painful transition to modernity. Will America, as model for the world's future, demonstrate that it has the dilemma of democracy and morals successfully in hand, as other nations look to us for guidance? Or will we remain paralyzed, unable even to formulate the problem, much less the response? If so, we will simply plunge ahead ever more deeply into a foundering amoral society—whose foundations were laid by democracy itself, but which can then also destroy that same democracy. If democracy cannot handle the dilemma of the collapsing social order, then more authoritarian forces are standing in the wings to do the necessary to preserve the social order. Does democracy have to sow the seeds of its own destruction?

NOTES

1. David Briggs, "Religion's Fading Role Leaves Many Adrift," *Los Angeles Times*, January 5, 1991.

2. Penny Pagano, "FCC Upholds 24-Hour-a-Day Ban on 'Indecent' Broadcasts," *Los Angeles Times*, July 13, 1990.

3. Barry Siegel, "Locking Up 'Sexual Predators,' " *Los Angeles Times*, May 10, 1990.

4. See Richard Rodriguez, "A Continental Shift: Latin Americans Convert from Catholicism to a More Private Protestant Belief," Opinion section, *Los Angeles Times*, August, 13, 1989.

NINE

Exporting the Blame

Greatness may be a burden, but it does a lot for your sense of self-confidence. Being a superpower had its burdens, but we loved it. After all, leadership is exhilarating. It thrusts Washington front and center. It provides creative opportunities, a chance to shape one's surroundings, indeed, to shape the future. America took on the economic, political, military, technological, and even moral leadership of the noncommunist world for nearly half a century. In the middle of the Cold War, much of the rest of the world was ready to accede to that leadership.

But now we are undergoing withdrawal pains. There is no way that the United States, in the post–Cold War era, can exercise the same monopoly on leadership in the world, in almost any field. If that is unsettling, we have the consolation that part of our decline is relative to the rise of other actors and nations in the world. For the Soviet Union, the news is much worse. Soviet decline is not relative but absolute. Moscow is now experiencing the trauma of watching its "superpower" status—primarily based on its military force and ideological pretensions—waste away in national trauma. Whatever our problems in America may be, we at least do not need to wonder if we have just spent seventy years marching down the wrong road, or if we are on the verge of total economic collapse.

While this book has focused more on the inherent dilemmas of modern democracy before us, there are obviously concrete and material facets to our own domestic crisis as well. An inability to make domestic savings, spending beyond our means, lethargy in facing a new world market, an educational system in tailspin, a huge trade deficit—all of these factors are well known.

As these signs of decline come upon us, do we have the self-confidence to reinvigorate ourselves? Can we look reality in the eye, or are we going to make excuses? Are we too busy satisfying our desire to have fun, lead the good life, and remember past glories to focus on many of the hard issues around us? Will we take a hard look at ourselves? Do we have the guts to put these failures of national character and will on the national agenda? Or will we end up exporting the blame?

Exporting the Blame, Part I: Drugging Ourselves

There is no better example of our current unwillingness to face hard-core social problems than the blight of drugs in America. We had better recognize that drugs are not simply a scourge of inner-city culture, but a disturbing and possibly growing virus in the national culture. Why should we not consider it a natural outgrowth of modern consumer culture? Why is indulgence in drugs not part of a culture of gratification, of the constant retreat of the borders of the licit? Clearly the widespread recreational use of pot in the sixties and seventies removed the stigma of drug usage among the middle class. A prominent drug specialist has told us that the human desire to drug oneself is an integral part of human culture and character, traceable from the dawn of recorded history. People do it to feel good.

With the elevation of "feeling good" as a culture fetish of modern American life ("I've been feeling good about myself lately," intones a yuppie at a class reunion in *Doonesbury*), can it be surprising that drugs are part of that cornu/pharma/copia? If stress is the modern affliction, where do we draw the line on stress relief? Most specialists agree that part of the drug problem is that the very decisions about what is legal are not always directly related to the virulence of the drug. Alcohol is more addictive than pot, and ranks at the top of substance abuse. Yet pot lands you in jail, alcohol not—except for DWI charges.

Where do we draw the line? Make it all legal? Or all illegal? And what of escalating needs for kicks? There can be little doubt that indulgence in almost anything gradually leads to greater quantities being required to maintain levels of excitement and gratification. Are not modern teenagers exposed to a constant barrage of neurological titillation, in music, foods, levels of violence, and the endless quest for novelty? The normative levels of boredom for the modern teenager already begin at such supercharged levels of sensate exposure that escalation increasingly taxes the inventive ingenuity of the marketplace to gratify demand.

Democracy has not created drugs. No country is free of narco-blight, not even the Soviet Union under the earlier police state. But the sweeping freedoms of democracy obviously facilitate both freedom of demand and the entrepreneurial stimulus to provide gratification. As the country grows more confused about its values, as individual rights come to receive greater emphasis, the state loses both the powers and the mechanisms to take prompt and effective action. We grow inured to the greater part of the drug problem, writing off the inner cities and focusing resources on its more manageable middle-class pathology.

And for all the *Sturm und Drang* in Washington over the issue, all the signs are that American society is avoiding the hard-core issue and the hard choices. Our government is one of the leading culprits in facilitating the great American cover-up, like the wife who protects her family and her children from her husband's alcoholism through denial of the problem. Discussion at the level of the national agenda still won't tell it like it is. Washington has fallen upon a less painful form of truth denial. We are exporting the blame—literally.

The Mysterious Law of Supply and Demand

America, the center of the capitalist world, deep in the embrace of the free market, is playing it coy about the law of supply and demand. This most elementary principle of the free-market economy is imparted to freshmen in the first day of Econ 101; yet Washington would seem to be smoking something itself in relating this principle to the drug problem. Successions of drug experts, blue-ribbon panels, drug czars, and White House directives are steadfastly gazing abroad in trying to end the drug problem: *cherchez l'étranger*. We are finding the villain for heroin supplies in such far-flung places as Laos, Afghanistan, Pakistan, Thailand, and Turkey. As a member of the American embassy in Afghanistan I have more times than I care to think gone off with other members of the embassy staff and my family on weekend jaunts to help count poppy fields on the back roads, so that the embassy could send in its semiannual drug report to Washington. American ambassadors all over Asia have marched resolutely in to speak to prime ministers and presidents about American concern for the poppies we know are being grown in the hills. Annual U.S. foreign aid budgets are brandished as potential casualties in the event of noncooperation by the local government.

That was in the sixties and seventies. Despite our poppy watch in Asia, the drug problem has moved from bad to worse. Meanwhile heroin has now been surpassed by cocaine as the recreational drug of choice. Our diplomatic operations now reach into new hemispheres, visiting Colombia, Peru, and Noriega's pernicious Panama in our ceaseless quest to export the blame. Our drug needs have brought Colombia to a virtual state of civil war against the *narcotraficantes*. We are getting ready to spray up dirt-poor Peruvian peasants in the highlands with helicopter-borne defoliants to stamp out a coke blight in New York and Los Angeles.

We have invested billions and billions of dollars in overseas efforts to locate, seize, destroy, intercept. And the domestic problem just goes on getting worse. We are hooked on exporting the blame.

Have we forgotten supply and demand? Why are we attacking the supply—which is potentially infinite—when the demand is creating the supply? In those few countries where we have been able to bludgeon some cooperation out of local governments, the supply has simply moved on elsewhere. When, at great expense and diplomatic cost, we have made a dent in supplies in one country, the result is like squeezing a balloon: supply mushrooms out from some new source, rising to meet demand. Do we, as card-carrying capitalists, seriously believe that we can wipe out supply while demand remains high?

Washington, of course, officially recognizes that the demand problem must be met as well. But why "as well"? The heart of the problem is demand. If demand goes away, so does the supply. The answer is that it is simply easier and more comfortable for us to deal with the supply. Washington can stay busy. We can make demarches to Third World governments, satellites can scan poppy fields, the CIA can report on the linkage of drugs and politics abroad, Air Force and Navy missions can scan the skies and seas for the drug runners. We can all stay busy. And we can regularly show on television spectacular heists of huge drug seizures inside the country and out. But the drug problem persists, and grows. Spectacular interdictions and seizures don't touch even 10 percent of the problem. We are like the drunk searching for his keys under the streetlight. That's not where we lost them, but there's more light to see by there.

Of course, the United States needs to work on the international level to try to reduce drug supplies where possible. But that is a modest part of the problem and should not be the focus of our efforts. We pursue our keys under the streetlight because dealing with the real problem—demand—is far harder. The politician hates failure. Talk about seizures, never about drug consumption figures. No wimpy Carterisms about "blaming America" here, no sirree.

The drug consumption problem gets to the heart of the national dilemma. It is an issue of morality, of self-discipline, of the ordering of society, and of limits on freedom. Why are we unwilling to crack down on the yuppie recreational drug users? Why is the effort to change the presentation of drugs on film and TV having such limited success? Why are we unwilling to suspend certain kinds of civil liberties on testing, searches, etc., if it will significantly help in nipping drugs in the bud? Or do we believe it just doesn't matter that much? We still seem to be "NRA liberals" in this regard as well: as if tighter interpretations of some civil liberties related to drug usage in a period of national drug crisis somehow automatically leads to loss of all civil liberties—the slippery slope to totalitarianism. The plain fact is that the country does not yet have the guts to face the problem. Or else the problem is not so great as to merit exceptional efforts. We can't have it both ways.

If the importance of the drug problem is not sufficient to warrant some hard thinking about the use and abuse of civil liberties, then we are also taking a greater step toward the perpetuation of a permanent underclass—already nearly a reality. That is tantamount to saying that we can cope with the problem in the well-heeled suburbs, but that we consign the inner cities to perdition. Let's bust the rappers on the street corner but avoid the hassles of stopping recreational usage by yuppies. Why shouldn't we be attacking yuppie drug usage with particular vigor? This surely is the least justifiable use; a potential elite of the country is helping foster the problem. To pursue the ghetto more vigorously than the yuppie is classic class and even race discrimination. We need a lot more yuppies going to prison and having their lives crimped before people start to get the message. Tom Wolfe's *Bonfire of the Vanities* could be a classic yuppie drug usage story as well.

The ghetto problem is of course bound up with the broader problem of the underclass—and sheer police power is not enough. It will require, among other things, a concerted act of will on the part of the black and ghetto communities and a political and economic empowerment of those classes to start to make a dent. But the first step is to give up the *Star Wars* approach to the supply problem and start dealing with the demand problem as the absolute heart of the issue. It is morally offensive that we should find it easier to whomp Peruvian peasants and submit Colombian citizens to waves of domestic terror because we lack both the guts and the imagination to deal with the problem here at home. It augurs poorly for our own future that the policymakers in Washington and the public at large conspire in the moral cop-out of exporting the blame.

Exporting the Blame, Part II: Trading Japanese VCRs for Blame

Atavistic whiffs from World War II are back with us in the now decade-long struggle of the United States with Japan over trade balances. While Japan is in many ways an infuriatingly impenetrable society for foreigners, and has been unwilling to address American trade concerns as fully as it should, our basic problem is that Japan is beating the pants off us in areas that have traditionally been American areas of know-how. Every year has seen at least one more major product slip out of the American column and over into the Japanese column— almost totally on the basis of quality. Americans who are up in arms about Japan's refusal to do anything about our trade balance are the first to rush out and buy that Honda instead of a Chrysler.

Nobody is forcing us to buy Japanese products. We simply find them better-made, more thoughtfully engineered, and often more attractively produced. Yet, in a way, things have gotten so bad that we are being forced to buy Japanese products. We still have a choice when it comes to buying a car. But when you go to buy a VCR, try to find an American one. How many cameras can you find that are still American? Or TV sets? American products are becoming endangered species—partly because we won't buy them ourselves.

This is a pity, for the suggestion would be that the Japanese are simply superior to Americans as a society. The ultimate horror was articulated by the Democratic presidential hopeful in the last primary campaign who conjured up the image of American workers doomed to a future of sweeping up around Japanese robots. Right now Japan would indeed seem to be a superior society in the economic race. But we are frequently reminded that the United States still has major reservoirs of unique talent as a society that are critical to our own economic and technical future. Foremost among those talents is ability at pure research. This is demonstrated vividly in the area of software, in which the United States still has 70 percent of the world market, but needs to keep hustling.

> To some analysts, the consistent inability of the Japanese to crack [the software] market is proof that they lack the creativity and imagination critical to a process many liken to art.
>
> "You can't pick it up and imitate it so easily. You can't carve it, measure it, you can't even see it. You need more creativity, and we may have the edge there for a long time." . . .
>
> "We tend to be very tolerant of strange people with long hair and bad eating habits who produce things of genius. And

the Japanese don't quite understand that. The Japanese sala-
ryman syndrome is not one that fosters artistic, aesthetically
oriented creativity. . . ."[1]

Yet we seem to be blowing our lead, and blaming the Japanese rather than ourselves for some of the deeper systemic
problems of our society. Meanwhile the Japanese have begun
to rent our long-haired and unconventional software boy
geniuses as well.

The Japanese Juggernaut

Many volumes have been written over the past decade on
the question of Japanese competitiveness, pointing up divisions among professional Japan watchers. Japan has clearly
created a new kind of state-to-industry relationship that poses
severe challenge within the free-market system. The Japanese
industrial structure is not directed by the Japanese state, but
represents a high degree of partnership between government
and industry. As several Japan experts have pointed out, the
major problem with Japan is that its policies within the market
system aim at strengthening the producer's power rather than
meeting the consumer's needs; in less corporately structured
American industry, the system involves more competition and
works more to the consumer's than the producer's benefit.
This all may be so, but the fact remains that Japanese goods
are still faring better in the marketplace than many American
equivalents, even when the American product should have
the price edge.

At the same time, Japanese society is capable of saving
more, and investing more, than American society, which is
actually going into debt to preserve its "life-style." The urge
for quick profits in the quarterly board report is destroying
any prospect of far-reaching industrial policies in which investment and long-range planning play a role. The Japanese
investment rate vastly exceeds the American. Little wonder
that Japan is now poised to surpass America in almost every
arena.

The staggering American scandal of leveraged buyouts is
allowing capitalist predators to cannibalize our national indus-

trial capacity, in which a handful of robber barons are able to leverage a firm deep into debt to pay for the junk bonds it has been saddled with. This devastating process destroys the ability of any firm to invest, to plan for the future, to pursue creative R&D policies, to take risks, and to compete effectively in the marketplace because of the crippling rate of debt servicing. The entire process—while destroying industrial capacity in the process—creates no national wealth whatsoever. The American media have failed to investigate and publicize the rapacious and corrosive characteristic of leveraged buyouts that are on the way to consuming our very industrial and commercial resources.

Ironically, it may be that the Japanese will save us from ourselves: the vast hold Japanese banking now maintains over the American financial market is increasingly restraining the financing of leveraged buyouts, which are bad business for America, and hence bad for Japanese investment in America's long-range future.

Japan vastly exceeds America at producing technically educated workers. This cannot be attributed simply to the Japanese state's providing unfair advantage to industry. Japanese society is obviously possessed of an internal discipline that encourages greater commitment to education and greater worker loyalty to employers. The extraordinary ethnic homogeneity of Japan and its continuous, undiluted cultural tradition preserved on an island contribute greatly to the cohesion of the country.

The Japanese phenomenon thus raises the urgent question once again: the degree to which ethnic homogeneity of the state is a desirable feature—however much it is vanishing in this world. Crude and insensitive remarks by even the top Japanese leadership about what they perceive as the drawbacks of mixed ethnicity in America reflect the depth of Japanese conviction in the benefits of racial homogeneity. The benefits of homogeneity are obviously considerable in creating a disciplined and organized society. But such homogeneity is also not the wave of the future anywhere, as the world continues to be buffeted by cross-cultural change.

As we noted in the field of education, the vaunted Japanese qualities of self-discipline may be giving way to a "greening" of Japan, an "Americanization" of Japan to the extent that its culture is beginning to pursue lines of mass culture already pioneered by America. Cultural homogeneity weakens—slightly—as Japan's need for outside labor continues to grow well into the next century in order to offset the "graying" of Japan. Japanese are traveling, studying, learning foreign languages, living and working overseas more than ever before, creating sharp new pressures on Japanese values and society. Desire for a better life-style will counter the traditional self-sacrifice. These factors are likely to gradually weaken Japan's productivity and intensity of focus, and may also contribute to a more flexible, diverse, and creative society. Japan is one of those countries destined for major change in the future, and change will come hard, for it will mean accepting greater ethnic and cultural diversity and greater interchange with the rest of the world.

Democracy and Bad News

In the interim, America must examine the roots of its own economic weaknesses if our own society is not to wallow in self-indulgence and founder in social confusion and doubt. Our tendency to export the blame in the key areas of drugs and failing industrial policies is disturbing. In principle, democracy should be good at self-criticism, because of the freedom to point out these shortcomings openly and the ability to focus political attention on them via the ballot box. On the other hand, no one knows whether the *freedom* to address these issues necessarily produces the actual public exacerbation of all these problems before public attention focuses on them sharply.

It is not in the character of democracy to excel at acting on long-range trends or pursuing farsighted policies. To some extent, democracy is doomed to be a reactive system, responding only to those concerns actively on the public mind. Expecting the public to make sacrifices early on for problems that have yet to touch the public heart or pocketbook is not realistic. The public will sacrifice, but the challenge must be palpable first. America is capable of "blood, sweat, and tears," but only when crisis is impending and the sacrifice not too lengthy. Apparently the American crisis has not yet attained those dimensions in most of the areas of life we have discussed in this book. How would we fare if we were confronted with the problems that face the Soviet Union today?

Does democracy tend to be a "fair-weather" system of government, one that works well as long as conditions are not desperate? One body of democratic theory says that that is precisely the case. Yet America came through the Great Depression fairly handily, although not without producing an impressive amount of radical politics at the same time. We should have some confidence in our ability to explore our societal dilemmas in our politically conscious and educated circles. That does not automatically transfer to national debate—so often trivialized into twenty-second sound bites. We need only fear that American political leadership will find it politically advantageous to continue to export the blame rather than talking straight with the public. If that's the case, is this the system that we are now urging our newfound Russian friends to adopt—in order to cope with the most intractable political and economic transition in the history of the human race?

NOTES

1. See Teresa Watanabe, "Japan's Trying Hard to Catch U.S. in Software," *Los Angeles Times*, July 8, 1990.

TEN

Democracy and the Intellectual

Democracy: The Ambiguous Value?

The relationship between the intellectual and democracy is often one of profound ambivalence. Yet how could this be? On the face of it, any tension at all between democracy and the intellectual seems paradoxical, for who might seemingly profit more from the freedom of expression accorded by democracy than the intellectual?

While nearly all intellectuals welcomed the fall of the Berlin Wall and the Gorbachev Revolution, for many there is also an ambivalence. For communism—while historically dealing harshly with any resistance to the state by intellectuals—in another sense empowered the intellectual, granting him a role in society greater than almost any other political system does. The intellectual's role was, of course, to serve the state—in no way comparable to the function of the intellectual in Western democratic, capitalistic societies. Given the divergence of function between intellectuals East and West, let's see how the emergence of democracy has brought new dilemmas for the freshly liberated intellectuals. The intellectuals' own misgivings about democracy reveal some of the internal weaknesses of democracy, but also the paradoxical attitude intellectuals of most societies maintain toward democratic government and authority.

The term "intellectual," of course, carries a broad variety of meanings; it could perhaps be replaced by the word—taken from nineteenth-century Russian society—"intelligentsia." Intellectuals include not just artists, but nearly all those who use primarily intellectual resources in the conduct of their work. The concept is a broad one, and naturally the observations of this chapter cannot be applied to all intellectuals universally.

Creativity and Perestroika

Creativity may have been one of the first victims of perestroika. The complicated, all-consuming process of political democratization and economic transition in the Eastern Bloc and the Soviet Union has already cut into the creative and artistic impulse. Disquieting features, possibly only temporary, can already be perceived in the exciting passage out of the old system and into the new. In the late Brezhnev-Chernenko period, the growing richness of Soviet literature was impressive as the censors grew sloppier and wearier. Clearly, writers and filmmakers were taking greater liberties than ever before in their fiction: Valentin Rasputin and his extraordinary tales of the destruction of both the Russian countryside and the Russian cultural patrimony by the rootless, mindless internationalism of communist "planning"; Chingiz Aitmatov and his evocation of the passion of Christ and a dialogue with Pontius Pilate on the nature of the Soviet system; Yuri Trifonov and the anguish of the university intellectuals in having to play Communist Party politics in academia to survive. The really exciting prospect was what the literary genius of the Russian people would do once it entirely threw off the strictures of seventy years of stereotyped and choreographed literary commissar-style thinking. Yet several years have gone by now since the advent of glasnost, and we see no new masterpieces emerging yet. Rasputin has dedicated himself to the pursuit of right-wing Russian nationalist politics. Aitmatov has gone off to the Good Life as ambassador to Luxembourg. Film has so far not done much better. Eastern Europe presents the same picture.

One reason for this deafening literary silence is the simple fact that people are utterly preoccupied with the incredible political process swirling around them. The press is filled with the continuing, astonishing revelations about the Russians' own suppressed past and the extraordinary iconoclasm of contemporary politics. As the wags had it—in the land where history used to get rewritten with each new ruler—"the difference between communism and capitalism is that under communism nobody can tell what the past will be, but everybody knows what the future will be." The Russian public, caught up in the daily revolution of glasnost, has become utterly consumed with reading newspapers—a chore once quickly dispensed with in the old days of party-dispensed Truth. As one Russian said, comparing the early daily bombshells in the press to the unchanged grim economic realities of the streets, "It's more interesting to read than to live!"

Yet there is already a price to be paid. Russian literary talent is getting involved in politics. Writers, liberal and conservative, are lining up to influence the battle for the destiny of Mother Russia and her Empire. There may not be a lot of time for Russian masterpieces for a while.

Too Free to Write?

More than politics is affecting the arts. Indeed, it is a truism that art often flourishes under adversity; immense challenge often brings out the best in people. With the end of communism and harsh political adversity, can the moral and political challenge ever be quite the same again? What will the grand issues be, now that everyone has free license to write as he or she wishes? What will become of the brilliant and artfully constructed satires and treatises that regularly came out of the Eastern Bloc to spite the censor and the system? Whence will come the driving, focused quality of *samizdat* literature, so powerfully impelled by political and legal repression? What moral cause can ever arise that will match the epic struggle of freedom against a seventy-year-old totalitarian structure? Could it be that the total freedom of democracy constitutes a trap for creativity? Surely Russian writers will eventually respond with great art, but the initial artistic response to the new freedoms is so far slow in coming.

The Trivialization of the Intellectual Under Democracy

Ironically, one of the "gifts" previously bestowed upon the aspiring Communist Bloc artist and intellectual was the party's very political repression. This kind of repression was a unique spur to genuine artistic inspiration, passion, commitment, and creativity. Indeed, the creative stimulus of political adversity is a well-known cultural phenomenon in which the artist may take on the powerful voice of opposition and resistance to repression. This phenomenon stands in sharp contrast to a phenomenon on the Western intellectual scene that some observers—especially Eastern Bloc intellectuals—have described as the "trivialization" of the intellectual in the West. While the universal role of the intellectual is to serve as social critic and public conscience, that function is less easily fulfilled in an American society in which the views of the intellectual class do not enjoy broad social respect. Even the term "intellectual" in American society does not carry with it much distinction; nearly any politician would rather be tagged as anything else than an intellectual. William Buckley once noted that he would rather be governed by the first forty pages of the Boston telephone directory than by the faculty of Harvard University. This arch statement, which angered so many intellectuals, is of course profoundly democratic at heart, as well as a rebuff to elitism, especially intellectual elitism. It is also a profoundly anti-intellectual remark, from an intellectual.

But Western democracy, especially when combined with the capitalist free-market system, is not necessarily kind to intellectuals. To be sure, it provides the formal freedom to pursue what the intelligentsia wills, but our system does not provide the hard cash, the automatic state funding and perks that are also important to the intellectual. Democratic capitalism instead casts intellectuals rudely out upon the marketplace. But more than that, the public—at least the American public—seems to distrust the intellectual and does not regularly offer him high place in the power structure. We don't want intellectuals to be president. This is a source of frustration to intellectuals, often driving them into positions harshly critical of—even alienated from—the system in which they live.

Worse, democracy does not even officially accord to intellectuals a formal role in the conduct of society. Yet, ironically, communism does. As Hungarian dissident Miklos Haraszti noted in *The Velvet Prison*, a brilliant book about the role of the intellectual in Eastern European communist society, the communist system needs and seeks out the intellectual for the functioning and legitimization of communist society.

All alienated artists dream of living in a world where noble values rule. . . . This dream is shared by the diverse currents of intellectual opposition to commercialism. [The artist] finds it more painful than most that, in the eyes of society, he is not valuable except to the extent that he is marketable. . . . Socialism succeeded in seducing artists from the past into the future only with the promise of a powerful and honorable incorporation. . . . Socialism offered solutions to their material and spiritual problems. How could they object to a future state that *needed* artists and whose tastes artists would dictate?[1]

Communism is nothing if not a system run on an idea, a rigid philosophy and world outlook that justifies everything in the name of the revolutionary vision. The intellectual under communism is inherently flattered to be asked to be part of the system. If the intellectual does not fight the system outright, she is accorded a major role in the well-endowed structure of state-supported arts. The theoretician is an essential pillar of the communist regime. Thus is the intellectual seduced by the system. Once the terror of Stalinism was past, the intellectual who conformed found a fairly comfortable, undemanding system under the limp-wristed ideological requirements of Brezhnevism. For the price of paying lip service to the state and its goals, the intellectual could be richly supported as a central, honored, and subsidized element of society. That is the Velvet Prison of Haraszti.

The Intellectual Patriarchate

Beyond that, many intellectuals have found the idea of a planned and organized structure to be deeply gratifying to their own sense of intellectual order. Society *should* be planned, and it is the intellectual who should be doing it. Stalin, for whom aesthetics were not exactly the first priority, made the utilitarian observation that the writer is the engineer of the soul. Even if communism has been a monument to brutality and misplanning, at least it was an attempt in the right direction—toward employing the intellectual in the planning process.

The intellectual thus often feels a profound sense of ambivalence toward the planned "socialist" societies and economies of the world. While Western intellectuals have no particular admiration for communism, many share a deep and implicit animus against a capitalist system that accords the intellectual almost no value if it cannot be measured in dollars.

While many Western intellectuals often speak of "the people," they do not really like the people, who both fail to appreciate intellectuals and foist a popular, mass, crass culture upon society, to the discomfiture of the discriminating intellectual elite. It has been this love-hate syndrome toward the people that has created a tendency among some intellectuals to be very forgiving of communist ("socialist") systems compared with other systems, for at least the communist system is seen to have its heart in the right place—even if the errors of implementation have been egregious.

It is such intellectual alienation that Hungarian-born Paul Hollander, now at Amherst, described as the trivialization of Western intellectual life.[2] Hollander judges the issues over which the Western intellectual can truly exert significant influence to be minimal, provoking the intellectual to rebel against almost anything as a nominal gesture against the system. Given the luxury in Western liberal societies of being able to say anything—literally anything—with impunity, without fear of incurring any cost to himself, the American intellectual feels free to take an unconsidered, unreasoned (or unreasonable) position on almost any issue. This situation Hollander contrasts sharply with that of the Eastern European intellectual, who must carefully weigh every word he utters to be sure it is wise, considered, and worth paying some inevitable price for. In the absence of ever paying a price for the consequences of his or her utterances, the American intellectual is thus trivialized. This is the reason, according to Hollander, why Western intellectuals often find elements of meaninglessness in their existence, unlike Eastern Bloc intellectuals, who are engaged in an intensely meaningful existential struggle in defense of powerful ideals. It is for this reason, for example, that the arts in the West tend to gravitate toward increasingly trivial, nonrepresentative, self-consumed, personal obsessions and statements—the quest for the perfect orgasm in Scarsdale, or the bullwhip protruding from his anus in one of the photographs of the gifted Robert Mapplethorpe. Are these the most profound issues on the mind of the aspiring artist in the West today?

The Cold War at least had the virtue on the American side of potentially galvanizing Western intellectuals in the struggle against totalitarianism. To be fair, a large number of intellectuals, regardless of any ambivalence they have toward failings of Western capitalism, were under no illusion about the tender mercies of the totalitarian state. But with the passing of that grand ideological struggle, to what great cause will the Western intellectual turn his attention, or will he retreat ever further into the private vision, or the lure of the marketplace, or just sheer personalized trivia?

Democracy and the Third World Intellectual

Intellectuals of the Third World share much of their Western counterparts' ambivalence about democracy. For it has been in the emerging Third World that the intellectual has played a supremely important role in the nation-building process. It is the intellectual who has first defined the essence of the newly emerging nation, or who has established the ideology of the new state in the modern order—often in opposition to the West. In a state of often severe underdevelopment, it has been the intellectuals who, in principle, were best situated to understand the nature of the problem and to do something about it.

Unfortunately, the intellectual has not had a great track record in actually bringing about the development of the Third World state. Intellectuals have usually been attracted to the concept of the planned economy and society, systems that quintessentially call for the participation of the intellectual—in distinction to a free-market system in which the intellectual loses position. Thus the bane of state planning and, worse, the cruelties of social engineering have emanated above all from the intellectual at the helm of the Third World state. In these states the concept of paternalistic authoritarianism is deeply pervasive—for the intellectual always knows best. The people are not yet ready for democracy, they are not well enough educated, they must be guided. And who should guide them? The intellectual, of course.

In China, one of the neoconservative thinkers currently backing the discredited Communist Party in the wake of the Tiananmen Square massacre, Wang Huming of the International Politics Department at Shanghai's Fudan University, smugly informed us in 1990 that most Chinese are not knowledgeable enough to cope with the choices a democratic system would offer. "To carry out democracy, the majority of the people must know what their interests are," he says—which apparently the Chinese people do not.[3] You see, it takes an intellectual to know that the peasant should not have his own land to till for himself, and should not plant crops on the basis of crass profitability, or decide whether the party chief in the village is doing right by the village, or whether the national leadership of the country has been on the right track for the last forty years.

The curse of paternalism runs rampant through most of the Third World. Even if the intellectuals and the elite did have a better sense of where the country should go than the majority of the populace, the argument has also been extremely self-serving. It is predicated on the perpetuation of intellectuals in power, perhaps indefinitely. The dilemma of the Third World intellectual will remain a serious one in the decades ahead. While everyone believes deeply that education has a critical role to play in the advancement of developing nations, the question is whether the educated elite has the right, by virtue of education, to maintain paternalistic, uncontested power because of its supposed inherent wisdom.

In most of the Third World, the concept of real democracy is therefore profoundly dangerous to the status quo, however "revolutionary" the ruling party may be. Democracy is more revolutionary than many Third World intellectuals would like. The recent democratic revolution in the Communist Bloc has therefore exacerbated the dilemma of many Third World intellectuals. In fact, most revolutionary intellectuals do not really want "the people" in power, or passing judgment on their leadership. Yet the only way to guarantee that the considerable intellectual skills of the intellectual class will be used to the best interests of the people is for the leadership to face the trauma of periodically rendering account to the people at regular elections, particularly at the local level. Thus the dilemma of democracy for the emerging Eastern Bloc states, and for the Third World as a whole, is how to wean the intellectual off the institutionalized power trip that so many of them have enjoyed under communism or Third World authoritarianism.

Third World Intellectuals and the Collapse of Communism

The collapse of communist rule still reverberates among other authoritarian socialist movements. The unrepentant communist classically seeks refuge in the belief that the Russians "didn't do it right"—as indeed, it so happens, neither did the rest of Eastern Europe or China, or Cuba, Nicaragua, Afghanistan, Ethiopia, Cambodia, etc. Yet typically we read that a conservative Communist Party leader in Italy, Pietro Ingrao, argues that if communism is on the run in Eastern Europe, "it is because dictatorial regimes there were Communist in name only."[4]

If it were only a matter of the intellectuals' self-interest, the truth of the matter would be self-evident. But a further subtle snare is also involved: ideology is a great substitute for the hard, complex process of choosing among a great variety of gray, unsatisfying alternatives. Politics rarely consists of the clear-cut decision, the unambiguous choice just waiting to be taken. As societies grow more complex, the trade-offs become ever more complicated, harder to expound readily on a TV screen, and less gratifying to make. Ideology is great because it helps eliminate the need for thinking. It is always there, ready to be plugged in, instant touchstone to action. Among the less thoughtful intellectual elements of the Third World, ideology is particularly attractive, for it offers a clear-cut, handy pocket explanation of the world and what is to be done. It explains enemies and friends, both foreign and domestic. It spares the need for agonizing choices.

The disappearance of communist ideology has left gaping holes, leaving nothing yet in its place. In China, for example (where the Communist Party has not yet been overturned, despite its total discrediting), the weakening of a central ideological concept has been devastating, and not just at the intellectual level. The *New York Times* reports:

> An age of secular faith appears to have collapsed in China, turning into a time of despair and doubt in which many people have no heroes and nothing to believe in. . . . A university student in Beijing said some of his friends were turning to Christianity and Buddhism as a new source of moral values. "Without doubt there's a spiritual crisis in China," he said. "I don't have any friends who believe in Marxism now." . . ."It's very serious when people don't believe in anything," said a business executive in his thirties. "Even my friends who are foreign-trained intellectuals do nothing but play the game mahjongg all day. It's disastrous for the long run, and the central leaders know it."[5]

America and Its Enemies

America is a phenomenon about which almost no one can be neutral. America's aspirations, ideals, power, influence, heavy-handedness, wealth, interventionism, idealism, generosity, openness, egalitarianism—all of these qualities immediately spark reactions among a wide cross section of foreign observers. Intellectuals in particular feel an ambivalence because so many of their cherished ideals and interests are threatened in the American phenomenon. Intellectuals nourish resentment toward America for its implicit popular hostility to leftist authoritarianism, within which intellectuals can often thrive.

The Leftist Ideologists

Intellectuals often have a predisposition toward left-wing ideology, because it is more systematic in outlook, more cerebral and theoretical by nature, more comprehensive in scope, more idealistic in its aspirations, more oriented toward the "people" as an abstract concept, and affords an important role to the intellectual for its implementation. None of this means that the ideological preferences of intellectuals have any monopoly on truth, reality, or success.

America, as the symbol and center of world capitalism, is a major reason for intellectuals' hostility to America. Capitalism is distasteful to intellectuals because it is founded on the reality of greed rather than idealism. Capitalism extols the role and opportunities of the individual rather than the masses. Those whom capitalism blesses are not at all necessarily cultured, worthy, or intellectual; it is impartial in sharing its benefits only with those who have the best sense of the market and its needs. Capitalism, far from being an ideological vision, is practical and result-oriented. Its success can only be judged by results rather by theory. Capitalism demands that government largely keep hands off the market process if it is to work at all effectively, eliminating the need for intellectuals to direct and order the process. And capitalism's aspirations are never utopian but rather concrete and materialistic in nature. Capitalism, too, lacks systemic explanations of the world order and the course of history. While it enriches more of the population than other systems, it also tends to produce a greater disparity between haves and have-nots, leaving a higher proportion of the population that must be satisfied with some kind of support from outside of the market system. Lastly, the very concept of a free market is deeply rooted in the political counterpart of capitalism, democracy. The collectivist mentality is thus deeply uncomfortable with America and its system.

The Anti-Imperialists

Other grounds for intellectual dislike of America also abound. "Imperialism" is more than just a left-wing abstraction to the Third World. Most Third World states at some point have direct experience with Western imperialism, either under occupation or colonization or as a protectorate of one Western state or another; nearly all have emerged from a struggle against it. Other Third World states have usually felt the impact of great power politics swirling around them, in which they have usually been helpless to resist. Many ills of those states, some real, others spurious, are also attributed to Western imperialism.

Intellectuals, who have invariably played a major role in the national liberation struggle, and who often have led the post-independence state, bear special resentments against the colonial heritage. While America has never maintained any significant major colonies—except the Philippines—it has nonetheless come to be identified as an "imperialist state" in the eyes of leftists and intellectuals in the Third World. This charge is based on close American association with the European allies after World War II, as well as on American support during the Cold War for many authoritarian figures whose major virtue was that they were anticommunist in policy (and often dealt peremptorily with outspoken intellectuals). Complex intellectual theories—mostly neo-Marxist or neo-Leninist in character, such as dependency theory—all propound the doctrine of American neo-imperialism, based on America's capitalist character. American efforts to suppress a number of communist or procommunist guerrilla movements in Vietnam, Cambodia, Angola, Nicaragua, El Salvador, etc. further placed America in the "reactionary" camp in the eyes of many.

Envy of Power

American wealth, often profligately displayed on American TV programs and films aired abroad, carries the image of a rich and hedonistic America. It cannot help but excite a certain degree of envy among the have-nots. It is hard to root for General Motors. Closely related is resentment of American power, both military and civilian. Many countries have specific experience with American efforts to impose military solutions on a variety of situations, from Vietnam, Korea,

Lebanon, Iran, and Iraq to Libya, Angola, Afghanistan, Grenada, Panama, and Nicaragua. This is not to say that American policy was necessarily unjustifiable in many of those situations. American political and economic power has also been used often to support friends and weaken enemies on the international scene. America is not unique in this exercise of power; the exercise of any power by one nation regularly brings resentment in its wake. Third World intellectuals have been in the forefront of formulating opposition to aspects of the exercise of American power abroad.

America thus often emerges as a key target of intellectual resentment abroad. While American military power and interventionism are hardly a function of democracy—the Soviets exercised them too—the democratic, pluralistic, and egalitarian features of American life do not always evoke positive response among intellectuals abroad.

Despite their setbacks, communists and other left-wing authoritarians in the twentieth century have generally maintained greater longevity in power in the Third World than have the right-wing authoritarians. But now Gorbachev has betrayed them; perestroika has already traced original sin back to Lenin, and Marx is next. Third World leftists are profoundly uncomfortable with Soviet developments, feel deeply threatened by them, and for the moment have nowhere to turn. As an article of faith, they are not ready to turn to Western capitalism. They associate it with colonial exploitation and modern dependency theory.

These, then, are the problems of democracy and the intellectual. There will be a constant tension here. Indeed, intellectuals know they are, indeed often pride themselves on being, the gadflies of the system, the professional observers who are quick to point it out whenever the emperor is not wearing clothes. Is this adversarial role a sufficiently satisfying one? If our Western intellectuals have become "trivialized" as a result of their noncentral role in society, can they accept such a diminished role as the price to pay for freedom? Or will they long for a more central role, even in a velvet prison that grants them authentic powers as long as they cooperate?

And what of the Eastern Bloc intellectuals who did not compromise with the system and instead maintained a glorious tradition of opposition, of art turned to the task of dissidence, the social consciences of their land and time? A large number demonstrated passive resistance, even if only a small handful really had the courage and the strength and endurance to pay the price of continually bucking the system. That price was often high: under Stalin it was almost a mandatory death sentence, only later shading off to the lesser horrors of Siberian gulags, or simply life under house arrest somewhere, or later yet, simply deprivation of any formal role in society and its official institutions.

Will these intellectual leaders from within the communist world—like Vaclav Havel, Miklos Haraszti, Czeslaw Milosz, Adam Michnik, Andrei Sakharov, Milovan Djilas, Fang Lizhi, and Liu Binyan—find it easy, or satisfying, to function in the new democracies? Having rid their nations of crude totalitarian power, will they not find themselves professionally slipping into the trap of feeling that they alone understand how to guide their people in the right direction? Will they happily accept the transmission of leadership to ruder, less profound men, politicians who excel at the manipulation of the crowd and at the art of political logrolling? Will these intellectuals still have meaningful roles accorded them in the new democracies of Eastern Europe and the Soviet Union? Or are they gradually condemned to move toward trivialization themselves as the truly grand issues begin to fade, giving way to the more prosaic tasks of fiscal policy, gradations of taxation, tariffs, and the exasperating trade-offs of ecological legislation?

It would be a pity to think that all these brave, glorious voices of the Eastern Bloc that kept alive the notions of freedom—indeed, of national existence—for forty or even seventy years will now retreat to the wings. What will become of their art? Will they now be able to turn their artistic skills to biting critiques of the new society? Will the new societies present quite such a ringingly negative target against which all might rally? Or will the new artists only be able to pillory in partisan fashion one political party in the service of another party? It may be a rule of life that as the grand issues become less clear, less ringing, the less room there will be for the charismatic role of brave, clear-sighted intellectuals. As the new freedoms move into place, the risks of speaking out are vastly reduced, leaving more room for the off-the-wall judgments that so often pass for profundity of thought in politics and art in the West.

Or perhaps has the ordeal of Eastern Europe vouchsafed to it a certain wisdom, certain types of insight into the velvet prison and the trap of ideological thinking—at least for a few decades? Have they been indefinitely immunized against the mistakes of communism, and inoculated with a permanent appreciation of the benefits and blessings of true liberty? If so, we might witness the extraordinary phenomenon of greater political wisdom and profundity emerging from these erstwhile Marxist-Leninist automaton states than we are used to witnessing in the West, where democracy has so long been taken for granted. Daniel Hamilton, a longtime student of the two Germanys, writes:

> Believe it or not, East Germans are also likely to spark a more individualistic grass-roots style of democracy than has existed in West German society. . . . The East German citizens' movements have been strident supporters of local democracy and popular initiatives and referendums. They are quite skeptical of West Germany's political machine, which is dominated by the major parties and oiled by mutual favor, loyalty and tight discipline. East Germany's embryonic brand of participatory democracy could spread westward.[6]

Having been steeled in adversity, they will take their liberties seriously for a while, so close are they to their painful acquisition.

Thus democracy and the intellectual are eternally destined to coexist uncomfortably. The intellectuals' role will often lie at the very heart of the democratic process, often creatively, often as gadfly, often as harsh critic—with their own interests as a professional class always at stake as well, preventing them, too, from pure objectivity on the workings of the democratic process. Many others, particularly in the West, are cynical enough about any political process to want to remain aloof from it entirely. Whatever personal and ideological agendas intellectuals may carry with them, their participation in the process is essential to the yeasting process of democracy.

NOTES

1. Miklos Haraszti, *The Velvet Prison* (New York: Basic Books, 1987), pp. 24-25.

2. See Paul Hollander, "Intellectuals East and West," *Society*, May/June 1990, pp. 82–89.

3. See Ann Scott Tyson, "China's Neoconservatives Step to the Fore," *Christian Science Monitor*, May 15, 1990.

4. Clyde Haberman, "Some Italian Communists Fight Tide," *New York Times*, March 9, 1990.

5. Nicholas D. Kristoff, "When Marxism Died, It Left a Vast Emptiness," *New York Times*, May 18, 1990.

6. Daniel Hamilton, "Unification Is Not a One-Way Street," *Los Angeles Times*, March 7, 1990.

ELEVEN

Democracy and Foreign Policy: Is There an American "Mission"?

The American Mission

Is there an American "mission"? Indeed, should we have a mission? The very term "mission," of course, smacks of ideology, evoking near-religious overtones—a calling to purvey a deeply held conviction to the world. And yet the term is not entirely out of place for Americans. We have always felt that our nation had a calling. That calling has been our *raison d'être*, the unique conviction that our constitutional freedoms are the very basis of the nation. These freedoms transcend any pride of ethnicity—in distinction to nearly every other nation in the world. We also believe in freedom's economic corollary: the free-market system that celebrates, in concrete terms, the quality of individualism economically empowered. We not only believe in these ideals, but are convinced that they have worked in America and that they will contribute to a better world and better life for all abroad.

Cold War Compromises to Our Ideology

The Cold War presented us with a paradox. On the one hand, the ideological struggle compelled us to articulate and embrace our own philosophical ideals more firmly. Ironically, it also pushed us to tactically compromise those same ideals. American thinking became entrapped in an ideological framework that was the mirror image of the ideological structure created by the Soviet Union. The ideology of anticommunism as a guiding principle of foreign policy came to overshadow an emphasis on democracy and freedom. While democracy and anticommunism are hardly mutually exclusive, they are also not the same, and at times tactically conflict.

The anticommunist struggle, therefore, immediately predisposed Washington toward a preference for stability and maintenance of the status quo. Only preservation of world stability and order could contain the Soviet Union and its ideological hosts around the globe. Enlightened American policies did frequently recognize that the struggle against communism also required meeting the needs of Third World peoples so that they would not turn to communism in despair. Nonetheless, there was an implicit notion that containment of the USSR must inevitably "contain" a great deal else going on in the world as well.

The task of Soviet foreign policy in some ways was easier than our own in much of the Third World. The radical ideological character of the communist offensive enabled Moscow to take a nominally "progressive" position on most world issues—encouraging "change," as opposed to the American preference for preserving the status quo. The Soviet rationale was simple, and limited: "change" implied changing what was on our side. Changing the status quo, or fomenting political turmoil through subversive guerrilla or local communist party action, automatically worked to Soviet advantage—as long as that "change" extended to "the rest of the world" and not to the Soviet Empire or the "socialist world."

In ideological terms, of course, the "socialist states" were by definition already "advanced," hence any change implied retrogression, an attempt to "reverse history." This ideological framework worked fine until the Soviet Empire acquired a variety of Marxist-Leninist allies of its own in the Third World, a development that suddenly required the USSR to become a "status quo" power itself to preserve its own empire. Once genuinely progressive forces in those countries began to challenge the Leninist repressions and rigidities of local ruling communist parties, the Soviet Empire itself could not last long, except through massive infusions of force from within the socialist bloc. Turmoil in the Marxist-Leninist states of Afghanistan, Angola, Cambodia, Ethiopia, and Nicaragua, to name a few, could now only work to severe Soviet disadvantage. The Soviet overseas empire was doomed, along with the hollow protestations that the Socialist Bloc represented progressive forces moving with the flow of history.

But many Americans, including numerous policymakers, were uncomfortable with the paradox that Washington, standing for freedom and the establishment of democracy, had somehow found itself often more closely wedded to preservation of the status quo in the evolving Cold War. The communist challenge posed another genuine problem as well: how do you champion "moderation"? American policy might have preferred, and indeed often supported, truly moderate forces in parts of Latin America, Asia, and Africa. But these moderates were often ineffective in sustaining their policies against zealous right- or left-wing groups that were unfettered by any constraints of moderation. It is hard to be "militantly moderate" against extremist foes on the left and right who see benefit for themselves in destabilizing any efforts at moderation or reform. For such radicals, reform programs by moderate governments undercut the potency of their extremist slogans and tactics—especially in countries where social and economic problems were already severe.

Actually there were many neoconservatives who argued during the early eighties that the United States had allowed itself to be corrupted by the mindless pursuit of anticommunism. Figures such as the Hudson Institute's Max Singer argued that the United States must remain true to the goal of furthering democracy around the world, that our anticommunist crusade had ended up costing us dearly in ideological terms by requiring us to cast in our lot with a spectrum of unsavory authoritarian and often corrupt leaders who oppressed their peoples nearly as much as communists did. These authoritarians, so the argument went, were not only the most efficient mechanism for giving the West a bad name, but served to drive these nations more quickly into the hands of communist guerrilla "liberators"—or else more extreme right-wing apostles of "social order and tranquillity"—in places such as Nicaragua, Vietnam, Chile, the Philippines, South Korea, Portugal, Iran, and El Salvador. The Kennedy administration, too, had showed an early recognition of this dilemma.

Change vs. Stability

We have now been released from this ideological bind—one of the great gratifications of our new post–Cold War era. Political and social changes no longer need to be seen "to work to the advantage of the Soviet Union" or to be automatically fraught with peril. Indeed, "change" is in essence a neutral, nonideological concept: some change is for the better, some is not. Indeed, the very essence of the philosophical debate between conservatives and liberals is not over the importance of change, but over the alacrity with which it should be embraced. The virtues of change are counterpoised by virtues of stability and continuity. That is the classic dialectic.

Now that we can once again feel less anxious about the concept of change on the international scene, where do the trade-offs with stability come? We have consistently encouraged greater democracy—with varying or only limited success—in friendly countries such as Iran, South Korea, Taiwan, Turkey, Chile, Mexico, El Salvador, the Philippines, Zaire, Jordan, Argentina, and Peru. We were not at all slavish to the status quo in recognizing the need from time to time of removing oppressive right-wing dictators whose policies had come to be counterproductive: Ferdinand Marcos in the Philippines, Baby Doc Duvalier in Haiti, Syngman Rhee and later Chun Doo Hwan in Korea, Ngo Dinh Diem in South Vietnam, Somoza in Nicaragua, and others. But often these moves occurred when those countries were already on the brink of revolution, and represented too little too late from the perspective of the citizens of those countries; they considered that the United States had long helped support such figures in earlier years (when there was often reasonable justification to do so) and that we had delayed in assisting in their departure.

These bold policy steps to remove friendly dictators nonetheless represented an exception and not the rule in our overall comfort with the status quo and preference for stability. Yet stability is only one desideratum for the modern world, not the only one, and it cannot be the highest measure of social value. (Indeed, the Soviet Union itself was the single greatest paragon of stability for most of the twentieth century, until, like the one-hoss shay, it fell apart all at once.) America is therefore now faced with a complex task of reassessing the character and virtues of "stability" in our pantheon of foreign policy goals.

Democracy and Stability

If stability and retention of the status quo are the goals, then democracy is not the governance of choice anyway. Democracy does not seek to provide stability per se; instead, it provides a mechanism by which to channel and adjudicate conflict and instability. While comfortable Western democracies prefer the nonchallenging character of stability, we simultaneously must recognize too that the stabilities of authoritarianism are hardly healthy, and in fact are conducive to ultimately even more bruising political and social explosion.

But what should our foreign policy ideals be then, for an America that has often shown instinctive gravitation toward idealistic/ideological expression of its interests and worldview? How readily do the goals of democracy, self-determination, and human rights square with a preference for stability in the world? And what is the place for "revolution" in the mind of twenty-first-century America, whose own "revolution" is now so long past?

Revolution

As much as Americans hark back to the American Revolution, it was not a revolution in the modern sense, or even like the French Revolution. It was primarily a national liberation movement designed to win independence from foreign domination. It sought to implement those liberal democratic values that had already been conceived—if not fully applied—in England. There were unquestionably some class overtones to the revolution—there always are in such struggles—but the American Revolution did not need to shatter the existing class structure or launch an ideologically based military and guerrilla assault against the world in the manner that the French, Russian, Chinese, and Iranian revolutions have done.

Revolutions often bring a great deal more grief and suffering than they do good. The overturning of an established order brings immense turmoil, often civil war, widespread settling of private scores, license to violence among religious and ethnic groups outside the context of the revolutionary agenda, years of ruthless new jockeying for position by new leaders, campaigns to eliminate enemies in an atmosphere of violence, and an absence of any rule by law for long periods. Indeed, most of what passes for "revolution" is not revolution at all but simply coups d'état that exchange one set of oppressors for another, accompanied by only cosmetic social change. Understandably the United States has often felt less than fully enthusiastic toward those who call for revolution in the classic sense.

Democracy as the Vehicle for Modernization

It is democracy that is uniquely qualified in many ways to manage the tensions of stability vs. change by channeling, ordering, and controlling the process of change, a process of controlled fission rather than a nuclear explosion. It would seem important to invoke democracy, then, not as an ideal process, but as about as good a process as one could invoke to negotiate the treacherous shoals to modernization. For whatever its virtues and drawbacks, modernization is as inevitable as the tide, even if it sometimes can be momentarily delayed and channeled.

Even then, democracy has hardly been the world's only model by any means for economic and social modernization; many would argue that it is not necessarily the best. The experience of East Asia, in particular, suggests that at least as far as *modernization* is concerned, benevolent and wise authoritarianism has been a more successful route to reform, creation of capital and a requisite economic infrastructure, and the development of successful new high-tech industries able to compete on the global market. Japan took most of these steps in the nineteenth century, but twentieth-century examples abound. Singapore is probably the best model: Lee Kuan Yew brilliantly directed that tiny island republic's destiny for nearly forty years—tolerating very little opposition—to the point where Singapore is now an extraordinary economy for its size, and a model society of efficiency. Korea did admirably in the economic sphere under the "benevolent" dictatorship of several authoritarian no-nonsense leaders who brought the country to a position of major competitor on the international scene. Taiwan is now a major economy in East Asia with the second-biggest capital holdings of any state in the region—all under firm authoritarian rule until quite recently. Thailand has also economically progressed under nondemocratic rule. So has Chile. In all of these states, however, time is running out, or has run out, on the authoritarian structure. Korea has demonstrated explosive opposition to the government, and, through bloody confrontations, opposition forces have forced the government to major changes. Taiwan is now moving toward greater popular participation and free elections. Singapore is taking a few tentative steps, and the future without Lee is less clear, despite his position as revered founding father of the state. Pinochet has already lost his presidency in Chile.

But most authoritarian models have not been successful. Furthermore, there are several important provisos even in cases where it has succeeded. First, benevolent dictatorship may be the most "efficient" way to achieve modernization and create an internationally competitive economy, but clearly is not the best way to establish experience with democratic practice. It remains to be seen how these economically successful states will function democratically. And the hands of the benevolent dictator must invariably be pried off the levers of power: from the dictator's point of view, the people are never "quite ready" to assume leadership themselves.

More significantly, while the benevolent authoritarianism of many East Asian models may have been of genuine assistance in traversing the shoals to modernization, there is no guarantee at all that you get a Lee Kuan Yew. Russia got a Stalin to shepherd his people through the process, and they are probably farther away than ever. Cambodia got a Pol Pot.

China got a Mao Zedong, while Cuba got a Castro. Iraq got saddled with a Saddam Hussein.

In fact, it is an irony of ideology that the extreme left has generally been vastly more brutal and generally far more inefficient than the extreme right in overseeing the process of modernization. By definition the left tends to have a grander vision, and is willing to entertain means as commensurately drastic as the loftiness of the vision. The left tends to be more utopian and less willing to face the realities of social and especially economic laws of operation. Pinochet of Chile, who had very little time for the niceties of civil liberties and human rights, nonetheless is considered to have done an impressive job in developing the critically necessary infrastructure for the significant economic progress registered by Chile over the past decade. Facts like these are awkward to accept for those who tend for good reason to respond to lofty social ideals and who find the nitty-gritty details of economic construction to be slightly tedious and technical. With the far right you often get economic progress with oppression, even if no psychological or political satisfaction. With the far left, as Mick Jagger said, you can't get no satisfaction.

Lastly, it is interesting to note that the successful examples of benevolent dictators shepherding their countries through into a modern and competitive economic stage have mostly been in East Asia. There is something about the ancient and disciplined character of Confucian societies that seems to respond better than any other societies to the necessary self-discipline of nation-building and economic modernization. Those deeply rooted cultural, social, and philosophical roots cannot be exported. One only has to note how markedly different experience is in the Philippines—an East Asian country that entirely lacks the Confucian tradition.

The "Prerequisites" for Democracy

The classic argument of all autocrats—as noted earlier—is that the people are "not ready" for democracy. But what signal will flag such readiness? Democracy is rarely bestowed; it usually comes when people successfully wrest it from unwilling autocrats. But the trick is not so much in the process of the first elections as in the sustained process. The real crunch comes when those democratically elected to power must then relinquish power to successors who have just beaten them in subsequent elections. If America is to be interested in exporting democracy, then surely the question of the "prerequisites" for democracy must be understood as well. We are already spectators at the fascinating process of learning whether Russia is "ready" for democracy.

In principle, of course, there are important—or at least desirable—prerequisites for democracy. One would like some historical experience with democracy or political pluralism. A reasonably well-educated population is important. A fairly homogeneous population in ethnic and religious terms facilitates the establishment of a rough national consensus. A promising economic basis and the existence of a solid middle class is very valuable. A stable international environment in the region also helps. Economic growth and stable international commodity prices can make a major difference in the resilience of the political order. All of these factors greatly assist in the creation of a functional, durable democracy.

The problem is, you don't usually get all of this at once. Often you get very little of it. And you have to make do with what you've got. No would-be democratic reformer will delay implementation of democracy in the absence of theoretical preconditions. And you have to begin somewhere to build the process, to undergo the experience. Most political scientists will agree that there is no one formula for successful democratization: nearly every case is different.

In simplest terms, however, it does not take an educated populace to know that what they've got right now is intolerable and must be changed. They are ready to vote, today, to throw the bastards out. Hence the fate of the Sandinistas in the 1990 elections, for all the populism of that ideological regime. Hence the fate of Pinochet two months earlier—even though the economy had done well. The ability to remove the offending leadership is the first critical step of empowerment of the people.

In later phases the restraint of national leaders is the next critical element. Will a ruling leadership accept the results of elections that then throw them out of office? Can parties accept defeat? Can they be forced to compromise dramatically with opponents and enemies? Do the parties merely represent uncompromising blocs of conflicting ethnic and religious groups, or are they based more on class and economic interests? Here is where homogeneity of population and a reasonably large middle class become nearly indispensable. The more the cleavages in the society, the more the choice of leadership becomes a zero-sum game—where my gain automatically becomes your absolute loss. When the economic interests of different groups differ absolutely, the victory of one party is an absolute setback to the interests of the other.

The United States is a classic case in point. It does not really and truly affect most of us significantly whichever party wins the election. Our society is sufficiently homogeneous that the policies of one party over another will not usually make critical differences to our personal lives. Indeed, two reasonably similar political parties—by world standards—manage to cover most of the political spectrum desired by most Americans, despite massive ethnic differences. In most Third World countries, however, immense disparities of wealth and position and ethno-religious differences pit radically different interests against each other. Usually a plethora of parties are required to cover the spectrum of political interests where one's gain is always the other's loss. Under these circumstances one might well take to the barricades when one's own party loses power. The name of one former political party in Peru said it all: the Intransigent Radicals. It is not that Third World voters are necessarily less tolerant than Americans—it is just that the stakes in elections are vastly higher. We might feel differently in America if we had six different parties, running a spectrum from Wall Street interests to farm interests and including a black party, a Hispanic party, an industrial workers party, and a white-collar bureaucrats' party.

It is only when the gut interests of most of the society are able to be meaningfully encapsulated within two or three parties that elections cease to represent such winner-take-all contests and the machinery of democracy has a better chance of functioning with broad acceptance.

The last key criterion, education, while important, should not be given overwhelming weight either. Most issues of modern democracies are extremely complex, especially in the legal and economic areas. In California, a voter is presented with a hundred-plus-page booklet in which the pros and cons of electoral "propositions" are set forth for referendum at each election. I usually feel humbled by most of the issues on which I am asked to vote, often overwhelmed by the complexity of trade-offs involved, ones that are often not even fully articulated. Even an educated electorate is still in no position to fully understand the intricacies of a vast number of issues; indeed, major experts split down the middle on the same questions themselves. In the end, one votes by gut, often uncomfortable at the decision. One thing is for sure: in California voters know when they think things have gone wrong, and they say so. That is the bottom line of democracy, as valid in Ouagadougou as in Walla Walla.

Corruption is a vice we all love to excoriate, but it plays a disproportionately large role in our thinking about the character of foreign regimes. In reality, corruption is endemic to the human condition, under communism, capitalism, socialism, tribalism, democracy, and dictatorship. It is a minor peccadillo compared to the horrors of mass killings and gratuitous wars that mark many Third World and all totalitarian states. Nonetheless, corruption is indeed gradually corrosive and engenders undesirable cynicism among the populace; sentiments emerge, even in jest, that "America has the best Congress money can buy." Perhaps corruption is yet another face of participatory democracy—especially in big-city machine politics. It should be combatted, but it should not be elevated to a prominent place among reasons for the failure of democracy where it is present. Perhaps only Stalin, and Saddam Hussein could be reasonably sure that their politburos were not on the take.

Exporting the American Revolution

How much should America be in the business of encouraging democracy overseas? Should the installation of democracy now be the centerpiece of our foreign policy? The question cannot be answered strictly on its own merits: many other factors need to be considered as well. The United States went in to protect the autocratic rulers of Saudi Arabia from Iraqi aggression in 1990 because the potential of an Iraqi grab of

Saudi oil far transcended concern over lack of democracy there. There will always be additional mitigating factors—especially economic—in any foreign policy equation, apart from the establishment of democracy.

Americans themselves tend to be divided into two camps on this issue. We can discern a general ideological prodemocracy tilt on the part of many neoconservatives and strong liberals, who see the spread of democracy as highly desirable for the world, and who are indeed willing to make it the centerpiece of American policy, other things being equal. They would probably agree, too, that economic liberalism and a free-market economy flow from, and are essential to, political democracy. This school of thought has furthermore been liberated by the end of the Cold War, because it is no longer forced to make choices between security and stability on the one hand and democracy on the other.

The opposing school—more classically Realpolitik—eschews ideological commitments in foreign policy and looks to the fulfillment of American interests. While this school would see democracy as desirable, all other things being equal, it would insist that all other things are never equal. It is equally uncomfortable with any kind of commanding ideological principle in foreign policy that complicates concrete, tactical decisions—where the injection of ideological considerations serves only to muddy. The State Department is also more comfortable with Realpolitik, partly because the natural inclination of diplomats overseas typically is to maintain good bilateral relations and get along with those in power, rather than complicate their own lives by delivering unpopular demarches.

The realpolitik school also has reservations about the ethics of American interventionism in attempting to dictate to, or otherwise pressure, foreign states about the character of their political systems. In effect, who are we to be telling the world how to live? How much can America play policeman to the world. This view, which had a great deal more relevance during the extreme pressures of the Cold War era, now has less to justify its position. Its proponents would also probably fall back onto the argument that many states are not "ready" for democracy either—a point that always has a modicum of validity, even if it is not truly persuasive. As noted above, we cannot be hung up on theoretical "prerequisites" for the establishment of democratic procedures—it is never too early. To claim otherwise is both condescending and dilatory.

The Question of Means: American Interventionism?

The question of means is paramount, whatever our chosen ideological path. We have grown accustomed to the role of leadership in the world; few other nations have had the wherewithal or the will to intervene consistently in the interests of the world order. ("Shucks, ma'am, somebody had to do it.") But the habit has stuck. Put in its most simplistic form, do we wish to remain policeman of the world?

In the Iraq-Kuwait crisis of 1990–91, the United States moved quickly to defend Saudi Arabia and went to war to restore the existence of the state of Kuwait and cancel its annexation by Iraq. There were important reasons, grounded in international law and the international economy, for action to be taken. But why America? Because we are the strongest Western power? Out of sheer habit? Because we believe our unilateral action is more efficacious than other international mechanisms? Or was there also a concern that we had better demonstrate to ourselves and to the world that America can be relied upon, that we have a "commitment" to maintain the values of freedom, that we still have the right stuff when it comes to international action?

Yet today we are entering a qualitatively different world that includes a truly functional United Nations. Under those circumstances, where does American unilateralism fit in? And can we financially afford it? Some pundits have suggested that we will turn into a hired gun paid by the Japanese and the Germans to meet their security needs and to preserve a world order for their markets, and to enable them to keep their own hands clean. Or maybe an American Rent-an-Army on permanent call to the UN, with occasional side gigs around the world on our own?

The post-Kuwait reckonings are not over. While many nations will be grateful that the United States took the initiative to deter an ugly expansionist dictator like Saddam Hussein, not all nations will approve the strong unilateral character of the action. President Bush deserved credit for attempting to create a broad international consensus about the need to use force, but many powers of the world may not want to see the exercise repeated in this same fashion the next time around. Too many states are likely to see behind the war over Kuwait a uniquely American agenda aimed at securing distinct American strategic interests that do not fully tally with the interests of other states in the means or extent of the conflict. We may in fact have witnessed the great swansong of the era of American unilateralism. The "new international order" is likely to be less enthusiastic about such American policies in the future, if indeed the American public itself is up to them.

Third World Fears of a Unipolar World

The question is not only what role America wishes to play, but what the rest of the world thinks about it. The Soviet Union is now *hors de combat*, no longer in a position to exert major influence on the course of international events. The United States is the immediate international beneficiary of this windfall. America still remains unchallenged as the preeminent international force likely to intervene on behalf of challenges to the international order. While this role may be gratifying to Americans who worry about the end of the Cold War, such American preeminence does not bring universal joy to all the world. Iraqi President Saddam Hussein, in a speech six months before his attack on Kuwait, made the observation about the new international correlation of forces that

> suddenly the situation has changed in a dramatic way. . . . It has become clear to everyone that the United States has emerged in a superior position in international politics. This superiority will be demonstrated in U.S. readiness to play a role well beyond what might have previously been expected of it. . . . We believe that the U.S. will continue to depart from the restrictions that govern the rest of the world throughout the next five years until new forces of balance are formed. . . .[1]

These observations by Saddam Hussein undoubtedly echo the observations of many other leaders in the world, whether they have articulated the thought or not. For Saddam, of course, the observation was prophetic—and he did not heed it.

But nature abhors a vacuum, and a bid by the United States, however unlikely, to fill the gap left by the Soviet Union will not be welcomed internationally. The international order will indeed grow uncomfortable with unfettered American ability to exercise unilateral military support—even in the defense of the international order, and however benign or wise many of these American actions might seem to be. It was not Saddam Hussein alone who took exception to the role of the United States as international policeman. Many countries have goals that often differ from those of the United States, or simply feel their own relative power and influence to be threatened by the existence of a single superpower in a policed international order. These states will not support the continued centrist role of America in all international crises.

Other emerging powers will also have increasing desire for greater voice on the international scene. Europe, the "new superpower," will be one of those forces—although there is considerable doubt as to whether it can ever get its political act together. Japan is another. Regional "superpowers" such as India, Brazil, China, Iran, and South Africa, will also see their own international power circumscribed by excessive American projection of unilateral power into distant places. They too will seek to limit the future American role to some extent.

The Soviet Union itself will be the single greatest champion of discouraging any American tendency toward unilateralism. Having given up or lost its own claim to major international clout, the USSR does not want to see the role pass exclusively over to the United States. The Soviet Union is thus emerging as a champion of the United Nations and of the use of multilateral power to achieve international security goals. It will consistently oppose U.S. unilateralism in the decades ahead.

In all likelihood, then, America's newly acquired monopoly of international power is likely to be contested and probably short-lived, sought neither by the majority of the American public nor by the international community. Yet the Kuwaiti crisis gives pause for thought. It was indeed American military power that proved uniquely capable of responding quickly to the need to block Iraqi expansionism with convincing array of force. It is arguable whether any other state or combination of states would have proved as capable of responding as quickly and as fully as the United States did in moving force to Saudi Arabia. But did the international community truly vote for war? Or for the date when war should start? Or for how it should be fought? Or ended?

It is very possible that the next crisis will entail yet more international and less American action. The war over Kuwait may be an exception. It is hard to imagine another region in the world which would draw such an overall surge of international interest as the Persian Gulf. We may then be witnessing a transitional period of unpopularity in international affairs which is already giving way to a new multilateralism.

This multilateralism may not sit easily with all elements of the American government, for it inevitably suggests a waning of American world preeminence in the security field. Indeed, U.S. military force might be a critical part of any new international force that might come into being. There is furthermore no doubt that unilateral force is more efficient and effective than international mechanisms. There may, too, be cases of such urgency that they cannot be entrusted to slower-moving multilateral forces. One such case might involve the need for a preemptive strike against the nuclear facilities of another country about to launch nuclear war on a neighbor. But the gain in international legitimacy through the use of mechanisms like the UN may make up for some loss in efficiency.

But can the United States live with this? Are we prepared to accept a diminished role on the international scene? Are we prepared to submit our military forces to the command of some Finnish or Nigerian general? Or are America and the UN better off without the politically volatile presence of American troops as part of an international force?

A major role for American future unilateral interventionism is further complicated by an American public that seems increasingly less interested in playing the international policeman, largely because of the expense in treasure and blood. Democracies simply prefer to place their money and lives elsewhere unless the threat is grave indeed. America itself thus may ultimately decide to lead the way out of a unipolar world and into a multipolar, multilateral one.

The debate, of course, is partly theoretical. In fact most policy choices are made on the individual merits of each case. Washington rarely maintains any sustained grand vision in the conduct of policy, but moves tactically and often reactively. We may or may not be inclined to intervene in a given situation depending upon the general outlook of the administration and the mood of the Congress and the people. No policymaker will want to be saddled with restrictive ideological commitments.

The next decade will thus be a critical turning point for the future of American foreign policy. American democracy will complicate the formulation of such policy—indeed, one foreign policy observer, Alan Tonelson, has halfway seriously suggested foreign policy by referendum. Such is enough to send shivers down the spines of the professional diplomat, but it is a reality that the public may well have—may already have—increasing daily say in foreign policy formulation. Witness the growing power of Congress in foreign policy deliberation. The national mood and even the national interest may be increasingly affected by the changing demographic character of the country and the role of immigrant groups from Asia or Latin America that will have different ideas about how American policy should be conducted in those regions.

Facing Third World Problems

And there is no getting around it: America faces serious problems ahead in its encounters with the Third World. Ethnicity will be on the rise, seeking full expression, and angered at great-power efforts to control it, channel it, or deny it its goals of greater self-determination. The economic problems of many countries are unlikely to get any better, and perhaps will be getting worse, more systemic and insoluble. These countries will turn in anger upon the West—especially America—in demanding either relief or solutions.

The expectations of the post–Cold War world have dramatically risen. For starters, the exhibition of a dozen states overthrowing their communist regimes and seeking democracy raises expectations that the same process should emerge elsewhere as well. Democracy is now felt to be a movement whose time has come—even if it will be frustrated in many countries in the implementation.

Countries now look too to some kind of "peace dividend" within their own societies and from the West. America will be perceived as the country that should be able to provide greater assistance than ever before, even while we protest that we are less able to do so. The smell of a new era is in the air; new political alignments and formations are emerging that whet the hopes of most countries that the new order will bring them something too. Yet, as in any period of change, inevitably there will be numerous winners and probably more losers.

Haves vs. Have-Nots in the Next Millennium

We are on the threshold, not just of a new century, but of a new millennium. The end of the last millennium, in 999, was celebrated apocalyptically, in the expectation that the end of the world was not far off. At that time neither nuclear weapons, nor AIDS, nor junk food had been invented, but the Huns, the Plague, and fatty ox roasts were no less threatening. In the next millennium there will be new ideological challenges to liberal democracy, though perhaps none so systematic and global as the challenge of totalitarian communism. But whatever the next ideological challenge will be, it will surely also be phrased in global dimensions—how could it not, given the global network of instant communication and knowledge? Very surely the next challenge will come from the have-nots against the haves. They will speak in apocalyptic terms of a small minority squandering for their own satisfactions the resources of the world, both ecological and monetary. The struggle will be about participation and share in the global bounty. This time there is no "East-West" pull to disorient the compass of the "North-South" struggle. These issues were a constant undertone in the Kuwait war.

Democracy had better have some good answers about these North-South challenges early on, rather than after new global fault lines appear. If democracy in the West continues to fuel the good life only for the minority of world haves, then it will surely be our undoing. If our own democracy enables us self-ishly to choose not to involve ourselves deeply in the welfare of the rest of the globe, that too will be our downfall.

The New Sensitivity

The emerging era will pose new demands by the less developed countries that they be treated on a basis of greater equality and dignity—a demand that is inconsistent with the philosophy and style of American unilateralism that is predicated on the primacy of American interests. Most of the less developed world holds deeply ambivalent feelings toward the advanced countries of the world—combining envy, rising expectations and despair at meeting them, a sense of power-lessness and humiliation before the developed world, and a desire to be masters of their own destinies. These aspirations involve an increasing demand for greater economic equity in the world order, a greater role and voice for the Third World in world politics, and a deepening resentment of great-power interference in their affairs. With the end of the Cold War the traditional kind of ready external intervention at the whim of the great powers will be increasingly less acceptable, and seen as less justifiable. The scars of the Iraq-Kuwait war run very deep as the ultimate expression of white men massively bombing non-Western men in unequal combat, regardless of the sins of Saddam Hussein. A demand for a new spirit of equity and equality in the world will emerge. This demand, ironically, is intensified by the collapse of the Soviet Union, which for seventy years spearheaded—entirely for its own ends—a selective campaign of rhetoric on behalf of the "downtrodden" against the "imperialists" (read Soviet allies vs. American allies). The vacuum left by the USSR could well hasten the emergence of some other champion of the cause of the downtrodden, from a country as yet uncertain, to serve as a Pied Piper to a world of Third World equality. That role could even be played by Russia itself.

We, of course, are in some senses poorly equipped to demonstrate full understanding and sympathy toward these aspirations of the Third World. Nations possessed of great power do not usually need to be endowed with great sensitivity toward other smaller nations of the world. Great nations act out of power, and power is persuasive, either positively or negatively. It speaks its own language. Small countries, on the other hand, enjoy no such luxury. Lacking the persuasive power of great force and influence, they must live on their wits, develop exquisite sensitivity to the moods of the great powers, and seek to influence them through subtler means. The art of compromise, negotiation, and accommodation is far more masterfully conducted by the small power, to which such skills are part of a survival kit, than by the large.

The demands of the new era will require the United States to develop greater understanding of and sensitivity toward the rest of the world. The groundwork for such new American policy sensitivity has already been laid in our domestic policies; we now contemplate the extension into international affairs of a domestic process in which we already demonstrate increased compassion toward our own poor, disadvantaged, and underprivileged. The welfare of our own economic, social, and ethnic minorities and the underprivileged is perceived as a critical part of the national weal. This concept will come to be increasingly projected abroad as nation-states grow less exclusivistic in their view of their interest. As we use less and less force domestically to meet the needs of the frustrated and disadvantaged and seek to alleviate root causes, so too, internationally we may be less inclined to resort to costly force to deal with errant nations.

Two Faces of American Democracy

In reality, our democratic culture speaks with two tongues, as we have seen in this book—one conservative and one revolutionary. On the one hand, our democratic system and its free-market system have produced immense boons to our lives; these blessings have caused us to grow comfortable with the status quo and to seek stability in the world so that it does not intrude too deeply into our comfortable, nondemanding lives. We believe in orderly procedure and due process. We believe that stability is an important virtue in allowing people to live orderly lives under a rule of law— impossible if there is instability.

On the other hand, we are all born of a revolutionary and idealistic legacy that envisions democracy as the desirable goal for all men and women. Ours was not a revolution of means; it was a revolution of ideals and concepts implemented—the celebration of the existence of fundamental rights, the rule of law, the equality of all before the law, and the right to establish a government responsive solely to the people.

Those ideas are still revolutionary. They are still not operative in most of the world. But our culture and society remain revolutionary, involving a constant process of change, permanent reordering of political and social relationships, and the empowerment of ever newer groups, and the weakening of traditional sources of power. We are restless, bursting with new ideas, creativity, change. New arrivals in the country constantly transform our way of life, shape our sensitivities, affect how we think, even what we eat and wear, and the music we listen to. There is almost no dead weight of tradition. We are encumbered by no system of class which limits our upward progression. By now, skilled blacks, Hispanics, and females in America possess remarkable professional options that they did not have before. We are in general open as a society to consider almost any idea.

But this revolutionary and dynamic spirit is often threatening to much of the rest of the world, certainly to those societies in which a traditional elite seeks to maintain the status quo, in which one ethnic group feels it cannot afford to permit the gain of another group. But these American ideals also represent their own hopes, for they too aspire to much of what we have in both material terms and availability of opportunity. Our cultural and social message to the rest of the world is thus intense and disruptive, whether we always realize it or not. Americans living abroad usually reflect these values of equality and informality in dealing with other societies, often to the annoyance and discomfiture of those societies.

It is now the task of American policy to determine which of the two voices—the idealistic or the realpolitik—speaks more authentically for our nation, which of the two speaks for the future.

This book does not call for a choice between liberalism and conservatism, for both are critical elements to political and social balance. Preference of one over the other is like saying

one prefers the accelerator to the brakes in a car; neither is
an optional feature and each has its critical function on the
journey. Supporting "change" just for its own sake can be
mindless and trendy, just as preservation of the status quo for
reasons of comfort is thoughtless and dangerous. The emplace-
ment of the lowest social order into power by revolution is no
more virtuous, moral, or progressive than is retention of the
old and traditional elite. Individual talent and skills must win
out over preconceived notions of position accorded by race,
religion, class, gender, or age. The revolutionary vision of our
principles still lies at the heart of the American idea. We want
these ideas to prevail, not because they are American, but
because they are universal, and have withstood the ravages of
twentieth-century politics.

The Virtues of "Exporting the Revolution"

Our own society faces many dilemmas inherent in democracy—"Democracy Traps" as talked about in this book—not
the least of which is the danger of our losing sense of what
democracy was all about in the first place. But there are civics
lessons for us out of the ashes of communism. Witnessing the
renewal of our democratic ideas abroad in other cultures
should help make us more aware of these traps. Involvement
in their experience should help us remember the active dialectic, the trade-offs of democracy, that often get forgotten in
the complacency of our long-established, relatively successful
political and economic system. This involvement will help
renew our own ideas and ideals as we become engaged in
the struggles of other peoples to implement similar ideas and
concepts. This is a key argument for our support of an American policy that "exports the revolution."

Realpolitik, on the contrary, is a profoundly Bismarckian,
nineteenth-century, Central European concept—as the word
and its German origin suggest. Of course, politics must always
acknowledge the real; the national interest must always be
the critical determining factor in policy formulation. But as
the world progresses, the concept of self-interest evolves and
broadens. The circle of human beings with which we identify

constantly expands. (The ecologists say that these values extend to the environment and all species as well.)

Some Americans will object that all of this is ideological in character. It is. But if we are not mindful of our own values and ideologies, they will rapidly fall into meaninglessness in the trivia of our own daily self-focused, introverted, safe lives. We need to participate vicariously in the constant replanting of the tree of democracy elsewhere in the world to keep the concept alive for ourselves. Adversity in the democratic experiment that we experience vicariously abroad can also help us better to focus on the nature of our problems at home. Fortress America, insular America, self-satisfied America, spells death for our own democracy.

The "traps" of democracy thus exist most dangerously in the absence of reflection. Democracy at home and abroad complicates our personal, social, political, and international lives. For it calls for a sense of discrimination—constantly—about who we are and what we are about. If democracy is taken simply as a benign environment in which we can all go about our business and our pleasure, then we are in trouble. The exercise of democracy implies responsibilities—privileged burdens not possessed by the citizen of autocratic regimes under which everything can be left to Big Brother. It implies participation in the great and small issues that affect our lives and the lives of others.

Yet the nonvoting patterns of the American electorate suggest that we are already weary of complex problems unless they are urgent enough to come up in local referenda—where they generate greater passion than presidential politics or the new international order. The democratic politicians who do not raise the hard issues—because it is "smart politics" not to—also contribute to the creation of a rudderless ship. As Richard Reeves pointed out, it is almost as if Americans don't want leadership in Washington, they just want to fine-tune policies by direct referenda, as it were, when the big questions come up. If that is the future stuff of our politics, then democracy will not likely fare very well in the twenty-first century.

Have we come this far on the human odyssey over tens of thousands of years to suddenly rest on our laurels now? Democracy will not run on automatic pilot. Ideas about the "end of history" only represent a complacency or ignorance about the "internal challenge" of democracy that is more dangerous than the totalitarian communist enemy it has so recently vanquished.

The techno-optimists who write cheerily of the coming Third Waves and G-forces of the world—all suggestive of a better living through rational technology—are actually pushing us to the brink of the Democracy Trap. They are peddling the comforting thought that science and rationality are the key to the future in our technologically evolving future. In fact, the main problem of society is not its technology, but its values—where we are all going and why.

The very "success" of American democracy encourages us to drop out of active contention with the issues, to leave it to the system—however cynically we may refer to it. It encourages us to pursue our own paths with relative impunity, and perhaps without regard for the moral, ethical, and spiritual framework of human life. It is often only those who live in adversity who come up with the spiritual reserves to survive and improve. We need to anticipate future adversity early on so as to release our capacities to think about it.

Conclusion

I do not presume to suggest that there is any master moral plan or code of values that will solve all these problems. But it is a central thesis of this book that the values and the practice of modern democracy are demonstrably of a higher order than the values and practice of any other system could be. Some traditional societies like those of the Native Americans or Trobriand Islanders may too have possessed rich and fulfilling social orders, within the context of a static, insulated, and nondemocratic society. But once the virus of change—rapid, sweeping change in the twentieth century—touches them and any other culture, there is no going back, whatever the idyll may have been. No system—a few occasional benevolent dictatorships aside—other than liberal democracy is more systematically reliable in bringing about the well-being of society.

But this belief, this faith, does not guarantee that the path will be permanently sustainable. It has also been the cardinal thesis of this book that our democratic values are creating increasingly severe operational dilemmas in their wake. Particular social problems, including the handling of race and ethnicity, morality, and maintenance of the social order are daunting; they may even be exacerbated by the systematic furthering of democratic practice. These dilemmas will challenge American society as never before, and all other societies of the world, too, as they traverse much of the same economic, political, and even cultural ground pioneered by America—good as well as bad. We simply cannot know where this path will take us.

Ideally, the democratic path will provide self-correction as need arises. But it may not, and certainly not in every society, perhaps not even in our own. If the social problems become critical enough, and the democratic order becomes paralyzed, it may result in a sharp pendulum swing toward an authoritarian solution in order to preserve society.

This book basically attempts to look into the future implications of these trends and to sound certain warning bells. When dangers can be anticipated, when warnings about possible problems looming ahead can be made, we may be ready for them should they actually materialize. That is the whole point of the warning process: not to predict, but to anticipate potential problems sufficiently far ahead so that corrective steps can be taken. If none of the darker problems raised in this book ever fully materialize, I will be delighted. I don't even mind being wrong. I just don't want to be wrong about our faith in democracy—in its ability to handle the unique new challenges of the post–Cold War world, in which our greatest enemy is no longer overseas but lies in the inherent contradictions of ourselves and our system.

NOTES
1. Speech by Saddam Hussein at the Fourth Summit of the Arab Cooperation Council in Amman, February 24, 1990.

INDEX

269